...AISE FOR *DEFI... DESIGN*

"Many elem... ...signed, silly, and even da... ...argues that these designs are effectively biased, discriminating against those of different genders, ages, and body types, and creating real barriers to equality. In the crusading spirit of consumer-rights champion Ralph Nader, Anthony makes a polemical argument for change and offers practical remedies to achieve it. A transformative and agenda-setting book."

—Barbara Penner, PhD, Bartlett School of Architecture,
University College London

"Finally, someone other than me, a small woman, understands that one size doesn't fit all. Anthony gives a comprehensive look at gender, body, and age biases built into all types of consumer products and buildings, describing the harm that they cause. She goes even further by challenging us with a call to action, supporting products and legislation that are gender, body, and age neutral. A thoughtful read for those pursuing product and architecture development."

—Beth Brykman, author of *The Best of Both Worlds:
How Mothers Can Find Full-Time Satisfaction in Part-Time Work*

"With warmth but a keen eye, Anthony dissects the everyday world, from small children's toys to the urban setting. This is a must-read book not only for design students who want to know about inclusive design but also for anyone looking for better-quality products. From the first pages dealing with micro-scale personal products up to the last pages covering buildings and public transportation, this book is full of examples that make us look again at our preconceptions and point us toward design solution... make our day-to-day lives better, regardless of gender, a... and condition."

—Sun-Young ...

Defined by Design

*The Surprising Power
of Hidden Gender, Age, and Body Bias
in Everyday Products and Places*

Kathryn H. Anthony

Ⓟ Prometheus Books
59 John Glenn Drive
Amherst, New York 14228

Published 2017 by Prometheus Books

Cover images © iStock Photo
Cover design by John Larson
Cover design © Prometheus Books

Trademarked names appear throughout this book. Prometheus Books recognizes all registered trademarks, trademarks, and service marks mentioned in the text.

The Internet addresses listed in the text were accurate at the time of publication. The inclusion of a website does not indicate an endorsement by the author or by Prometheus Books, and Prometheus Books does not guarantee the accuracy of the information presented at these sites.

Inquiries should be addressed to
Prometheus Books
59 John Glenn Drive
Amherst, New York 14228
VOICE: 716–691–0133
FAX: 716–691–0137
WWW.PROMETHEUSBOOKS.COM

21 20 19 18 17   5 4 3 2 1

Library of Congress Cataloging-in-Publication Data

Names: Anthony, Kathryn H., author. | Schmidt, Eric, 1955 April 27- writer of
    foreword.
Title: Defined by design : the surprising power of hidden gender, age, and body
    bias in everyday products and places / by Kathryn H. Anthony, PhD.
Description: Amherst, New York : Prometheus Books, 2017. | Includes index.
Identifiers: LCCN 2016036580 (print) | LCCN 2016036697 (ebook) |
    ISBN 9781633882836 (paperback) | ISBN 9781633882843 (ebook)
Subjects: LCSH: Design–Human factors. | Design–Social aspects. | BISAC: DESIGN
    / General. | DESIGN / Product. | ARCHITECTURE / Buildings / Public,
    Commercial & Industrial.
Classification: LCC NK1520 .A58 2017 (print) | LCC NK1520 (ebook) |
    DDC 745–dc23
LC record available at https://lccn.loc.gov/2016036580

Printed in the United States of America

CONTENTS

ACKNOWLEDGMENTS

*D*efined by Design took about a decade to write. So I have many, many people whom I must thank. It takes a village to write a book.

Special thanks to my longtime friend Eric Schmidt for taking time out of his fast-paced schedule to write the foreword to this book. Each and every day, through his leadership as executive chairman and former chief executive officer at Google, Eric and his colleagues are continuing to make the world a better place for all of us. Thanks too go to John Musnicki, who has been an outstanding host at Google Chicago to my graduate seminar for many years. Google's meticulous attention to design that meets the demands of a diverse worldwide clientele never ceases to amaze me.

Hundreds of people shaped this book by entrusting me with candid insights about their experiences with everyday products, places, and spaces. Their stories ranged from comedies to tragedies, and everywhere in between. Each of their tales was amusing, entertaining, and enlightening in its own way, ultimately taking this book in directions I would never have thought of on my own. To all of these individuals who remain anonymous, I am enormously grateful.

Another round of thanks goes to journalists Lisa Anderson, Ceri Au, Laura Bliss, John Branch, Josie Delap, Levi Fishman, Maria La Ganga, Mike Pesca, Rachel Martin, and John Sutter for including my comments in earlier print and broadcast interviews at the *Atlantic*, CNN, the *Economist*, the *Guardian*, National Public Radio, the *New York Times*, *Time*, and elsewhere, alerting audiences to the pressing need for gender equity in design.

My deepest thanks to all those who made my dream come true to see this book published. At Prometheus Books, Vice President and

Editor in Chief Steven L. Mitchell recognized this book's potential, and Editorial Assistant Hanna Etu skillfully saw this project through to fruition. Will DeRooy provided a thoughtful copyedit. Working with the staff at Prometheus has been a pleasure every step of the way.

Olga Kontzias Psillis believed in my book from the get-go and after a circuitous path eventually pointed me in the direction of Maryann Karinch. Had I not intercepted Olga just days before she retired, chances are I would never have discovered Maryann. Maryann Karinch believed in this project from the first time she saw it and ushered me through several iterations of my book proposal. Without her, *Defined by Design* may never have seen the light of day. For both of us, patience, persistence, and perseverance were the name of the game—until we finally found the perfect match.

Enormous thanks to Jean McDonald, my colleague who teaches journalism at the University of Illinois at Urbana–Champaign, and who proved to be a spectacular editor. Her timely insights at critical stages improved this book in countless ways, including working with me to shrink it almost in half. I'm indebted to Rich Martin, former head of the Department of Journalism, who steered me in Jean's direction.

Over the past decade, many colleagues invited me to speak about my ongoing research for *Defined by Design* in places both near and far: Ankara, Bangkok, Champaign-Urbana, Chicago, Chongqing, Moscow, Nicosia, Philadelphia, Salzburg, Seoul, Shanghai, Venice, and even a congressional testimony in Washington, DC.

A warm thank you to all my hosts and colleagues: William Cope, Chunlan Du, Meltem Ö. Gürel, Sylvia Hahn, Haesong Je, Mary Kalantzis, Heping Li, Zhi Liu, Feng Lu, Wei Lu, Kathryn Marshak, Anne Marshall, Stan Nadel, Jay Peters, Pani Pyla, Sun-Young Rieh, Joanne Royce, Jack Sim, former US representative Edolphus Towns, Alexander Wolf, Leiqing Xu, and Hua Yue, as well as to my long-time friends and colleagues at Chicago Women in Architecture. With each speaking engagement came new encounters with new friends who inspired me to delve into this topic even more.

Historian Emeritus of the United States Senate Donald Ritchie generously provided me with a memorable behind-the-scenes tour of the US Capitol, where he pointed out fascinating gender issues in design.

For their pioneering advocacy work to usher in a new era of gender-friendly public restroom designs, I am grateful to Robert Brubaker, Tom Keating, Mary Coakley Munk, Steven Soifer, and especially to Jack Sim, an international leader on this issue whose efforts led to the official recognition of November 19 as World Toilet Day by the United Nations.

Former chancellor Nancy Cantor and former provost Linda Katehi invited me to serve in key leadership positions at the University of Illinois at Urbana–Champaign to advance gender equity on campus, providing special opportunities and modest financial support to put into practice gender issues in design. I was privileged to work with colleagues Mark Barcus, Deanie Brown, Anita Kaiser, Timothy McCarthy, Kelly Sullivan Milburn, Gale Summerfield, Barbara Wilson, and Brad Ward, who helped bring our design ideas to life.

David Chasco and Peter Mortensen provided a supportive working environment in the Illinois School of Architecture that enabled me to teach my graduate seminars on gender and race in contemporary architecture and social and behavioral factors in design, allowing me to work together with scores of talented students and plant the seeds of *Defined by Design*.

Many former students and colleagues provided valuable research assistance with various stages of this project. I am most grateful to Gloria Colom, Ron Corniels, Nai-Wen Kuo, Natalya Falk Lee, Heidi Hagen Lightner, Wambaa Mathu, Terrence McMahon, Christina Mooney, Joanne Muniz, Sudipta Rakshit, Neha Rane, Aparna Saligrama, Muhammad Taimur Sarwar, Sana Hafeez Taimur, Shannon Tucker, Chia-Hui Wang, and Crystal Whiters. Special thanks go to Meghan Dufresne, who worked with me for a number of years and became one of my favorite coauthors.

Two of my former students, Andrea Stafford Cecelia and Jon Cecelia, graciously provided photographs of their young daughters, Annalise and Madeleine, as they are routinely disadvantaged by design, as did my niece, Anastasia Lewis, and her infant son, Ethan.

Beth Tauke, Korydon Smith, and Charles Davis invited me to write a book chapter about gender issues in podium design for their textbook, *Diversity and Design*, stirring me to reflect on my experiences.

Thanks as well to Susan Grossinger, Greg Moore, Joi Sumpton,

Paul Sumpton, and Nicholas Watkins, who introduced me to products that do an exceptionally good job designing for diverse genders, ages, and body sizes.

Good friends, neighbors, and nearby colleagues provided fascinating discussions, great leads, refreshing walks, scenic drives, and nourishing meals. In Champaign-Urbana and Chicago, these included Charlotte Arnstein, Sylvia Arnstein, Walter Arnstein, Leanne Rodgers Barnhart, Sara Bartumeus, William Cope, Beth Finke, Victor Font, John Garner, Wendy Greenhouse, Spring Harrison, Sharon Irish, Mary Kalantzis, Darlene Kloeppel, James Kloeppel, Joy Malnar, Melissa Mitchell, Lubitsa Nenadov, Bea Nettles, Carole Rebeiz, Tino Rebeiz, Nate Schmitz, Gisela Sin, Amita Sinha, Beth Stafford-Vaughan, Lionel Suntop, Rachel Suntop, Michael Trenary, Frank Vodvarka, Trish Wilkinson, and Kostas Yfantis. While based in La Jolla, these included Eve Allen, Jerry Allen, Greg Lambron, Barry Levich, Mike Maynard, William McGill, Betsey Monsell, Craig Monsell, Erys Phillips, Gillian Pinsky, Paul Pinsky, Helga Stark, and Paul Stark.

Three lifelong academic mentors provided an intellectual grounding that inspired my career as an educator and an author: Clare Cooper Marcus, Galen Cranz, and Robert Sommer. The years I spent as a graduate student at the University of California at Berkeley's International House helped to spark my interest in diversity.

I am especially grateful to colleagues who provided thoughtful comments and critiques, from its very early stages as a book proposal, to manuscript drafts, to its near-final form: Beth Brykman, Colleen Casey, Clare Cooper Marcus, Diane Ghirardo, Clara Greed, Meltem Ö. Gürel, Dolores Hayden, Maggie Jackson, Ryuzo Ohno, Barbara Penner, Sun-Young Rieh, Susan Schulman, Jack Sim, Dan Stokols, and Despina Stratigakos, as well as scores of students.

My good friend Stefanos Katsikas provided terrific company, delicious food, and illuminating travel experiences, all the while serving as a strict taskmaster encouraging me to focus and finish this book. Ever since our visit to London where I first received news about my book contract, he has become my good-luck charm.

From the book's inception to its completion, I had countless conversations with John Smith and Mary Anne Anthony Smith about what it meant to be defined by design.

A few special women, now deceased, inspired me in writing this book. The first was Katina Boretos Skoufis, my maternal grandmother. When she was a young girl in her native Greece, her father forbid her to attend school. Knowing that she would never be allowed inside, she sat out on the front steps and sobbed as her friends entered the schoolhouse. Although she never learned to read or write, her wisdom surpassed that of many. The afghans she wove and the recipes she cooked remind me that she is always with us. The second was my paternal grandmother, Maria Ftoulis Antoniades, who raised five children on her own on a remote Greek island. As was then the custom for widows in that part of the world, she mourned the loss of her husband by wearing only black for over forty years, nearly half her life. Were my grandmothers alive today, they could only marvel at the sea change of opportunities now available to women, especially their granddaughters.

My three beloved aunts, Georgia Paul, Helen Rozos, and Helen Skoufis, who passed away within just six weeks of each other, were three of my closest friends. They always loved hearing about whatever I was writing and were happy to engage with me in lively discussions about anything and everything related to this book. I will miss the chance to share it with them.

Finally, perpetual thanks go to my parents, Anne Anthony and Harry Anthony, two surviving members of the Greatest Generation who supported my dreams to pursue my academic career and become an author. They have always been my biggest cheerleaders, my biggest fans, and my biggest role models. A fellowship from the French government allowed my father to escape extreme poverty in war-torn Greece to study architecture and urbanism at the Sorbonne. In Paris he worked for the world-renowned architect LeCorbusier, and in New York he headed the urban-planning program at Columbia University. In contrast to my father, who steered clear of the digital revolution, starting in her eighties, my mother defied ageist stereotypes, enjoying the challenge of surfing the Internet and learning how to master three computers, two iPads, e-mail, Skype, and Facebook.

Our overseas trips to visit family in Greece starting when I was only three years old instilled in me a love of travel and curiosity about the world that has been a source of great pleasure throughout my life. And from what my parents told me, they put up with a very fussy customer who, even then, carefully chose which restrooms she was willing to use. For even as a three-year-old, I was already being defined by design.

FOREWORD

Eric Schmidt, PhD,
Executive Chairman and
Former Chief Executive Officer, Google

Design has the capacity to inspire, delight, and empower us. Whether we see it face-to-face or online, an eye-catching product, a stunning piece of fashion, or a beautifully designed space can captivate us. At Google our constant attention to design, down to the smallest details, has been one of the hallmarks of our search engines, our websites, our workspaces, and our ways of life.

Yet, secret biases in design have the ability to disadvantage and disempower us in ways that the rest of us must now recognize and remedy.

I am pleased to see the release of Kathryn Anthony's latest book, *Defined by Design: The Surprising Power of Hidden Gender, Age, and Body Bias in Everyday Products and Places*, one that is long overdue. It offers a wealth of information about how to make wiser choices about designs that affect you every day in ways that you may never have realized before. From parents concerned about how hidden hazardous designs impact the health and safety of their children, to chief executive officers committed to creating environments that offer fair and equitable treatment for an increasingly diverse, global workforce, *Defined by Design* is guaranteed to strike a chord.

Becoming aware of hidden gender, age, and body bias in daily designs that surround us makes us smarter consumers. Avoiding exposure to these biases whenever possible makes us smarter still. Learning about sensitively designed products, places, and spaces that recognize our differences and prevent bias altogether is frosting on the cake. *Defined by Design* does all this and more.

In her previous books, *Design Juries on Trial: The Renaissance of the Design Studio, Designing for Diversity: Gender, Race, and Ethnicity in the Architectural Profession,* and *Running for Our Lives: An Odyssey with Cancer,* and even in her doctoral dissertation *International House: Home Away From Home,* Kathryn Anthony has opened the eyes of thousands of readers to voices that are rarely heard: students pulling all-nighters in a design studio; architects whose gender, race, and ethnicities are underrepresented in their profession; and patients and their families struggling to survive life-threatening illnesses.

Here, too, in *Defined by Design,* she exposes readers to voices of people who are rarely heard yet have important things to say. *Defined by Design* is the culmination of the author's decade of research listening to hundreds of people share their stories about how everyday designs affect them in profound ways. And in her usual style, rather than just identifying pressing problems, she points the way toward innovative solutions that empower people to make better choices about the clothes they wear, the products they buy, the homes they live in, and the spaces where they work and play.

Kathryn Anthony's powerful testimony before a US Congressional Committee led Hillary Clinton to value her "leadership in addressing gender issues in design."

Here is how others have described Kathryn Anthony and her writing: "surprising and groundbreaking," "an insightful, informative, and delightful read," "not only a scholar but a pioneer," "one of architecture's leading social consciences," "a distinguished teacher because of the transformative impact she has had . . . on how the profession looks at itself as an engine of social change," "invariably the most mesmerizing contributor to dialogue not only about what impediments exist . . . but also about what concrete solutions exist . . . to become more diverse in sustainable ways," "she has given voice not only to her own critical assessment but importantly to those individuals . . . who have been marginalized . . . and often silenced."

As I've written in my book, *How Google Works,* one of our stated values at Google has always been to "Focus on the User." Our users come from a diverse pool of people from all over the world. Designing virtual search engines that respond to millions of diverse users across the globe and designing workspace environments that respond to thousands of diverse Google employees have always been important to us. Our sensitivity to designing for different cultures, genders and ages is a key reason for Google's widespread appeal.

Throughout Kathryn Anthony's lengthy career as a highly acclaimed author, educator, and advocate for designing for diversity, she personifies the values we both share to "Focus on the User."

Defined by Design does what I believe Google does best: uses information to open up new windows into the world around us. And once you open this particular window of Kathryn's, you will be amazed at what you see.

INTRODUCTION

Take a good look at your surroundings. Unless you're out in the wilderness right now, someone planned and designed most of what you see. You may rarely think about the reasons why the things you use every day look and work the way they do. Perhaps the designers had someone like you in mind. If so, you may appreciate the things they created that make your life go smoothly. You may absolutely love them and wonder how you ever lived without them. Or you may not even notice them at all. But perhaps the designers had a vision that, for some reason, excluded people like you. At best, the products, spaces, and places they created may annoy you, making you feel as if you don't fit the mold. At worst, they may injure or even kill you.

Beautifully designed fashions, products, spaces, and places seduce consumers and clients into spending lots of money, time, and energy. Yet all too often, these investments turn out to be huge mistakes. We may be mesmerized by a brilliant design but unaware of the psychological or physiological impact it has on us. The design of the products we use, the neighborhoods we inhabit, the schools our children attend, and the buildings we work in every day are only the backdrop to our lives, yet they play an integral role in our health and well-being.

Defined by Design spotlights how design shapes our lives, revealing how gender, age, and body biases affect everything we feel, think, and do. It offers valuable insights, guidelines, and tools for taking charge of everyday encounters with designs of all kinds so that you can make smarter decisions about what you wear, where you live, where you work, how you commute, and what you buy for your children. It will empower you to become a more critical consumer and will show you stellar designs that work exceptionally well for the people who use them. No matter who you are—parent, teacher, student, employer, or employee—and no matter where you are—in bed, on a plane, or even in your bathroom—*Defined by Design* will forever change how you experience your world.

Defined by Design examines the countless ways in which the design of clothing, products, and buildings affect people's daily lives. Over a period of ten years, I recorded the comments of hundreds of ordinary people: men and women, young and old, short and tall, thin and plus-size. I heard many great stories about personal struggles with everyday spaces, places, products, and things. Petite people like me couldn't reach the top shelf in the grocery store or climb on a barstool without fear of falling off. Short men couldn't find a tie that didn't hang in the wrong place. Tall people banged their heads on overhead compartments in airplanes. Large people couldn't find a car that fit them. Young children couldn't reach the bathroom sink. New mothers couldn't find a place to nurse their babies or change their diapers. Each conversation alerted me to a hidden bias, often one that I had never thought about before. That, in turn, motivated me to research what, if anything, had been written on this issue. I was shocked by what I found.

I wrote this book for people who are forced to deal with poor designs that drive them up the wall: women tired of waiting in long lines for the ladies' room, parents desperate for diaper-changing stations in public places, and new mothers struggling to find a private lactation space in the workplace. This book is for parents fearful of hidden health hazards in toys or furniture, people who have hurt themselves trying to pry open hard plastic packaging, and workers stuck in an indoor mall or a windowless workplace. It's for anyone who's curious to learn about innovative, cutting-edge designs that work for all genders, ages, and body sizes, as well as what we all can do to prevent design disasters.

As a citizen and consumer, you have a far greater ability to harness the hidden power of design in your everyday life than you might imagine. This book will show you how to wield that power to design a world for you and your family that is safer, happier, and more comfortable than before.

Laundry and dishwasher detergent pods hit the US consumer market in 2012. Designed to be colorful and convenient, they sped up the tedious routine of loading up the washing machine or the dishwasher, even making it more fun. Yet, two years later, a study based on nationwide data from 17,230 children younger than age six reported that "laundry detergent pods pose a serious poisoning risk for young children."[1] Almost three-quarters of the cases involved children under three years of age who started eating the pods by mistake. Many ended up in the hospital. By 2016, every forty-five minutes, a poison control center somewhere in the US received a call about a child who had ingested or been exposed to a laundry-detergent packet, according to Gary Smith, director of the Center for Injury Research and Policy at Nationwide Children's Hospital in Columbus, Ohio. "Concentrated detergent packets may be good for sales but not for children. . . . Packets often resemble candy or juice, and are the perfect size for a young child to grab and put in their mouth." In fact, said Smith, the Consumers Union recommended that people stop using detergent pods altogether—the second time in its history that it has made such a strong statement.[2] The colorful pods had proved to be a deadly design.

Six-year-old Karl Clermont of suburban Chicago was killed instantly when the family's thirty-two-inch television fell on him. He was one of more than 360 children age ten or younger killed by falling TVs from 2000 to 2013.[3] According to the US Consumer Product Safety Commission (CPSC), in 2010 alone, emergency rooms in the United States reported an estimated twenty thousand injuries related to unstable TVs. "We view it as one of the most dangerous hidden hazards in the home," said Scott Wolfson of the CPSC.[4]

An article titled "Killer Chairs: How Desk Jobs Ruin Your Health" in the October 14, 2014, issue of *Scientific American*—based on eighteen studies over sixteen years, covering eight hundred thousand people—asserted that "we live amid a sea of killer chairs: adjustable, swivel, recliner, wing, club, chaise longue, arm, four-legged, three-legged, wood leather, plastic, car, plane, train, dining and bar."[5] The design of our homes and work environments can contribute to obesity and have dramatic effects on our health. Sitting is the new smoking.

The Acropolis Museum in Athens, Greece, attracts more than four thousand visitors a day.[6] Climbing along transparent stairways and glass-floored galleries, museum patrons marvel at archaeological treasures below. The design reflects the architects' concept of bathing the 150,000-square-foot exhibition space in ambient natural light, a quality hailed by critics and visitors alike. But those glass-floored galleries and stairway promenades provide visitors with another spatial experience omitted from the designer's fact sheet: a sneak peek up the skirts and dresses of women and girls.

A similar problem with a glass stairway in a $105 million Columbus, Ohio, courthouse made CNN headlines in 2011. According to Judge Julie Lynch, who wears a dress under her robe almost every day, "When you stand under the stairwell, you can see right up through them."[7] Security guards had to warn women about taking the stairs.

At the University of Iowa in the 1970s, football coach Hayden Fry, a psychology major, ordered the visiting team's locker room painted pink. The "sissy color" sent a message about the masculinity of the opponents. As part of Kinnick Stadium's $88 million renovation in 2005, university officials took Fry's idea to a new level, splashing pink across the brick walls and shower floors and installing pink lockers, pink carpeting, pink sinks, pink showers, and pink urinals.[8]

What were these designers thinking—or were they? Why do certain designs create "points of pain" like these—and what can we do about them? Why are some people unfairly disadvantaged by the design of particular spaces, places, and products, while others are not? On the flip side, what innovative designs create level playing fields that advantage us all?

Our built environment and the products that we use every day contain many biases so familiar to us that we don't even recognize them. Most of us take for granted the design of spaces, places, and things. If we have problems using them, we tend to blame ourselves. Design affects the quality of our lives in profound ways. From the largest to the smallest of spaces, from the most public to the most private, subtle design distinctions perpetuate human inequalities.

Many of us are plagued by the biases—intentional or not—that went into the conception, development, or production of certain fashions, products, or buildings. Insensitive designs can widen psychological, social, cultural, and generational divides that privilege one gender, age, or body type over another. At one end of the spectrum, poorly designed products, fashions, and spaces can cause minor annoyance and frustration. At the other end, they can cause serious injury—or death.

Defined by Design explores the mysteries behind gender, age, and body biases in fashion, product, and building design. Some gender biases in design, such as toy preferences for babies, may reflect innate differences between the sexes. Other designs, such as the layouts of department stores and shopping malls, are architectural and design responses to culturally determined gender roles. And others, such as the planning and design of public restrooms, impose inequality by treating genuine differences as if they didn't exist.

Some age biases in design reflect the fact that young children and senior citizens aren't the ones designing the products they use and the spaces and places they inhabit. Some body biases reflect an outmoded physical environment that hasn't kept pace with the proliferation of oversized people and the increasing diversity of body types, both large and small.

Not all biases in design disadvantage people of one gender or the other. But when they do, the burden tends to fall disproportionately on women. Not all biases in design disadvantage people of a certain age group. But when they do, the burden falls disproportionately on children or the elderly. Not all biases in design disadvantage people of a certain body type. But when they do, the burden falls disproportionately on the petite or oversized, in addition to those with physical disabilities, both visible and invisible—anyone who is "not average."

As French sociologist and philosopher Henri Lefebvre argued, "Space is not a scientific object removed from ideology and politics; it has always been political."[9]

Malcolm Gladwell's insightful analyses in his 2000 best seller *The Tipping Point: How Little Things Can Make a Big Difference* changed the way we think about selling products and disseminating ideas. Gladwell devoted two chapters to "the power of context," how tinkering with the smallest details of our immediate environment can have major effects on our lives, how "in ways that we don't necessarily appreciate, our inner states are the result of our outer circumstances." Building upon *The Tipping Point* by zeroing in on the power of context, *Defined by Design*, too, will change the way you view your world.

Part 1

FASHION DESIGN

Chapter 1

SKIN TIGHT:
CLOTHING AND FASHION DESIGN

"I have problems looking for clothes because I'm short. Finding a blouse is hard. It may fit, but it's way too long. I'm hoping that they have a petite size in the blouse that I want. I have to find a specialty store that may have my size." (Female, white, age 61, 4′ 11″, 200 lb.)

"A few things about fashion and my personal frustrations with most retail stores: First, retail stores (especially boutiques or niche fashion) generally have very limited clothing options for men, as well as for larger men and women—rather surprising considering the fact that such a large portion of the US is overweight. Second, most of the clothing options for larger men and women seem rather conservative and usually not very 'sexy.' Third, rarely do I see dignifying or alluring in-store advertisements or representations of larger men or women. Finally, men's clothing is overwhelmingly advertised/promoted to appeal to affluent heterosexuals (the football- or polo-playing, yacht-sailing Hemingway-esque man's man), raising questions about advertising and social normalization. These are some of the reasons that I tend to shop at thrift stores or order clothes via the Internet." (Male, white, age 39, 5′11″, 230 lb.)

It's commencement day. Hundreds of family members and friends are in the audience. All eyes are on the graduates as they walk across the stage in their caps and gowns, one by one. As each student's name is called, tension mounts. As one of them climbs the stairs, she trips and falls. All eyes land on her shoes: four-inch pumps.

The decisions we make every day about which clothes and shoes to

25

wear affect us in ways that most of us don't think about—until disaster strikes. The consequences of clothes and shoes whose designs are mismatched with our bodies may not be readily apparent, but they can have long-lasting effects on our health and well-being. The most obvious cases of disadvantaging by design may occur at the smallest scale of all: clothing. The fashion industry dictates our appearance, which clothes we wear regularly, and which clothes hang listlessly in our closets. Both women and men are subject to the whims of the fashion industry, yet because of the importance of clothing and body image from girlhood and beyond, women are often more adversely affected.

MENSWEAR

Some clothing designs can prove disadvantageous to men's health. While men's pants pockets, in front and in back, are deep enough to hold a wallet—offering men flexibility and security that women do not have—routinely carrying wallets in back pockets can lead to serious back pain. The problem is not from carrying wallets but rather sitting on them for eight to ten hours a day.

Just as a crooked building foundation can cause structural failure, years of sitting on wallets can cause an imbalance in the pelvis, the lowermost part of the spine. Improper alignment of the pelvis can damage a man's hips, his lower back, and even his neck. A report in the *New England Journal of Medicine* first referred to this problem as "credit-carditis."[1] It's also known as wallet sciatica. When the position of the pelvic bones is shifted, tissues on one side of the body are stretched while those on the other side are contracted. The rest of the body compensates for this change in balance. Continuous pressure on the piriformis muscle in the buttocks, connected to the sciatic nerve, results in pain radiating throughout the back and hip. It may also affect one's gait and standing posture. Men are better off carrying money in a money clip in a front pocket, or in a thin wallet in an inner front jacket pocket. Emptying out-of-date cards and clutter and carrying a lighter load can also help.

Many men who don't fit the average mold struggle to find

clothing that fits them. The search can be both demeaning and demoralizing. Short men, many of whom are Asian or Latino, find fewer options in clothing designs. The same is true for tall men, who may find clothes that are long enough but too wide. Men whose feet are smaller or larger than the norm can also find shoe shopping to be a frustrating experience. Despite today's limitless opportunities to order shoes over the Internet, many men (and women) refuse to buy a pair of shoes without trying them on.

Men's ties come in only one size. But men come in many different sizes: tall, short, fat, thin—all of which affects where the tie ends up resting on their bodies. Short, thin men are at a special disadvantage. As one friend put it, "Neckties are too long for short men. You can't position them right. So instead of going to your belly, they end up way below the belt." As his wife said, "Neckties are the stupidest things ever invented! Men's belts come in different sizes, but why not ties?"

FOOTBALL HELMETS AND CONCUSSIONS

"In the United States, professional football is the most popular sport by a landslide. People love the history, competitiveness, and mostly the hard hitting of the sport. It is so popular because you can see the world's greatest athletes compete with one another on such a physical level. But such an extreme physical level also shortens the careers of the best athletes of the game. It is hard for me to understand why there is not more money and time spent on the design of the helmets. This year, a team spent $1.2 billion on a stadium while one of the best quarterbacks in the league, Ben Roethlisberger, got his fourth concussion by taking a knee to the top of the helmet. This does not seem right. As a spectator, I want to see the best possible athletes on the field. I do not want inadequate equipment design to hinder the game." (Male, white, age 23, 6′, 180 lb.)

Sports-related concussions affect 1.6–3.8 million people each year in the United States, and nearly 30 percent of these concussions happen to children between five and nineteen years of age.[2] Male and female athletes in a variety of sports—football, hockey, base-ball, softball, cycling, speed skating, horseback riding, and skiing, to name a few—wear helmets for protection. Yet the design of football helmets, an item worn nearly exclusively by male athletes, makes the players of this high-contact, dangerous sport especially vulnerable to injury.

Each year in the United States, roughly 1.1 million high school students play football, 3 million play youth football, and 100,000 combined play in the National Football League (NFL), college, junior college, Arena, and semipro.[3] According to *Sports Illustrated*, eleven high school football players died before the end of 2015 during in-season and preseason incidents, and more than half the deaths were caused by head injuries. The *Sports Illustrated* article features heart-breaking profiles of each of the players struck down on the field.[4] In 2014, eleven people died from high school football injuries; eighteen died in 2013. Data from the University of North Carolina's National Center for Catastrophic Sport Injury Research revealed that more than one hundred children died from high school football–related injuries in the last decade.[5] The dangers of suffering concussions while under the football helmet have prompted extensive national media coverage.

According to Dr. Douglas Casa, chief executive officer of the University of Connecticut's Korey Stringer Institute (KSI), named after the NFL player who died from heat stroke in 2001, states and schools aren't putting the right policies in place to protect their athletes. "The best practices are not being followed. . . . I'm kind of mystified, but people are just not implementing evidence-based medicine and policies at the high school level. I'm not saying they're not interested in it, but they're just not doing it."[6] KSI tracks states that meet basic standards for safety in sports. According to an October 2015 *Huffington Post* article, no state had met KSI's minimum best practices when it came to concussion management, emergency action plans, and defibrillators.[7]

According to an analysis of peer-reviewed studies on head trauma in high school sports, high school football players are nearly twice as likely as college players to sustain a concussion; they suffered 11.2 concussions for every ten thousand games and practices, while the rate for college players was 6.3. The authors of the analysis urged caution in interpreting the results, because many concussions go unreported and data is limited.[8]

Researchers at Purdue University discovered brain damage in high school football players who had suffered concussions—as well as those who had not—and that repetitive hits to the head can cause as much damage as concussion-causing hits. The average high school football lineman receives one thousand to fifteen hundred shots to the head during a single football season.[9]

Another study, from the Colorado School of Public Health at the University of Colorado Anschutz Medical Campus, was the first national football concussion research to evaluate how helmets performed when worn by young athletes actually playing the game, rather than how helmets performed in impact testing in a laboratory. It revealed that all approved helmets evaluated in the study performed similarly, regardless of cost, and that older, reconditioned helmets performed similarly to new helmets as long as the reconditioning had been done recently (within twelve months prior to use). Yet players wearing old helmets that had not been recently reconditioned suffered longer concussion symptoms than those who wore new helmets.[10]

Many of these concussions result in traumatic brain injury, the effects of which can last a lifetime. A significant impact to the head causes the brain to move about inside the skull and bump against bone. This can cause the brain to stretch and twist, breaking nerve fibers and blood vessels. Research suggests that even though professional football players—being bigger and stronger—collide with greater impact than younger players, children and teenagers may be even more likely to suffer from prolonged brain swelling after a concussion. High school athletes may take longer to recover than college or older athletes and may be more susceptible to complications. A team of researchers from Vanderbilt University School of Medicine, whose results were published in *Surgical Neurology International,* examined recovery from sports-related concussions among high school and collegiate athletics and found that athletes age thirteen to sixteen took longer to return to their neurocognitive and symptom baselines than athletes eighteen to twenty-two years of age.

They discovered statistically significant differences between the two age groups on verbal memory, visual memory, reaction time, and postconcussion symptom scale.[11]

Concussions vary in severity, and symptoms can include headache, dizziness, nausea, vomiting, confusion, blurred vision, tinnitus (ringing in the ears), double vision, and loss of consciousness. Athletes who suffer repeated and severe concussions may experience long-term effects such as depression, memory loss, dementia, and other serious neurological problems.

Some NFL players suffering from chronic traumatic encephalopathy, a degenerative brain disease caused by repeated blows to the head, have ended up homicidal or suicidal. In 2011, former Chicago Bears star Dave Duerson committed suicide by shooting himself in the chest, in order to leave his brain to science. In 2012, Ray Easterling, former defensive back for the Atlanta Falcons, killed himself with a gun. In an interview with Fox Sports, his widow, Mary Ann Easterling, said: "He felt like his brain was falling off. . . . He was losing control. He couldn't remember things from five minutes ago."[12] Just a few weeks later, former San Diego Chargers and New England Patriots linebacker Junior Seau put a shotgun to his sternum and pulled the trigger. Easterling was the lead plaintiff in one of the player lawsuits against the NFL and had been well aware of the perils of concussions.

Roughly one hundred former NFL players filed a federal lawsuit, claiming that Riddell, NFL's official helmet maker from 1989 to 2014, made false claims about its helmet's ability to protect against concussions and brain injuries. In 2013, more than twenty thousand former NFL players sued the league, arguing that not enough was done to inform players about dangers of concussions in the past and still not enough is being done to care for injured players today.[13]

In 2016, an appellate court affirmed the settlement in the $1 billion lawsuit, providing up to $5 million to individual players with severe neurological diseases.[14] In the deal, the NFL admitted no fault and, according to a *New York Times* article, insisted that *all* retired players be included in the settlement, not only those who originally sued the league. Under the terms of the settlement, players will be paid up to $5 million if they develop Alzheimer's, amyotrophic lateral sclerosis (ALS), Parkinson's, or severe dementia or if they had developed chronic traumatic encephalopathy (CTE) before the settlement was approved. The payment amount to each player is based on his age and number of years in the league. As the *New York Times* reported: "The emphatic decision by the appeals court on Monday moved the N.F.L. a step closer to ending one of its most contentious, embarrassing and expensive legal challenges. The spectacle of thousands of former players suing the league for lying to them, and the prospect that some players might have testified in court about the harm they suffered, led the league to promise to pay potentially hundreds of millions of dollars to former players in dire straits."[15]

The concussion crisis was the centerpiece of the 2015 film *Concussion*, which tells the story of forensic pathologist Dr. Bennet Omalu (played by Will Smith), who discovered chronic traumatic encephalopathy while autopsying the brain of former Pittsburgh Steelers All-Pro Mike Webster. A PBS Frontline documentary, *League of Denial,* reported on football, the brain, and the NFL's unethical behavior.

Yet as Ken Reed has argued in the *Huffington Post:* "As a society, we need to take the attention this film will generate and move it off the NFL and refocus it on youth and high school football. There are less than 2,000 players in the NFL. The number of youth and high school players in this country is greater than three million."[16] Many high school athletes just use whatever equipment is available and suffer the consequences.

Parents of football players should ask their coach or athletic director about the type of helmet that their team currently uses and its safety record. They must learn to recognize the symptoms of short-term and long-term brain injuries that can often go unnoticed as a result of concussions. Two excellent resources for parents and players are the Brain Injury Association and the American Academy of Neurology.[17] In addition, as professor Dawn Comstock, senior author of the study at the University of Colorado, urged: "Many parents don't think to ask if the helmet issued to their child is new or previously used or, if not new, when it was last reconditioned. Parents should be asking questions and not assuming that the helmet assigned to their child is safe."[18]

In 2015, three members of the US Congress introduced the High School Football Safety Study Act, which would require the Centers for Disease Control and Prevention to examine the causes of football-related deaths and make recommendations about how to prevent them. As Rep. Cedric Richmond (D-LA) stated: "It is our responsibility to ensure that we leave no stone unturned to make the game as safe as possible for young people and prevent these tragedies from happening in the future. Moving forward, I hope this legislation will start that process and begin a national conversation about how to better protect youth in football."[19]

HIGH HEELS AND HIGH MEDICAL BILLS

> "I don't understand why women have to wear heels. I feel that it's targeted for the opposite gender. Otherwise why wouldn't men wear high heels? It gives stature, but after three hours on my feet, I am ready to die." (Female, Pacific Islander, age 32, 5′5″, 135 lb.)

> "I usually wear heels when I go out at night or on the weekends. Drainage grates, snow grates, or really any and all grates on sidewalks are especially annoying when wearing heels. Stilettos get caught in the openings, making it very difficult to walk and sometimes even cause women to fall. When walking over a large grate, women usually have to walk on the balls of their feet. In the event that the design calls for a grate, designers should make sure there is adequate space for one to maneuver around it." (Female, white, age 25, 5′4″, 120 lb.)

Women's fashions have long called for high heels, especially since the 1950s, when stiletto heels were first introduced. Named after the stiletto dagger, stilettos range in length from about one inch to eight inches or more if atop a platform sole. The most slender Italian-style stilettos are less than a quarter of an inch in diameter. They have been associated with images of femme fatale and seduction.

Yet, as many women and their doctors can attest, high heels can prove dangerous and costly. Research based on data from the Consumer Product Safety Commission's National Electronic Injury Surveillance System, published in the *Journal of Foot and Ankle Surgery*, showed that emergency-room visits for injuries associated with wearing high heels nearly doubled between 2002 and 2012. During that time, a total of 3,294 injuries, representing an estimated 123,355 high-heel related injuries, were treated in US emergency departments. Most injuries, over 80 percent, were to the ankle or foot, and just under 20 percent involved the knee, trunk, shoulder, head, or neck. Women in their twenties, followed by those in their thirties, were most likely to suffer an injury. White women had the largest number of heel-related injuries, yet the rate of injury for black women was double that of whites. Nearly half the injuries occurred in the home. As lead investigator Gerald McGwin, a professor in the Department of Epidemiology at the University of Alabama School of Public Health, noted, "Some historians suggest that high-heeled shoes have been around for nearly 300 years, and that medical professionals have been warning wearers about the dangers of such shoes for the same amount of time."[20]

Short-term shoe-related problems include ankle sprains and breaks, yet the damage from these injuries can result in symptoms that haunt women even years later.[21] Some designs—stilettos, steep wedges, and thick platforms—can interfere with driving, with the heel getting wedged under the pedals or caught under floor mats. Drivers wearing high heels have a tendency to press the pedals with just the tips of their toes, which may not provide enough force when needed to slam on the brakes in an emergency.[22] According to Adrienne Savoy, a driving instructor for DriversEd.com, the higher the heel the more a person is in danger: "When you're wearing high heels, it's nearly impossible for the heel to stay steady on top of the mat, which would delay the reaction time between the accelerator and the brake. Sometimes you only have a second to react, so that could be a split second you have to prevent a crash."[23] Conceivably, in the case of a car accident, shoe style could affect insurance compensation. Although a different shoe style completely, flip-flops can be just as dangerous because they can also get caught under pedals. As *Consumer Reports* says, "Wearing appropriate footwear while driving is critical."[24]

Because of the tremendous pressure transmitted through the heel, stilettos can damage carpets, hardwood floors, and outdoor lawns. Indentations from high heels have also posed problems for aircraft floor panels (which have honeycomb sandwich structures).

Researchers in composite materials testing and design have shown that highly concentrated loads, such as those carried by high heels, cause the greatest damage to aircraft floors. In fact, during preflight safety demonstrations airline passengers are warned to remove their high heels when exiting the plane in case of an emergency because pointy heels can puncture the inflatable slide. Even on women of small build, heels create dynamic loads of more than one thousand pounds per square inch. Ironically, a full-grown elephant exerts about twenty-five to thirty pounds of pressure per inch because the weight is spread across its large feet.

Researchers have linked high heels to knee osteoarthritis, a painful, degenerative joint disease that involves the breakdown of cartilage around the knee. As one might expect, narrow stiletto heels can pose major problems, but, surprisingly, so can wide heels. Because wide-heeled shoes feel more stable, women tend to wear them all day long. They're better for feet than stiletto heels but equally bad for knees. Walking on high heels places undue stress on both the front and the back of the knee.

High heels also cause various other foot problems, such as meta-tarsalgia (pain in the ball of the foot). Heels can lead to Morton's neuroma, a condition ten times more common in women than men and caused by a thickening of tissue around a nerve between the third and fourth toes. Irritation and pressure from the weight high heels place on the ball of the foot are usually the culprits.

But high heels aren't the only problem with the design of women's footwear. Pointed-toe shoes, often in high style, can lead to bunions, calluses, and hammertoe. The same can be said for shoes that pinch or scrunch the wearer's toes.

The Framingham Foot Study, published in 2009, is one of the most comprehensive studies; based on 3,378 participants, it compared gender differences in foot pain and type of shoe.[25] Researchers found that women who in the past wore athletic shoes or casual sneakers with good fit, foot posture, and shock absorption characteristics were 67 percent less likely to report hindfoot pain, even after adjusting for age and weight. High heels or pumps, sandals, and slippers were associated with hind foot pain.[26] By contrast, researchers found no such association between foot pain and choice of shoes in men.

For women suffering serious foot pain who insist on squeezing into fashionable high heels with narrow toes, an increasingly popular trend is an invasive procedure called cosmetic toe modification, a surgical shaving down of the bones of the second and third toes. Some women have their pinky toes severed to help their feet slide into stilettos. Others use Botox injections to loosen up muscles pulling on the toe. According to Dr. Angelo Volandes, a specialist in internal medicine at Massachusetts General Hospital whose research addresses ethical issues in medicine, the incidence of such procedures is "skyrocketing . . . fashion tastes are what they are, and people are willing to go through extremes, and this is just one additional extreme." He refers to it as the Cinderella-type phenomenon.[27]

High heels can be hazardous in emergency situations. For example, during the September 11, 2001, terrorist attacks and evacuation of New York's World Trade Center towers, women wearing high heels and men in new dress shoes moved more slowly and were reported to have caused backups in stairs. Some discarded their shoes so they could escape more quickly, but they were confronted with large pieces of debris and broken glass.[28]

Spike heels can get caught in crevices in sidewalks, cobblestone streets, outdoor decks, sewer grates, and escalators. At Macy's flagship store in New York City's Herald Square, the vintage wooden escalators installed in 1902 have long been a popular tourist attraction. Yet to this day, women's spike heels can get trapped in the treads.

Summer footwear can cause problems too. According to chiropractors Todd and Sheldon Sinett in their 2008 book, *The Truth about Back Pain*, "Business in chiropractic offices skyrockets in the summer months when both men and women start wearing sandals and flip-flops."[29]

So what is the ideal shoe for overall foot and leg health? According to Enzo J. Sella, an orthopedic surgeon at Yale–New Haven Hospital, low heels of one-half to three-quarters of an inch are helpful for both the front and back of the foot. Shoes with a roomy toe box prevent pinching and scrunching that can lead to painful problems.

BIG PURSES SPELL BIG PROBLEMS

> "Lately, when a patient comes in complaining of these symptoms, I walk over and pick up her purse. Without fail, it weighs a ton."
> —Karen Erickson, New York City chiropractor and spokesperson for the American Chiropractic Association[30]

> "My laptop bag hits right on my hip bone. Combine that with weight, rubbing and dry winter skin, and my hip bone and side are raw." (Female, white, age 25, 5′2″, 120 lb.)

Large purses have been the fashion rage, and, in recent years, bags have become bigger and bigger. Fashion designers finally responded to women's complaints that tiny designer purses didn't have enough space. But the roomier the bag, the more stuff women tend to shove inside. Designer bags often feature heavy leather and ornate detailing, all of which make them heavy even when empty. Wallets, lipstick, keys, cell phones, sunglasses, bottled water, laptop computers, umbrellas, and an extra pair of sneakers for a lunchtime walk can weigh down bags even more.

Overpacked purses cause women to walk lopsided, distorting their posture and resulting in aching backs, shoulders, necks, and hips. According to physical therapists, an aggravated neck or shoulder can lead to long-term upper-back problems. Overstuffed bags can also cause tingling fingers, headaches, and possibly arthritis. A common side effect is that the wearer's shoulders become uneven, with one shoulder slightly higher than the other. And when women talk on their cell phones while carrying their bag, this exacerbates the problem. Not only are they balancing too much weight on one side, but they're lifting the shoulder at the same time.

In a piece in the *New York Times* titled "Ouch! My Bag Is Killing Me!" Robin Ehrlich, director of the Eastside Massage Therapy Center on New York City's Upper East Side is quoted as saying: "It's an epidemic. We're busier than ever before right now and big bags are the reason."[31]

Some experts recommend a three-pound maximum. The American Chiropractic Association advises women to carry around no more than 10 percent of their body weight. Some chiropractors suggest structured bags that provide specific spots for special items so that the weight can be distributed evenly. They advise avoiding long straps and chain handles, as well as slouchy, unstructured canvas bags that allow their contents to shift around, throwing off the wearer's balance.

DOUBLE-STANDARDS ON THE DANCE FLOOR AND ON THE BEACH

Women's clothing has become tighter and tighter, revealing more body contours and exposing more skin. Fashion that promotes women as sex objects has been in style for decades. By contrast, men's pants have usually been loose-fitting. While teenage girls wear skintight jeans, most teenage boys today favor baggy pants. Men's clothing is loose enough to contain deep pockets that can hold their wallets. Women's pockets are rarely large enough to hold a wallet, hence the need to carry a purse slung over the shoulder.

Women who enjoy dancing are disadvantaged by the design of clothing that makes it difficult to carry their money or identification with them onto the dance floor. Unless they enlist a friend to watch their possessions, they may return to find their wallets stolen. How many cases of identity theft may result from women leaving their purses unattended on barstools and alongside the dance floor? By comparison, how many male dancers are forced to leave their wallets behind?

The zipper in men's pants is designed to open easily to allow for speedy urination. The zipper in women's pants resembles that of a man's, requiring women to disrobe and pull their pants down in order to urinate. Some women have come up with a new design for women's pants that places the zipper underneath the crotch, enabling women to squat atop a toilet and urinate without the need to disrobe.

Differences in the design of women's and men's swimwear influences their recreational behavior at a beach or pool, as well as the safety of their possessions. Women's bathing suits cling tightly to the skin, with no air to spare, whereas men's swim trunks are loose-fitting and often include a small buttoned or zippered pocket allowing them to carry nonelectronic keys into the water. Women swimming alone have no option but to leave their belongings unattended, hiding their valuables with their towels on the sand, where they are vulnerable to theft. If women are with others, they must take turns swimming while one of them watches their belongings.

WHAT'S WRONG WITH WOMEN'S THONGS?

"I'm a size 14 or 40B woman who likes quality lingerie that's colorful and sexy (not cheap). But I can't find it, even online. Listen up, Victoria's Secret and Garnet Hill!" (Female, white, age 66, 5′6″, 160 lb.)

In 1939, New York City Mayor Fiorello LaGuardia requested that the city's exotic dancers and strip club performers dress in more appropriate attire, and ever since, the thong has been their attire of choice. In 1974, fashion designer Rudi Gernreich introduced the modern thong.[32] By 2005, thongs had catapulted to 25 percent of the US panty market.[33] Eliminating the visible panty line (famously nicknamed "VPL" in Woody Allen's 1977 Academy Award–winning film, *Annie Hall*), they provide an attractive, seamless look when worn under leggings, tight pants, or skirts.

The problem is that not only are thongs uncomfortable, but according to a review of scientific literature, some women who wear thongs report an increase in urinary tract or yeast infections because when a thong slides back and forth during movement, it can transfer fecal bacteria from the anus to the urethra.[34] In addition, some physicians recommend that women prone to vulvar irritation and vaginitis avoid wearing thongs.

Thongs can also cause trouble during pregnancy. The constant rubbing of a thong can tear the skin between the rectum and the vagina, causing tiny perineal fissures. These open cuts may become prone to infection, including sexually transmitted diseases.

Women wearing tight thong underwear or tight blue jeans (especially when worn without underwear) are also susceptible to urethral syndrome, a condition that increases the need for daytime urination to as often as every thirty to sixty minutes.[35] Synthetic fabrics such as spandex and acrylics in underwear can lead to allergic reactions. Wearing thongs only for special occasions makes women and girls less vulnerable to health problems.

Before the thong, the fashion in women's underwear had gone from "granny panties" (such as those immortalized in the 2001 film *Bridget Jones's Diary*) to bikini briefs to French cut. Ironically, today it may have come full circle. As of 2015, as reported in the *New York Times*, data provided by the research company NPD Group revealed that sales of thongs had decreased in the past year, while sales of briefs, boy shorts, and "granny panties" rose a collective 17 percent. As Bernadette Kissane, an apparel analyst at the market intelligence firm Euromonitor, remarked: "Within millennial and Generation Y consumer groups, it's considered cool to be wearing full-bottom underwear. . . . Thongs have had their moment."[36] Marshal Cohen, chief industry analyst at NPD Group, confirmed this trend: "The big surprise is young women moving to full coverage panties and migrating away from the thong." Innovations in "seamless" materials, younger consumers' demand for comfort, and the popularity of sweatpants, a loose style that makes VPL irrelevant, have contributed to the decline of thong sales. Increasingly, consumers are buying lingerie online. It's a good choice for consumers who feel uncomfortable shopping for intimate wear in public and makes it easy for them to repurchase favorite items.[37]

UNDER WRAPS: FEMININE HYGIENE TECHNOLOGY[38]

Throughout history and across cultures, certain clothing designs for women and girls have had negative impacts on their physical and mental health. In ancient China, upper-class women bound their feet to keep their shape dainty. The binding repositioned their bones, making the simple act of walking painful. In the Victorian era, women laced up corsets so tightly that they affected their breathing. And even in the late twentieth century, the design of certain feminine hygiene devices distributed to millions of women as part of a massive promotional campaign resulted in injury or death for some users.

The design of feminine hygiene technology historically disadvantaged women, restricting their participation in school, in the workplace, and in sports. Tampons are a relatively recent invention that liberated women. Before tampons became the norm, women used bulky sanitary pads. As historian Sharra Vostral notes in her 2008 book, *Under Wraps: A History of Menstrual Hygiene Technology*, the women's suffrage movement of the 1910s and 1920s, along with increased public attention to practices of sanitation and hygiene, helped set the stage for the purchase and use of sanitary napkins. Yet advertising of feminine hygiene products and women's use of them—concealed in purses, invisible to the public eye—has always been discreet. Vostral refers to this as the "technology of passing."

Before the invention of disposable sanitary napkins, women used cloth pads, which they would wash and reuse. During the nineteenth century, American women produced these cloths by hand, folding and sewing cotton, gauze, flannel, or rags into pads that they pinned into their underwear. Layered petticoats, rubber aprons, and bloomers helped protect outerwear from stains.[39]

In his 1873 book, *Sex in Education; or, A Fair Chance for the Girls,* Dr. Edward Clarke argued that a woman's body could not function properly when expending energy in two different biological purposes, such as using brain energy to study while using reproductive energy to menstruate.[40] He proposed the concept of "periodicity," requiring a mandatory rest week from school during menstruation.

Clarke's book became an instant best seller. Over the course of thirteen years, it was published in seventeen editions throughout the United States and as far away as Great Britain and the Middle East. Clarke's influence was so strong that during their menstrual periods, young women paid a price by missing school days, remaining on bed rest, and sometimes being excluded from co-educational schools.

In 1896, Johnson & Johnson introduced Lister's Towels, the first mass-produced sanitary napkins. But these disposable, gauze-covered cotton pads didn't catch on at first. Only toward the end of World War I, when medical practitioners discouraged women from producing their own menstrual hygiene products, did the use of commercial sanitary napkins become widespread. One noted advantage was that the commercial products did a better job of not only catching blood but also trapping odor.

During World War I, cellucotton, a material produced from cellulose wood pulp, was used as surgical dressing for wounded soldiers. Nurses began using cellucotton bandages for their periods, and based upon their feedback, Kimberly-Clark started developing cellucotton sanitary napkins. The brand name Kotex (Cotton-like TEXture) was the target of a successful 1921 national advertising campaign in the *Ladies' Home Journal.*

The development of tampons remedied the shortcomings of sanitary pads. Inserted directly into the vagina, they hid menstrual blood and scents; left no telltale outlines; required no belts, harnesses, or pins; and promoted mobility and freedom—and while wearing them, women could even swim and enjoy sports.

Members of some religious orders, including many Catholics, advocated against the use of tampons, arguing that they destroyed the hymen and that girls would no longer be virgins eligible for marriage. Others argued that tampons would be sexually stimulating and induce eroticism. A report titled "Sanitary Pads and Tampons" issued by *Consumer Reports* in 1949 refuted these claims, as did physician Robert Dickinson in his 1945 article in the *Journal of the American Medical Association.*[41]

Just as Kotex introduced sanitary pads during the 1920s as women obtained the right to vote, during the early 1970s, at the peak of the feminist movement, beltless sanitary pads emerged. New double-stick adhesives on the underside of the pad that could adhere to underwear made this updated design possible. With brand names like "New Freedom" and "Stayfree," they reminded women of their recent political and economic gains.

The 1970s proved to be a watershed decade when a new tampon design was introduced that redefined the industry but ultimately posed a serious health threat. With its mushroom, umbrella-like design, Proctor & Gamble's new Rely tampon expanded outward rather than vertically, for better leak prevention. Instead of traditional cotton fibers, Rely was made of polyester foam cubes and chips of carboxymethylcellulose, a thickening agent used in puddings and ice cream, all encapsulated in a polyester teabag-like pouch.

Between 1975 and 1980, forty-five million free samples of Rely tampons were distributed. Yet during this time, many women began to experience serious health problems that appeared to be linked to the materials used in Rely. When mixed with the bacterial strain *Staphylococcus aureus* harbored in some women's bodies, these materials had toxic effects: women experienced flu-like symptoms including fever, chills, hypotension, rash, and scaly skin.

The issue came to a head with the lawsuit of a husband, Michael Kehm, whose wife, a twenty-five-year-old mother of two, died on September 6, 1980, from what is now known as toxic shock syndrome. Patricia Kehm, whose sister had urged her to try Rely, had worn the tampons for only four days when she developed a high fever, vomiting, and fatigue. Michael Kehm was awarded $300,000 in compensatory damages, and although the jury found Proctor & Gamble guilty of negligence because executives had known about toxic shock syndrome in the summer before Patricia Kehm died, the company was not ordered to pay punitive damages.

By 1980, 814 clinical cases of toxic shock syndrome and 38 deaths had been reported. No doubt many other cases went undetected. More than 1,000 lawsuits were filed against Proctor & Gamble, which continued to send out 2.5 million free samples even in July 1980 when reports postulated a link between Rely and toxic shock syndrome. P&G removed Rely from store shelves on September 22, 1980. Public health officials required that inserts about safety and use appear in tampon product boxes, and thousands of women stopped using tampons altogether.[42]

WIDOWS' WEAR, VEILS, AND VITAMINS; SOS FOR SARIS

Recall the spectacle created by newly widowed Scarlett O'Hara merrily dancing away in her jet-black evening gown in Margaret Mitchell's famous saga, *Gone with the Wind*.

Wearing black clothing to signify a period of mourning is a custom dating back to at least ancient Roman times. Throughout the Middle Ages and the Renaissance, women in mourning wore black caps and veils. In nineteenth-century England, women in mourning were expected to wear an ensemble of heavy black clothing, black caps and bonnets, and black crepe veils known as "widow's weeds" for up to four years after the death of a loved one.

In the United States in the nineteenth century, etiquette manuals mandating the length of time and apparel required of mourners placed the heaviest burden on widows. Women were to wear full black for the first two years, nonreflective black Parramatta and crape for the first year, nine months of dull black silk heavily trimmed with crape, and three months when crape would be discarded. Widows could change into colors of half-mourning—grays, lavender, black and white—during only the final months. The widow's bonnet included a long black veil, and her handkerchiefs featured a black trim.

Failing to wear this apparel or engaging in inappropriate behavior while dressed in widow's wear demonstrated a lack of respect for the deceased, and it carried a high social cost.[43]

In many cultures, women in mourning wore black for years following the death of a loved one. Such was the custom in rural Greek, Italian, Spanish, and Portuguese cultures, in which women were the chief mourners, forced to wear black forever as a badge of their loss. By contrast, Greek widowers had minimal clothing changes beyond a black armband that they wore for about a year. Even well into the twentieth century, widows—but never widowers—in India were expected to throw themselves onto the funeral pyre in sacrifice after their husband's death.[44]

Many Muslim women throughout the world cover their bodies from head to toe, including their face and hands, a tradition long dictated by religious customs. Ironically, even if they reside in a sunny, desert climate, their skin rarely sees the sun. Numerous studies have shown that due to the absence of exposure to sunlight, veiled women suffer from greater deficiencies in vitamin D than other women. Because we receive most of our vitamin D from sun-induced physiological processes rather than from our diet, medical researchers believe that hypovitaminosis D due to lack of sunlight is a major contributing factor to vitamin D deficiency.

One study compared vitamin D levels in Turkish veiled women and (nonveiled) men, workers in Turkey, and migrant workers in Germany. Turkish women living in Germany had lower vitamin D levels than their female counterparts in Turkey, where sunlight is more plentiful, but compared with Turkish men, Turkish women exhibited lower levels of vitamin D because of their veils. Among the potential health consequences are increased rates of various internal cancers, including breast and ovarian; harmful effects on the cardio-vascular system; and susceptibility to bone frailty and hip fractures.[45]

On the Indian subcontinent, traditional women's clothing—the long, loose sari—can be fatal when women cook near open flames and when the stove is used on a floor. So-called kitchen fires have now reached epidemic proportions. Clothing fires have also been severe among children in Delhi, Pune, Hyderabad, and Bangalore. In warm coastal areas of Papua New Guinea, many patients requiring hospitalization for burns severe enough to merit treatment for shock and skin grafts were young girls injured when their grass skirts caught fire. Many of these young girls were burned because their parents had left them alone near an open cooking fire, and when their clothes ignited they panicked and ran.[46]

FASHIONS THAT ADVANTAGE BY DESIGN

A New Era of Clothing Design: 3D Body Scanners

An estimated half of the clothes bought online are returned to the seller, often because they're the wrong size. Clothes that are sent in the wrong size frustrate buyers and cost millions of dollars in extra shipping costs and warehouse fees.[47]

Some fascinating developments at the cutting edge of apparel research are revolutionizing the world of fashion design. Susan Ashdown and Suzanne Locker at Cornell University used 3D body scanners to study the complex problems of clothing design and fit and to address the reality that people of a single size come in various shapes and proportions. For example, although a group of women may all take size 10 clothing, each has a different hip shape, torso length, and bust measurement, all of which affect how their clothing fits them.[48] A single scan captures about three hundred thousand points on the body and provides opportunities for virtual try-ons, helping consumers identify clothing that fits them the best.

At Brooks Brothers' New York City retail store, customers are measured using a 3D body scanner, after which they consult with a sales professional about their fit preferences, such as loose or form-fitting clothing. The salesperson helps them select style, fabrics, and design features from a computer screen. The data from the scan and the patterns for each customer are stored for reorders.

At Alton Lane stores in New York City, Chicago, and Washington, DC, shoppers stand inside a dark booth to have their measurements taken for custom-fitted suits. Chris Gayomali tried it out for *Fast Company*. He described the dazzling array of lights and sensors that come to life inside the booth: "Immediately bright white lights begin to swirl around me in a sequence, firing off in a synchronized clockwise pattern around my body. A soothing piano concerto begins flowing from the booth's speakers. It feels like I'm having my mind wiped by one of those *Men in Black* memory zappers. Or maybe I'm being beamed up by a UFO."[49]

Each body scanner costs about $15,000. It has fourteen sensors at various heights to take more than four hundred measurements around the body, including height, circumferences, volume, lengths, and surface area. The scanning process takes only thirty seconds. As Gayomali put it, "What we're likely witnessing is the nascent beginnings of 3-D mapping in the clothing industry."[50]

Other retailers who provide 3D scanners for custom clothing include Indochino, Combat Gent, Suit Supply, Proper Suit, Black Lapel, and Bello Verde. Some smaller web-based companies now offer custom design and size choices for clothing such as brides-maids' dresses; fleece jackets; and military, school, and industrial uniforms. These include IC3D (Interactive Custom Clothes Company Designs), American Fit, and Beyond Fleece.[51]

Fit3D, Inc. takes yet a different approach. According to Greg Moore, the company's chief executive officer: "Our vision is to democratize 3D body scanning and then enable our users to receive customized products and services specifically crafted for their bodies. . . . We use only one single camera to capture a point cloud of roughly 500,000 vertices and 380 measurements on the body. . . . We have placed on average one system every two days since we started selling Fit3D ProScanners."[52] For a minimal fee, people can scan their bodies and then upload their data to an e-commerce portal, allowing them to buy clothes designed for a perfect fit, saving buyers and retailers both time and money. Regular use of the Fit3D Pro-Scanner also provides health-club members with detailed "before and after" body measurements, motivating them to continue with—and not give up on—their exercise routines.

Sensible Shoes for Work Become Killer Heels at Night: Adjustable High Heels

An innovative design allows a woman's shoe to transfer from a low heel that is good for walking into a more stylish high heel for more formal occasions. The lower half of the heel pulls down to disengage it from the locked high-heel position. The wearer can push the heel forward until it locks into place, recessed under the arch of the shoe. Other designs have detachable or replaceable heels. Already, several companies, such as Tanya Heath Paris and Nael Coce, have made these available.

Nasim Jahangiri and Pantea Shahsavani, two students at Simon Fraser University in Vancouver, British Columbia, have come up with an even more sophisticated take on the adjustable high-heel shoe, after one of them attended a wedding in five-inch heels that made for a painful experience. Their prototypic design for their "Head Over Heels" project at Simon Fraser's School of Interactive Arts and Technology featured interlocking parts in the heel that can be used to raise or lower the shoe's height. The wearer can switch from five-inch heels to two-and-a-half-inch heels by detaching the bottom portion of the interlocking heel and storing it inside the shoe's remaining heel. Interactive pressure sensors in the shoe's heel hidden inside a front panel of the shoe vibrate after two hours, a reminder that it's time to adjust the height of the heels.[53]

Part 2

PRODUCT DESIGN

Chapter 2

PLAY AT YOUR OWN RISK: DESIGNING PRODUCTS FOR CHILDREN

"It's sort of a hollow victory if the CPSC [Consumer Product Safety Commission] doesn't issue an alert. There are tens of thousands of playgrounds with this bad design all over the country. But the CPSC really needs to let people know about this."

—Scott Burton, president of Safety Play, Inc.[1]

Children's products are big business. Parents enjoy buying toys for their children, and children delight in receiving them. The experience should be a pleasant one. Parents want the best for their children and are willing to spend a substantial portion of their income on items that many of them will soon outgrow.

Infants, children, and toddlers require products that conform to safety standards. Although the vast majority of children's products on the market are safe, all too often something slips by and disaster soon follows. The design and mass production of unsafe baby equipment, children's toys, and car seats can make the difference between life and death. Poorly designed and manufactured children's products place our most precious cargo—those least able to speak for themselves and advocate on their own behalf—in greatest danger.

CHILDREN'S PRODUCT RECALLS

On Thanksgiving in 2005, twenty-month-old Kenny Sweet of Redmond, Washington, died after swallowing nine aspirin-sized magnets that had come loose from a Magnetix construction set. His mother rushed him to the hospital with flu-like symptoms, but within minutes Kenny had died before doctors could even diagnose him. The magnets were so strong that they had pinched his intestines, twisted his bowel, and perforated his intestinal wall, allowing deadly bacteria to leak into his bloodstream. An investigation by Seattle TV station KOMO prompted a nationwide toy recall.[2]

For almost a decade, product safety advocates, mostly mothers, waged a fight against the male-dominated, $22 billion toy industry and $7 billion baby-products industry. Faulty toys and baby equipment such as cribs, playpens, high chairs, and walkers injure 250,000 children each year.

In 2007, manufacturers recalled millions of popular toys such as Thomas the Tank Engine trains and Sesame Street figures. By the end of 2007, the Consumer Product Safety Commission (CPSC), the federal safety agency charged with regulating most items in American homes, announced 107 recalls for nearly seventeen million pieces of toys, jewelry, clothing, and other items—as many recalls in a single year as had been announced in the agency's entire three-decade history.[3] Toy manufacturer Mattel recalled nineteen million toys that had potentially dangerous magnets or lead paint. The recall made international headlines, forcing the US Congress to consider the most sweeping product safety legislation in thirty-five years.

Until that time, the CPSC's methods of recall had proved largely ineffective. Because few companies know exactly who purchased a particular product, publicity is often the only way to reach consumers. According to Rachel Weintraub, senior council for the advocacy group Consumer Federation of America, the system is fatally flawed. The CPSC sends out press releases with the hope that people will find out somehow. As Brian Imus, state director with Illinois Public Interest Research Group, recognized, "Parents and other consumers shouldn't have to rely on after-the-fact recalls to make sure the products on store shelves and in their homes are safe."[4]

Members of the National Association of Manufacturers, including companies such as Graco, Cosco, Fisher-Price, Safety 1st, and Hasbro, have paid fines for concealing the fact that their products designed for children have caused injuries or deaths. In controversial court cases, manufacturers of hazardous toys usually have relied upon one of two defense strategies: trivialize the hazard or blame the mother. In defending Magnetix, MegaBrands attorney Rick Locker pointed his finger at parents, blaming them for "inadequate supervision."[5] Nancy Cowles of Kids in Danger (KID), a nonprofit, product-safety group, replied, "According to Locker and other industry guys, there's just an army of incompetent mothers out there, refusing to supervise their kids."[6]

Two Chicago parents, Linda Ginzel and Boaz Keysar, professors at the University of Chicago, formed KID in 1998 after their son Danny was killed by a Playskool Travel-Lite Portable Crib that had been recalled five years earlier. A draftsman with only a high school education had designed the crib, and no evidence could be found that any safety engineer had tested the crib before it was sold. Their story sparked a groundbreaking investigation of the juvenile product industry chronicled by Marla Felcher in her 2001 book, *It's No Accident: How Corporations Sell Dangerous Baby Products*.[7] As Ginzel and Keysar warn:

> American families trust that the products our babies use, from strollers to cribs to swings, will keep them safe. Unfortunately we found out the truth in the most terrible way. . . . Ask yourself, why aren't American manufacturers required to safety test most baby products before marketing them? How can they be allowed to set their own voluntary safety standards? Why don't most parents hear about the tens of millions of unsafe children's products recalled every year? What is the CPSC and why can't it effectively protect our children from disabling injuries and death?[8]

Massive recalls of children's products shined a public spotlight on deficiencies in their design, testing, and safety certification. In 2007, a series of Pulitzer Prize–winning articles in the *Chicago Tribune* prompted Congress to pass the broadest reform of consumer-product safety laws in a generation.[9] The bipartisan Consumer

Product Safety Improvement Act (CPSIA) passed in 2008 resulted in stricter tests for toys, greater public access to complaints about products, and the most significant improvements to the Consumer Product Safety Commission since it was established in the 1970s. It was long overdue. The law is intended to make consumer products safer by requiring toys and infant products to be tested, as well as by banning lead and phthalates in toys. Although the CPSC had twice delayed implementation of the testing requirement, the standards went into effect January 1, 2012.[10]

The law authorizes the first comprehensive, publicly accessible consumer complaint database, which was launched in March 2011. It can be found at http://www.saferproducts.gov. It increases civil penalties that the CPSC can assess against violators of consumer product safety laws and protects whistleblowers who report safety defects. Before the CPSIA was passed, the CPSC had authority over products only after they were sold. If products were found to be harmful, the CPSC could recall them—but only after the harm was already in consumers' homes and in children's hands. The new law requires children's products subject to mandatory standards be tested for safety before they're sold.[11]

US Rep. Jan Schakowsky (D-IL) introduced legislation in 2001 calling for third-party testing of cribs and other juvenile products. Together with Illinois Attorney General Lisa Madigan and Kids in Danger, Schakowsky released *The Year of the Nursery Product Recall*, an annual study of recalled children's products, which was issued in 2010.[12] It documented that in 2009 nursery products—high chairs, infant carriers, strollers, and cribs—were the most-recalled children's product type. During that year, 143 children's products were recalled, a total of more than 21.1 million units. Recalled products together caused at least 198 injuries and nine deaths. Injuries included entrapment, falls, and choking hazards.

The new law has had a major impact on improving child safety, resulting in a substantial reduction in the number of toy recalls. That number fell from 172 in 2008, to 50 in 2009, to 46 in 2010, and to 30 in 2014.[13] Yet, in 2014, two Boston-area children died while playing hide-and-seek in a chest. They reportedly climbed into a Land hope chest that latched shut automatically, with no way to open the airtight chest from the inside.[14] A seemingly innocent old wooden storage chest lying around the house can prove deadly. No doubt design and manufacturing mistakes will continue to be made, and toys and children's products will continue to be recalled.

As one North Shore Chicago pediatrician recognized: "Faulty design is a huge issue for kids. Most parents refer to 'accidents' but really it's problems with design that are to blame. And thousands of children are injured each year. There's lots of competition among parents today. Designer strollers can cost up to $800. People assume that if they pay more the product is better and safer for their kids—but that is not always so."[15]

BACKYARD PLAYGROUND EQUIPMENT

Sometimes the design of children's playground equipment in homeowners' backyards places children at risk. Arsenic, a naturally occurring mineral that is carcinogenic, was once commonly used as a wood preservative in playground equipment, porches, and home decks. In 2003, wood preservatives with arsenic were banned from homes and playgrounds throughout the United States, but older structures may still have them.[16]

In 2006, four-year-old Wesley Cowan died in his Utah backyard; he fell off monkey bars and strangled himself on a trapeze hanging below. His father, Reed Cowan, a TV anchor and reporter, joined other advocates for playground safety to help create new industry standards for backyard playground equipment. The new standards, approved in July 2009, prohibit the flawed design that places swings and other equipment underneath monkey bars.

Yet a month later, when the *Chicago Tribune* spotlighted this tragedy on the front page of a Sunday issue, the federal agency charged with protecting the public from dangerous products, the CPSC, had not yet issued any alerts about the flawed design.[17]

The new standard calls for swings and other components to be attached to a beam, not monkey bars. Yet such industry standards are voluntary. Alerts help pressure manufacturers to abandon flawed designs, but they may continue to be sold. The *Chicago Tribune* reported that Toys "R" Us still had a "small percentage" of play sets with the flawed design for sale but planned to require its suppliers to comply with the new standard. The newspaper reported that Target was still selling the play sets with the flawed design online, even though a Target representative said that the chain was evaluating whether to discontinue them. The CPSC estimated that American backyards housed about 6.3 million play sets.

In November 2009, the CPSC issued a voluntary recall and advised consumers to stop using them.[18] Yet it was unable to provide statistics for injuries related to the flawed monkey-bar design. Scott Burton believes that Cowan's 2006 death is the only fatality, but since 1990, there have been sixty-one reported injuries. Many more injuries, however, are never reported to hospitals or to the government, and because information on child injuries reported by emergency rooms often lack key details, the true extent of the problem may be greatly underestimated, allowing manufacturers to argue that the number of injuries compared with the number of sets sold was statistically insignificant and did not reflect a safety threat.

Trampolines are popular in many suburban backyards, and to the unknowing consumer, they appear to be a healthy form of exercise. Yet in 2010 in the United States, there were an estimated 92,159 emergency-room visits for trampoline-related injuries.[19] In 2012, 95,000 trampoline users ended up in emergency rooms. Between 2000 and 2009, twenty-two families lost a loved one due to a trampoline mishap.[20] According to the American Academy of Pediatrics (AAP), trampolines' design makes them among the most dangerous of all play equipment.[21] Most injuries were on home trampolines; 30 percent of trampoline-related injuries were fractures requiring treatment in an emergency department, often resulting in hospitalization and surgery. Children have been injured on trampolines ranging from three feet in diameter to those as wide as thirty feet, and injuries are just as likely to occur on any size trampoline.

As a result, the AAP reaffirmed its recommendation first made in 1999 that "trampolines should never be used in the home environment, in routine physical education classes, or in outdoor playgrounds. Design and behavioral recommendations are made for the limited use of trampolines in supervised training programs."[22]

Another study, led by Dr. Randall T. Loder, chair of orthopedic surgery at Indiana University School of Medicine, the first to examine fractures related to trampoline use nationwide, discovered that over ten years, trampolines caused an estimated 288,876 fractures costing more than $400 million. Trampoline injuries led to more than $1 billion in emergency room visits. As Loder remarked, "I'm sure they're fun. There's no doubt about it that they're fun. They're fun up until the time they get the injury."[23]

DANGEROUS CHILD SAFETY SEATS

Child safety seats, also known as car seats, are the one children's product that every parent in the United States is legally required to use. Even though most parents consider children their most precious cargo, they often select child safety seats based on which product fits their budget or best matches the color of their car's interior. They do so because they don't know that car seats are not all designed equally and that not all car seats are safe. Although the government tests new vehicles in side-impact, head-on, and rollover scenarios, child car seats are subjected only to frontal tests in laboratory-controlled conditions.

Yet, at lower speeds, side-impact collisions are more likely than head-on collisions to result in dire injuries. In 2014, side-impact testing was proposed by the National Highway Traffic Safety Administration (NHTSA), and the comment period concluded.[24]

One of those organizations commenting—and doing its own testing on car seats in side-impact crashes—was *Consumer Reports*, which found the test dummy would be equivalent to a three-year-old child. It wrote: "Given the dummy size and limited potential for structural failure, we conclude that the proposed side-impact test, using only the Q3s dummy, has little value for assessing side-impact protection in infant seats. For infant seat testing, an alternative, smaller side-impact instrumented dummy should be considered for approval: one that represents real-world usage and more accurately measures potential injuries and side-impact protection features."[25] *Consumer Reports* sent its findings to the NHTSA and said it hoped for subsequent changes in the final version of testing. Meanwhile, CR recommends parents place their child's car seat in the middle position in the rear seat, not on one side or the other.[26]

As of 2016, although federal regulators did provide ratings for "ease of use" for child car seats, they had failed to develop safety ratings for car seats or to significantly toughen crash tests. The ease of use section says "all car seats rated by NHTSA meet Federal Safety Standards and strict crash performance standards," but the most rigorous test for a federal standard for car seats was a simulated front-end collision at just thirty-five miles per hour.[27] Car seats can pass this test yet have serious problems at higher speeds. Dr. Ricardo Martinez, formerly of the NHTSA, said, "We had seats where, if you turned [the test sled] up five miles an hour, the seat would disintegrate."[28]

Motor vehicle accidents are the leading cause of death for young children. In 2008, the NHTSA reported that 157 children age four or under were killed during car crashes while strapped into their safety seats.[29] The NHTSA estimates that, between 1999 and 2008, 30,388 children age seven or under suffered incapacitating injuries during motor vehicle accidents while strapped into child safety seats.[30] According to Patricia Callahan, staff reporter of the *Chicago Tribune*, "Making a safe product can clash with the realities of the marketplace. . . . As a result, the device designed to protect the most vulnerable passengers in a car is tested by the government in fewer crash scenarios than the car itself or its seat belts."[31]

The NHTSA's Child Safety Seat Ease of Use Ratings are based on evaluation of instructions, evaluation of labels, vehicle installation features, and securing the child.[32] The organization also encourages parents to register their motor vehicles and car seats or booster seats in order to expedite notice of recalls.[33]

Yet when it comes to safe car seats for children, as with so many other instances of disadvantaging by design, complying with the minimum standard requirements is simply not enough.

TV AND FURNITURE TIP-OVERS

A two-and-a-half-year-old boy and his four-year-old sister climbed atop a dresser and reached a flat-panel TV, causing both the dresser and the TV to topple over. The boy suffered two skull fractures, nerve damage causing facial paralysis, and a burst eardrum. He spent a week in the hospital and took another seven months to recover. The sister suffered minor abrasions. Their story was featured on National Public Radio.[34]

From 2000 to 2010, the Consumer Product Safety Commission received 169 reports of children ages eight or younger killed by falling televisions. "Sometimes a TV simply looks more stable than it is, and the desire to climb within a child creates a very serious risk," said commission spokesman Scott Wolfson.[35] When families upgrade to a newer TV, often the older, bulkier set is banished to basements or bedrooms. Rather than spend money on appropriate stands, families may just set them on dressers, which safety experts say causes a "double hazard."

Flat-panel televisions have now replaced the old-fashioned tube sets that dominated the residential market for decades. Compared with their predecessors, flat-panel TVs are much thinner, are more attractive, and occupy much less floor space. But their design is also less stable. As any parent can attest, newly mobile toddlers grab on to anything in order to steady themselves, no matter how unstable.

"TV tip-overs" occur when children knock over a television, such as one placed atop a high dresser or desk. Dr. Gary Smith, former emergency medicine doctor and head of the Center for Injury Research and Policy at the Research Institute at Nationwide Children's Hospital in Columbus, Ohio, and his colleagues analyzed federal data from the National Electronic Injury Surveillance System. They concluded that many injuries could have been avoided if the TV and furniture had been secured and if items weren't so high up, encouraging children to climb on furniture that might tip over. "Parents, with all good intentions, think it's a good idea to keep the remote control out of reach," Smith said.[36] But that merely tempts children to go for that remote control, wherever it may be.

The CPSC reports that based on data collected from 2011 to 2013, an estimated annual average of 38,000 emergency-room visits were due to TV, furniture, and appliance product instability or tip-overs. More than half (21,700, or 57 percent) of the victims of these injuries were under age eighteen, about one-third (35 percent, or 13,200) were ages eighteen through fifty-nine, and many (8 percent, or 3,100) were age sixty or older. When the age data is broken down even further, half (50 percent, or 18,900) of the injuries were to children under age ten.

For children, the most frequent injuries were contusions/abrasions, internal organ injuries, lacerations, and fractures, and most affected the head, legs, feet, and toes. Of the annual average estimated emergency department–treated injuries, more than half (56 percent, or 21,100) involved only furniture (such as chests, bureaus, dressers, shelving units, and bookcases) falling, more than a third (41 percent, or 15,400) involved televisions or TVs plus furniture falling, and a small number (4 percent, or 1,500) involved appliances falling. Of the estimated emergency department-treated injuries, two-thirds (66 percent) occurred in residential settings.[37]

Of the 430 reported fatalities between 2000 and 2013 associated with tip-overs, 360 (84 percent) involved children ages one month to ten years, 19 (4 percent) involved adults ages twenty-eight to fifty-nine years, and 51 (12 percent) involved those age sixty or older. Of these reported fatalities, two-thirds (65 percent, or 279) involved televisions falling (37 percent only TV; 27 percent TV plus furniture), just over a quarter (28 percent, or 120) involved only furniture falling (largest category was chest, bureau, or dresser), and the rest (7 percent, or 31) involved appliances falling (largest category was stove/oven). Of the reported fatalities, the vast majority (81 percent) occurred in residential settings; 42 percent occurred in bedrooms and 21 percent occurred in living/family rooms. As a result of these alarming figures, the CPSC sought to establish a public education and outreach campaign related to the prevention of death and injuries from furniture and TV tip-overs.[38] Bear in mind that these figures are from the United States only, so one can only imagine the figures worldwide.

In June 2016, furniture giant IKEA announced a massive recall and the issuance of refunds for more than thirty-five million chests and dressers after six children died from furniture tip-overs. The recall included its well-known MALM line of three-drawer, four-drawer, and six-drawer dressers manufactured between January 2002 and June 2016. These dressers, which retailed from only $70 to $200, are constructed of particleboard and fiberboard and have been popular in starter homes and apartments. The company's statement warned, "Consumers should immediately stop using any recalled chest and dresser that is not properly anchored to the wall and place it into an area that children cannot access."[39]

After two children died as result of toppled furniture, IKEA began offering free wall-anchoring kits for its chests and dressers in 2015. IKEA had received reports of more than forty-one instances of MALM dressers and chests tipping over, resulting in seventeen injuries to children. Other IKEA models of chests and drawers had also prompted forty-one complaints, claimed the lives of three children and injured nineteen others. Elliot Kay, chairman of the CPSC, summed it up: "Every two weeks a child in the US is killed in a tip-over related incident involving furniture or TVs. These are tragic numbers."[40]

CHILDREN'S PRODUCTS THAT ADVANTAGE BY DESIGN

No More Mattress Madness:
The Award-Winning Quick Change Crib

Mary Anne Amato, mother of two, designed and patented the Quick Change Crib and became the CEO of Innovative Crib Designs in order to end the wrestling match that she experienced whenever she changed the sheets in her children's crib. Instead of lifting the mattress up and over the crib, disturbing crib mobiles and toys along the railing, Amato designed a crib with a hinged panel at its foot that opens out like a door. The mattress slides horizontally, making it much easier to handle. Amato's design received honors in the 2008 National Parenting Publications Awards, as well as a Grand Prize award from the 2006 Whirlpool Brand Mother of Invention Grant.[41]

Toy of the Year Awards:
Fisher-Price's Smart Cycle and GoldieBlox

Although no longer in production, Fisher-Price's Smart Cycle Physical Learning Arcade System, designed for children ages three to six, combines a stationary bike, a learning center, and an arcade game system. It plugs into a TV so that as children pedal along, their favorite characters guide them along learning discoveries, games, and races. Multiple levels of play are available for different ages and stages as they drive, learn, and race. The Smart Cycle teaches children upper and lowercase letters, numbers and counting, spelling, problem solving, shapes, matching creativity, spatial reasoning, and motor skills. For its ingenuity, it received two 2008 Toy of the Year Awards: Educational Toy of the Year—the best toy that through play helps children develop special skills and/or knowledge—and Most Innovative Toy of the Year—the best toy that combines the most unique blend of innovative technology and play value for children today.[42]

GoldieBlox and the Spinning Machine won the People's Choice Award in the 2014 Toy of the Year Awards.[43] GoldieBlox's story and construction sets are designed to encourage girls to build, especially in a world where men far outnumber women in the fields of science, technology, engineering, and math. The company aims to disrupt the pink aisle in toy stores and inspire future generations of female engineers—by leveling the playing field—and the paying field. Just as the Society of Women Engineers, Black Girls Code, Girls Who Code, and others provide positive role models, GoldieBlox provides role models for young girls and boys.

GoldieBlox inventor and CEO Debbie Sterling graduated with a degree in mechanical engineering and product design. As she claimed in her TED talk, "I don't fit in, but I believe that our little girls will."[44] She recalled that in her first mechanical engineering classes at Stanford University, much to her surprise:

> We weren't fixing train engines. We got to invent and design things. . . . How empowering to be able to build whatever you want. . . . Like a lot of other girls, I had underdeveloped spatial skills. Our parents never bought us Legos or Erector sets or Lincoln Logs. We

all thought that those were boys' toys. I thought: Those toys have been marketed to boys for over one hundred years. And they get them interested in math and science. Meanwhile all we get are the dolls and makeup kits and it's not fair.

She started the business with a Kickstarter campaign, which reached its $150,000 goal in just four days.

Today GoldieBlox is sold worldwide, and the GoldieBlox website features a blog showcasing female engineers. Molly McDonald wrote in her blog: "At GoldieBlox, we want to give girls the skills and the confidence to follow their dreams. No matter what she wants to be when she grows up, she deserves to make as much as a man."[45]

Chapter 3

BIG TOYS FOR BIG BOYS AND GIRLS: HIGH-TECH AND HIGH-TOUCH

"Last year, I bought a new cell phone (the latest model) for my mom, but the button is too small to push for her and she hardly uses other functions than dialing and receiving a call." (Female, Asian, age 30, 5′7″, 140 lb.)

Many of us consider the gadgets we use and the vehicles we drive to be some of our most prized possessions. Whether we realize it or not, their design has an enormous impact on the quality of our lives. Consider the number of hours per day and the amount of money you spend on your smartphone, on your computer, and on your car. Keeping up with the latest and greatest gadgets amounts to a large chunk of our lives and a significant portion of our incomes.

Recall the instant when you first laid eyes on your most prized possession. For many of us, whether in a showroom, on a website, or gazing over a stranger's shoulder, it was love at first sight. We were starstruck, under the designers' magic spell.

Ironically, our lives have been transformed by the introduction of high-tech toys that we may never have heard of a decade or two ago but can't live without today. Smartphones in our hands and global positioning systems in our cars now seem indispensable. The high-tech revolution has proceeded so rapidly that a myriad of new products are placed on the market daily. Yet many of these products contain gender, age, or body biases that work against us. Some of these biases result in serious dangers not only to the people who use them but to society at large. And a large portion of our population feels as if the high-tech age has left them behind. Whether we're at home, at work, out on the road, or on the golf course, the digital world has opened up new possibilities for some but continues to disempower others.

SMARTPHONES, DIGITAL CAMERAS, PERSONAL COMPUTERS, HOME ELECTRONICS

Over the past two decades, the number of cell-phone users has sky-rocketed. The United Nations International Telecommunications Union reported that in 2015 the number of mobile cellular sub-scribers was over seven billion worldwide, up from less than one billion in 2000. While in 2000 the mobile penetration rate was only 12 percent, by 2015 it had reached a whopping 97 percent.[1]

The design and use of cell phones may affect men more adversely than women. While women are more likely to carry cell phones in their purse, men tend to keep cell phones in their pockets, perhaps dangerously close to their reproductive organs. Research has shown that when in the "talk" mode, cell phones may adversely affect sperm, especially among men who used cell phones for more than four hours a day. Studies have documented a wide spectrum of possible effects from the use of cell phones, ranging from insignificant effects to varying degrees of testicular damage.[2] Researchers at the University of Exeter in the United Kingdom led a meta-analysis of ten studies analyzing 1,492 total semen samples from experimental lab studies with sperm samples to observational studies in humans. They found a small but consistent drop in quality of men's samples that had been exposed to mobile phone radiation—but no link between mobile phone radiation and an actual drop in fertility rates.[3] Skeptics of the links between cell phone use and male fertility abound.[4] To date, the mode of action of electromagnetic waves emitted from cell phones on the male reproductive system remains unclear. Scientists are continuing to study this issue. And the jury is still out on whether long-term use of cell phones by men and women may lead to brain tumors or other forms of cancer.[5]

Today's typical cell phone design can pose special problems for the elderly and people with reduced dexterity. The compact keypad makes it all too easy for someone with large fingers to hit the wrong button. And many people with rheumatoid arthritis have trouble using cell phones. Small display screens and tiny font sizes strain the eyes of people with even minor farsightedness. Elaborate navigational menus and multiple-function keys can be especially confusing for elderly people. For the same reasons, many elderly people struggle to use other portable electronic devices, such as digital cameras.

Some designers are attempting to remedy these problems by creating cell phones designed specifically for the elderly. Some products offer bigger, backlit buttons; bright, large text; and a powerful speaker that sounds loud and clear. Other phones feature large spaces between adjacent keys on the keypad to reduce instances of pressing the wrong button and to optimize visibility of character digits on the key. They have large display screens, some jumbo integer keys, fewer technological function keys and a "HELP" key on the reverse side of the phone to call for medical or rescue service.

Cell phones have also been designed to improve women's health. The Grameen Foundation's Mobile Midwife Program sends women daily text messages and weekly voicemails to advise them during pregnancy and during the first year of a child's life. UNICEF's 1,000 Days program provides mothers with nutritional recommendations through pregnancy and the first two years of a child's life.[6]

Cell-phone safety while driving has long been a contentious issue. Increasingly complex smartphone designs allow users to watch videos, share photos, send e-mail and text messages, select and listen to music, and download applications and ringtones, as well as make phone calls. Such activities magnify the dangers of using a cell phone while driving. As of 2010, the National Safety Council estimates that every year at least 1.6 million motor vehicle accidents—25 percent of all accidents—involve drivers using cell phones, with a minimum of two hundred thousand accidents caused by drivers who text.[7] Research demonstrates that drivers talking on cell phones are four times as likely as other drivers to crash, and drivers texting on cell phones are eight times as likely to crash. Because cell-phone use in conjunction with accidents is highly underreported—police often rely on drivers to admit to using cell phones, and many drivers are not forthcoming; others are seriously injured or killed, so their phone use at the time of the accident remains unknown—the magnitude of this threat is probably much larger than we think, and current laws are likely not strong enough to protect the public from this deadly epidemic.[8]

Driving while speaking on a cell phone—whether hands-free or not—is a major distraction for drivers of all ages, but especially for teenagers and the elderly. The American Automobile Association Foundation for Traffic Safety conducted some of the most comprehensive research to date into crash videos of teen drivers and found that distracted driving is a much more serious problem than we had thought. Researchers analyzed the six seconds leading up to a crash in almost seventeen hundred videos of teen drivers taken from in-vehicle event recorders. Results showed that distraction was a factor in over half (58 percent) of all crashes studied, including 89 percent of road-departure crashes and 76 percent of rear-end crashes. Prior to this study, the National Highway Traffic Safety Administration had estimated that distraction was a factor in only 14 percent of all teen driver crashes. Of the distractions leading up to a crash, cell-phone use was the second most common, accounting for 12 percent of crashes, right behind interacting with other passengers at 15 percent.[9]

University of Utah psychology professor Dave Strayer and his research team have published numerous studies based on simulated driving conditions showing that hands-free cell phones are no less dangerous than handheld cell phones. They also found that talking on a cell phone impairs driving ability just as much as having a 0.08 percent blood alcohol level (the legal limit for driving in all states), and when young adults talk on cell phones while driving, their reaction times become as slow as those of senior citizens.[10]

As of June 2016, fourteen states, the District of Columbia, Puerto Rico, and the US Virgin Islands prohibited drivers from talking on handheld cell phones while driving.[11] No state completely banned all types of cell phone use—handheld and hands-free—for all drivers, but several prohibited cell-phone use by certain segments of the population such as novice drivers and school bus drivers. Forty-six states, the District of Columbia, Puerto Rico, the US Virgin Islands, and

Guam ban text messaging for all drivers. More than forty-five countries have banned handheld use of cell phones while driving.[12]

Cell phones aren't the only electronic devices that some men should be worried about. The heat generated from laptop computers may impact sperm production and development. Reproductive specialists at Loyola University Chicago Stritch School of Medicine warn that laptops can impair male fertility when used directly on the lap as opposed to on a desk. Forty percent of fertility issues can be attributed to males; high temperature in the testicles that can damage or kill sperm is a major culprit. According to Suzanne Kavic, director of the division of reproductive endocrinology at Loyola University Health System, "The heat generated from laptops can impact sperm production and development making it difficult to conceive down the road."[13] Future fathers may best play it safe by placing their laptops on their desks.

What about personal computers and children? Here ergonomic design problems abound. When working at a desktop computer, ideally one's eye level should be at approximately two-thirds the height of the monitor. Yet many young children play with their parents' computers, craning their necks and straining their backs to view the screen, possibly leading to long-term negative effects on their posture and physical development. The computer mouse is too large for tiny hands. Adjustable height monitors and child-size mice would help solve some of these problems.

DOLLARS AND CENTS

While the digital world has opened up new opportunities for people with physical disabilities—for example, visually impaired people can now communicate electronically through voice recognition software—the visually impaired continue to face daily problems with one of the most widely circulated objects of all: paper currency. While our American coins are all the same shape (round), they are different sizes. This allows blind people to distinguish one type of coin from another. But American paper bills are all the same shape and size.

When I went out to dinner with a friend who is blind, I was

amazed to see her open her wallet and ask me to identify the bills she had with her. Much to my surprise, when I asked what she did when she was alone, she replied, "I try to mark them ahead of time with a clip, but sometimes I just open up my wallet and ask the waiter to help himself."

SERVICE STATIONS AND PUMP HANDLES

For some drivers, gas stations can be problematic. With the exception of two states, New Jersey and Oregon, self-service gas stations have been the norm for at least two decades. Many able-bodied people with small or frail hands find it difficult to lift and squeeze heavy, wide gasoline nozzles. This is especially true for motorists in California and other urban areas where smog is a problem, and where use of a vapor recovery nozzle, with a bulky rubber boot that fits directly over the vehicle's fill valve, has been required since 1994.[14] In 2013, the US Environmental Protection Agency eliminated the requirement for vapor recovery nozzles, as all vehicles manufactured after 2006 have vapor recovery technology onboard. States have the option to do away with vapor recovery systems at the pump, but many gas stations still have them.[15]

For drivers with disabilities, who are legally entitled to receive full-service at a gas station, catching the attention of station attendants is not always easy. A US patent for a kit for gas stations to increase accessibility by people with disabilities was issued to meet this need. The kit includes a bell button to mount near a gas pump and a speaker for inside the service station store to alert attendants that refueling assistance is needed. The kit also provides signs indicating the availability of refueling assistance. Optional items include a doorbell switch for the doorway into the service station store, an access ramp, additional signs, a checklist, a tape measure, and a doorstop. The kit includes installation instructions as well as training guidelines for staff.

YOUR AUTO AUTOBIOGRAPHY, IF WOMEN DESIGNED CARS

> "If women were designing cars they would be better for other women. Because women know what women want. Men don't. Whenever I go to buy a car, the first thing I say to the salesperson is, 'This car better fit me. Because if it doesn't I'm not going to buy it.'" (Female, white, age 61, 4′11″, 200 lb.)

Think about your own auto autobiography: All the cars you've ever owned and all the cars you've ever rented. Which were your favorites, and why? How well did they fit your body, or didn't they? Was it the car or was it you?

Women are the primary buyers of traditional household and consumer products, and they are increasingly buying products traditionally purchased by men, such as computers and cars.

What's my personal theory about why Japanese-made cars have sold so well in the United States for so long? It's not just that they get better gas mileage. It's that compared with most American cars, most Japanese cars fit the size and scale of smaller women.

In fact, for that reason, I have never owned an American car. My first car was a four-door 1971 Datsun 510, which I shared with my mother. I loved it because it felt like it was made for someone just my size. I could reach everything in the dashboard, see over the windshield, and even could see clearly out all four windows when I test rode it in the passenger seats.

Next was a Datsun B210 that I shared with my sister. It had decent visibility from the front seat, but the view from the back was a stretch because it was a two-door model with low seats. It did work well for my sister, who is several inches taller than I am. After we discovered that sharing a car was no fun, my next car was a Nissan Sentra, another ergonomically correct vehicle for my five-foot-two frame, and then I drove two Honda Accords, which fit me like a glove.

My next car was a 2003 Toyota Prius. What sold me on it almost as much as the innovative hybrid technology and outstanding gas mileage was the terrific visibility out the front and back windshield and all four side windows. Yet over a decade later, when I was all ready to buy another Prius, I was heartbroken to find its design so deficient for someone my size that I had to rule it out right away. Even when standing on my tiptoes, I couldn't reach the hatchback trunk to close it when it was raised. Plus the trunk lacked a remote control. A bad design decision, bad for business!

My latest car is a 2015 Hyundai Sonata. Although I was once again attracted to the hybrid technology and the sleek design, plus the chance to finally have heated seats and two moon roofs in both the front and back seat, making it an unusually light and bright vehicle, only after I had the car for a few weeks did I discover a serious shortcoming. All my friends who were my size who sat in the passenger seat couldn't see out the windows. And when I finally sat there myself, neither could I. I didn't realize this when I bought the car because I only tested it out from the driver's seat, which could be adjusted for height. I have since found a passenger seat height kit from a third-party vendor that raises the seat about one and a half inches—for $70 plus shipping—but why doesn't this come as a standard feature on the car?

A growing segment of women buyers is influencing product design. Volvo invited hundreds of its female employees to create a vehicle that suited their needs. The result, revealed in 2004, was a roomy, 215-horsepower coupe that's easy to park, maintain, and keep clean.[16] The sporty, low-emission, gas-electric hybrid Your Concept Car required an oil change only every thirty-one thousand miles. When the engine needed inspecting, the car sent a wireless message to a local service center that notified the driver. The vehicle had no hood, only a large front end that could be opened by a mechanic. The car had dirt-repellent paint and glass, exchangeable seat covers with matching carpet, and sensors to allow for easier parking.

Yet that innovative auto design never reached consumers. Your Concept Car was exhibited in art museums but not sold in auto showrooms. Even its name reinforced its status as an abstraction rather than reality, unlike typical car names derived from swift animals (Mustang, Impala), human virtues (Focus, Accord), or harmonious neologisms (Sephia, Camry). Volvo's female designers were relegated to the realms of art and inspiration, safely segregated from the means of production and implementation.[17] And today, female drivers still grapple with mundane problems such as where to place their purse. Should it go on the passenger seat, where it's vulnerable to theft? On the passenger-side floor, where they can't reach it? Or on the driver-side floor, where it can topple onto the pedals and cause an accident?

SQUEEZING INTO CAR SEATS

> "One of my biggest challenges was when I shopped for a new car. I really wanted to be ecological and buy a hybrid electric vehicle, but they were all too small for me. It took lots of hunting around till I finally found just one model where I could fit comfortably in the driver's seat." (Male, white, age 32, 5′11″, 300 lb.)

The front bench seat is no longer an option on American-made sedans after 2013, but bucket seats disadvantage taller and larger drivers, both male and female.[18] Have you ever parked your car in a parking lot with plenty of room to spare, only to return and find yourself trapped outside the driver's side of your car, sandwiched alongside a large vehicle that wasn't there before, so that you can't even squeeze yourself in to open your door? On such occasions, the only way into your car is to climb over the passenger seat, no mean feat. With gearshifts and parking brakes in between bucket seats, this maneuver requires careful acrobatics. Ironically, compared with bucket seats, old-fashioned bench seats were much more user-friendly, as even tall men could slide across to the driver's seat. Bench seats are still offered in some larger pickup trucks.

Today's automobiles are designed such that an automotive computer is required to perform even the most basic diagnostics. As a result, most of us are locked into expensive service appointments at the repair shop. Instructions on changing oil and spark plugs used to be included in every owner's manual. Ironically, the 1920s Model T Ford required only a simple set of wrenches and screwdrivers to fix almost any problem. Contemporary automobile designs have become so complex that repairs require not only complicated equipment but also a high level of manual dexterity. By contrast, some motorcycles come with a bag of tools that fits in the bike and allows the driver to take it apart and fix it.

RISKY GOLF CARTS

Golf carts are routinely used to transport people not only at golf courses, but also at sporting events, college campuses, hospitals, airports, national parks, businesses, prisons, and military bases, where often they shuttle visitors, especially the elderly or people with disabilities, to and from parking facilities for special events. In some gated and retirement communities, they have become the primary means of transportation. Golf carts can be operated legally on public roadways in certain states. Most golf carts are not subject to federal regulation, and state and local regulations regarding their use vary. Children under age sixteen are legally allowed to operate golf carts on private property, but golf carts aren't designed for children and most provide no child safety features. Most lack seat belts, doors, or any means of child restraint, and yet infants and young children are allowed to ride in them.

Each year, thousands of people are injured riding in golf carts because of insufficient safety features, such as the lack of seat belts and front-wheel brakes. A comprehensive study of patients treated in US emergency departments as a result of golf cart–related injuries between 1990 and 2006 was conducted based on data from the National Electronic Injury Surveillance System. It was the first study to examine golf cart–related injuries in the United States using a nationally representative sample.[19] Primary causes of injury included falling or jumping from a moving golf cart (38 percent), being struck or run over by a cart (16 percent), and colliding with another vehicle or stationary object (10 percent).

The most common cause of injury was falling or jumping from a golf cart. Children were at greater risk than adults for falling from the cart, and their falls were more likely to cause head or neck injuries and hospitalization. Adults were more likely than children to be injured while entering or exiting the cart. Cart overturns injured many, because golf carts moving at speeds as low as eleven miles per hour can eject a passenger during a turn. Rear-facing golf cart seats had the highest rates of passenger ejection, and most golf carts do not have brakes on all four wheels. Rear-wheel-only brake design can cause instability and reduce braking effectiveness, causing carts to fishtail. Brakes can lock so that the driver loses control, a special problem on hilly golf courses.

A study by a team of researchers at the University of Alabama at Birmingham's Center for Injury Sciences focused on golf cart–related injuries between 2002 and 2005.[20] The researchers concluded that more effective safety features are needed, especially improved passenger restraints. Drivers need to brake slowly, especially on downhill slopes, and avoid sharp turns at high speeds, as increased radius of a turn greatly decreases the risk of ejecting passengers. Passengers should place both feet firmly on the floor, keep their arms and legs inside the cart, sit back in the seat to be protected from hip restraints, and use handgrips to prevent a fall. If available, seat belts and helmets should be used, especially if the cart is driven on public roads. Because golf carts are not designed for safely transporting children, children should be discouraged from traveling in them.

BIG TOYS THAT ADVANTAGE BY DESIGN

Segway Personal Transporters

Have you ever seen police officers, firefighters, or security guards gliding around town in strange-looking open-air vehicles that have two wheels but stay upright by themselves? If you live in a scenic location, have you seen groups of helmeted tourists gliding above the crowds? Did their big-wheeled electric scooters look as if they had been lifted straight out of the 1960s sci-fi cartoon *The Jetsons*? Chances are they were all riding a Segway Personal Transporter. When it made its debut on ABC's *Good Morning America*, it was touted as "the world's first self-balancing human transporter." It became available to the public in 2002.

The Segway was designed to be an eco-friendly alternative for short car journeys that are part of our daily routine. According to the Environmental Protection Agency, Americans make nine hundred million car journeys daily, but half of these trips are driven by solo drivers and are less than five miles long. Riding Segways reduces greenhouse gas output and consumption of imported fossil fuels. The Segway is eleven times more efficient than the average American car because it glides about twenty-four miles per charge.[21]

Anyone who weighs at least 100 pounds or less than 260 can ride them. So while they're not yet designed for children under age fourteen, they work well for most adults regardless of gender, age, or body size. Teenagers enjoy them. So do people over age seventy who have had hip and other joint replacements.[22]

Riding a Segway is somewhat of a cross between walking and being on a bicycle, only it's much faster, safer, and efficient. Its internal electronic gyroscope responds to your body movements, providing a sense of power and speed, safety and control. Lean slightly forward and it moves forward. Lean slightly backward and it moves backward. Gently move to the right or left and it turns instantly in the direction you want to go. Its sensors and accelerometers take measurements of the terrain and the rider's body position a hundred times a second.[23]

The Segway company recommends a three-component safety training regimen including reading materials, a video presentation, and hands-on training for all its users, whether they're purchasing a Segway or a first-time user renting one for a group tour by a Segway-authorized business. Tour groups require participants to wear helmets to prevent head injuries. Although relatively rare, accidents have occurred, primarily with inexperienced riders and tourists.[24]

Ironically, the only death report to date was that of a highly experienced rider, James Heselden, age 62, the owner of the Segway company. In 2010, he fell to his death off a thirty-foot cliff and into a river while riding a Segway near his home in West Yorkshire, UK.[25]

Nintendo Wii Video Games Wake Up Couch Potatoes

The Wii video-game console made its debut at the Tokyo Game Show in 2005, and its popularity soon soared. Almost 83 million Nintendo *Wii Sports* games have been sold around the world since it was launched in 2006.[26] Regardless of gender, age, and body type, the games—which use motion-sensing controllers—provide a fun way to play and get light exercise at the same time.

The Wii opened the door to gaming for a new range of consumers, especially women and the elderly. It soon became the most popular platform, preferred by 80 percent of female gamers in the United States.[27] Many senior centers and retirement homes used Nintendo's Wii systems to help elderly people participate in low-impact indoor exercise, including Wii bowling, tennis, and golf. Grandparents and grandchildren can play together without leaving home.[28] Healthcare providers have been using the Wii as a teaching aid to help seniors learn balance techniques that can help prevent falls.

The Wii may help treat symptoms of Parkinson's disease, a degenerative disease that impairs motor skills. In an eight-week pilot study, a research team at Medical College of Georgia led by Dr. Ben Herz followed twenty Parkinson's patients who spent an hour playing the Wii three times a week for four weeks.[29] Patients were all at a similar stage of the disease, where both sides of their body were affected but they had not yet suffered from gait disturbance. According to a report in *Science Daily*: "Participants showed significant improvements in rigidity, movement, fine motor skills and energy levels. Perhaps most impressively, most participants' depression levels decreased to zero."

Chapter 4

WRAP RAGE: PRODUCT, FURNITURE, AND INDUSTRIAL DESIGN

"Why are electronic plastic packages so hard to open? It always takes me five to ten minutes to open one . . . most of the time, I end up cutting my fingers. I understand they have reasons for packaging them in such a way, but they need to come up with an easy efficient way to open them. How are elders supposed to open them, if I am twenty-one and having difficulties?" (Male, African-American, age 21, 5'11", 170 lb.)

Accidental stabs, falls, amputations, lifelong injuries, and deaths can result from faulty product, furniture, and industrial design. Many products are designed with greater priority given to packaging, shipping, and storage than to customer-friendliness and ease of use. Their design is often biased in favor of average-sized, able-bodied people while ignoring the needs of smaller women or men, children, and the elderly. Some fashionable, expensive furniture designs may look appealing in home design magazines, but when used every day in your home, depending on your gender, age, or body size, they can pose serious dangers to your health. A right-handed bias on many products disadvantages those who are left-handed—at school, at work, and at home. Whether it be mowing the lawn or shoveling snow, we buy products to make our home lives easier. Yet due to poor design, we sometimes end up buying unforeseen problems. While attempting to solve one problem, we create another.

CLAMSHELL PACKAGING AND "WRAP RAGE"

How often have you struggled to open tamper-proof jars or medicine caps? Have you ever cut yourself while wrestling with shrink-wrap and hard, sharp plastic covers? Not only do product designs discriminate against certain types of users, so does the design of product packaging.[1]

As Fergal Barry from Arthritis Australia said about the clamshell, "When you buy something it should be yours—you shouldn't have to get into a knife fight with it."[2]

USA Today reported:

> Eric Kent made it through two tours of duty in Iraq and one in Afghanistan with hardly a scratch.
>
> Yet a Marine who took on terrorists and insurgents abroad turned out to be no match in one of the USA's most common domestic smackdowns: man vs. product package.
>
> Kent, 23, raced to a Pittsburgh hospital this summer after slicing open his left thumb with a military-grade KA-Bar knife trying to hack open a printer cable from Geek Squad, a division of Best Buy.[3]

Clamshell packaging was introduced in the 1980s primarily as a way to prevent theft, to make items visible to customers, and to make packages capable of withstanding the rigors of shipping from manufacturing plants overseas. According to the National Association for Shoplifting Prevention, shoplifting costs US stores more than $10 billion a year, or $25 million a day.[4]

Estimates are that by 2015, more than eight billion oyster packs were opened up, thrown away, and deposited in landfills. Hermetically sealed oyster or clamshell hard-to-open plastic casings surround a wide array of goods, such as MP3 players, webcams, USB drives, computer mice, headsets, batteries, electric toothbrushes, and many children's toys. They often come with hard plastic spikes, sharp wires, or cable ties, to pin the product down.

A phenomenon nicknamed "wrap rage" has erupted. The US Consumer Product Safety Commission (CPSC) estimated that in 2006, injuries from plastic packaging resulted in approximately six thousand emergency-room visits. Because clamshells are impossible to open with bare hands, attempts to open them with knives, box cutters, razor blades, and scissors have sometimes led to amputated fingertips, severed tendons, and injured eyes. As Randall Culp, a surgeon at the Philadelphia Hand Center at Thomas Jefferson University Hospital explained, "I think it's a real health issue."[5] Emergency-room doctors report that the week after Christmas is one of the peak times for such injuries, although they see them all year long.

Along with the potential health hazards, environmental concerns have prompted calls for the elimination of clamshell packaging. According to the US Environmental Protection Agency, about one-third of consumer garbage is packaging, and plastics comprise 12 percent of US waste each year. Although the European Union attempts to regulate packaging design and waste, and California's Rigid Plastic Packaging Consumer Law encourages use of recycled plastics, such rules are rare in the United States, where businesses rather than the government rule the day.

In the United Kingdom, researchers at Nottingham University were asked by the Department of Trade and Industry to investigate the potential dangers of badly designed packaging. They found that each year more than sixty thousand people require hospital treatment after injuring themselves while opening difficult packaging—not just clamshells but also food cans, jars, glass bottles, spray bottles, and other tightly packed goods. More than nine thousand people injure themselves removing sharp lids from cans of corned beef. Injuries from other food cans sent 17,671 people to the hospital. More than two thousand people suffer wrist strain while struggling to pry lids off jam jars. About sixteen hundred people are injured when they accidentally spray the contents of spray bottles and aerosols in their eyes while trying to open the product. *Ironically, eighty-eight people were injured using a knife to open the packaging containing a new knife.*

Such injuries cost the National Health Service 12 million pounds a year. All of this prompted Beverley Norris of the Occupation Ergonomics Department to conclude, "What we found was a lack of design when it comes to consumers opening items." A spokesman for the Department of Trade and Industry called the results "staggering." David Jenkins, Product Safety Investigator for the Royal

Society for the Prevention of Accidents, said: "We receive regular complaints from consumers who have injured themselves trying to get at a product. This is a serious problem and the industry should be doing more."[6]

Alternatives to clamshell packaging are being developed.[7] Some big-box stores are considering using different packaging as part of their efforts to achieve sustainability goals. In 2006, Walmart launched an initiative to reduce packaging in its stores by 5 percent, estimating that doing so would reduce carbon-dioxide emissions by 667,000 tons a year. Retailers such as Costco and Home Depot are beginning to display products in a new type of packaging called Natralock, which is easier to open and uses less plastic. Some stores keep pricey products behind a counter while showcasing samples, reducing the need for so many plastic casings.

Some online retail establishments have taken the lead in combating this problem. Amazon's Certified Frustration-Free Packaging, launched in 2008, is easy to open, uses recyclable packaging, and is ready to ship—no need to put the product in a bigger box.[8] It started with just nineteen items, but as of 2014 more than eighty thousand goods are free from wires and plastic and instead are shipped in a plain brown box with minimal protective filling.[9] Kudos to Amazon. Now if only the rest of the packaging world would follow suit . . .

STEAMING OVER SODA CANS AND CRYING OVER SPILLED MILK

Most products are designed and packaged for able-bodied persons, not for the elderly or frail. A high level of manual dexterity and the ability to press hard are essential to opening pressure-sealed jars, bottle tops, and other food and beverage containers. Some elderly people with arthritis or other hand issues may give up altogether, resorting to frozen dinners or Meals on Wheels, even moving into assisted living facilities when everyday grocery shopping, cooking, and handling packaged items become too much of a challenge.

The elderly do not have a say in the design and packaging of everyday items. Their voices are marginalized or absent from the design process. Ironically, child-resistant pill containers—which require the consumer to pierce stiff foil, pull on a tiny tab, or pressing on a safety cap—can be among the most frustrating products for elderly people to open. Yet the strength of some elderly persons may be no greater than that of a young child.

Opening soda cans and jars can pose a major obstacle for many older people, rendering them helpless in their homes until a younger, stronger person comes to their rescue.

"Before my grandmother passed, I remember she always asked for my assistance when she wanted a soda pop with her meal. I basically had to open these metal cylinders . . . because of an inherent design flaw—the dexterity required to flip a small metal tab is too difficult for elderly people with arthritis and poor vision. Having none of these ailments, I too sometimes struggled. I suppose men are also disadvantaged by this design because they normally do not have long fingernails, which can be used as leverage to pry the top open." (Male, white, age 23, 5′8″, 160 lb.)

A change to the design of the gallon milk jug underscores the lack of attention paid to diverse milk-drinkers.[10] In 2008, Walmart and Costco adopted the new square jugs, which are cheaper to ship, require less energy to ship and store, provide fresher milk when it arrives in stores, and cost less. But the unusual shape poses special problems for children and the elderly. Because the jugs lack a real spout, first-time users find it awkward to pour. Unless the jug is tilted gently and poured slowly, the result is spilled milk!

BEDS ON STEROIDS

Today you can spend thousands of dollars to sleep in a high poster bed, a canopy bed, or even a sleigh bed. Crafted in swirling designs of cherry, mahogany, or oak trimmed with dark leather or scroll carvings, these luxurious beds boast exotic, regal-sounding names: Barcelona Bonnet, Bellewood Queen Mansion, Brompton Hall, Camelot, Casablanca, Dynasty, Hills of Tuscany, King Street, Louis-Philippe, Merlot, Nottingdale, Rivage, Sonoma Queen, Timber Heights, and Wanderlust. Add an extra-tall mattress to the bed frame and voilà, you're perched up high in the air with a panoramic view of your bedroom. Some beds are so tall that they require spending another few hundred dollars on matching bed steps so that you can climb in and out.

When you read product descriptions listing the dimensions of these lavish home furnishings, you will usually find the length and width of the bed along with the height of the headboard (sometimes up to seven and a half feet tall) and footboard. But what's often missing is the most critical dimension of all: the height of the bed itself when complete with the mattress of your choice. However fashionable it may be, oversized furniture in the bedroom can sometimes prove dangerous. If your bed is too high, you may fall out of it.

The US Centers for Disease Control and Prevention (CDC) reports that every year, millions of people age sixty-five and over fall; over 2.5 million elderly people are treated in emergency departments for fall-related injuries, and over 250,000 people are hospitalized for hip fractures, more than 95 percent of which are caused by falling, usually by falling sideways. Falls are the most common cause of traumatic brain injuries.[11] Many of these injuries occur simply from falling out of bed. The rate of fall-related deaths among the elderly rose sharply from 2004 to 2013. The popularity of high-fashion tall beds may be just one reason why.

But when it comes to residential injuries and falling out of bed, the CDC and hospital medical records don't keep track of one of the most important details of all: the design, model, and make of the bed that led to the fall. And where are the warnings—especially for short and elderly people—that should accompany these beds when they are sold? Falls can result in hip fractures, traumatic brain injuries, and even death. Medical conditions, mental impairment, and medications combined with bed height, mattress firmness, floor type, and footwear are among the factors that can cause problems when getting out of bed.

For people with Parkinson's, Alzheimer's, or other debilitating diseases, getting out of bed can be even more dangerous. The CDC publishes the guide *Preventing Falls: A Guide to Implementing Effective Community-Based Fall Prevention Programs*,[12] which contains a link to *Check for Safety: A Home Fall Prevention Checklist for Older Adults*. This useful checklist acknowledges that "falls are often due to hazards that are easy to overlook but easy to fix." The bedroom section calls for placing lamps close to the bed and using night-lights but makes no mention of the height of the bed.[13] The American Academy of Orthopaedic Surgeons' Home Safety Checklist for fall-proofing each room in the house advises: "Use a normal height bed. Sleep on a bed that is easy to get into and out of."[14]

BUNK BEDS

> "Growing up, my brother and I shared a bunk bed. My life growing up revolved around sports, so, naturally, while I was sleeping, I would dream about them. One night while sleeping on the top bunk, I was dreaming that we had to run sprints for basketball. My body took this to mean that I should be moving as fast as I could and rolled me off the edge of the bed. The bed had maybe a two-inch rail, but it was not high enough to stop someone from rolling over it. I went flying over the edge and woke up right as I left the bed. For the second I was awake and in the air, I had no clue where I was and became even more confused when I smashed into the ground. I am very lucky that I wasn't injured." (Male, white, age 24, 6′1″, 200 lb.)

Although older people are unlikely to sleep in bunk beds, many children do. Parents often team up siblings in bunk beds as a way of building camaraderie and saving precious floor space.

Estimates based on the European Union (EU) Injury Database show that every year in the EU about nineteen children age zero to fourteen are injured by bunk beds, requiring a trip to the emergency room. Leading causes of bunk-bed injuries are falls from the top bunk during sleep or playing and falls off the ladder while climbing.[15]

A study by Ohio State University researchers tracked emergency-room bunk bed–related injuries across the United States from 1990 to 2005, examining injuries to an estimated 572,580 children and adolescents under twenty-one years of age.[16] It was found that boys and young men were more likely to suffer from bunk-bed mishaps (61 percent) compared with girls. Most common injuries were cuts (nearly 30 percent), bruises or scrapes (24 percent), and bone fractures (19 percent). The head and neck were the most common body parts to be injured in all age groups (27 percent of all injuries), and 93.5 percent of mishaps happened at home.

Among the bunk-bed safety tips the researchers suggest: use guardrails on both sides of the upper bunk, use a proper-sized mattress, don't allow children younger than age six on the top bunk, use night-lights to help children see the ladder at night, and keep bunks far away from ceiling fans or fixtures.

Perhaps the Japanese, who sleep on tatami mats on the floor, know best.

MEN AND WOMEN: SEPARATE SPHERES

Historically, taste was ascribed to women while design was ascribed to men. Women decorated their homes, whereas men were paid to design and build them. Age-old stereotypes about interior designers versus architects reflect the fact that interiors were the domain of women, while architecture remained the arena of men. Today, the design of products, furniture, and industrial equipment pose an intriguing juxtaposition of diversity issues.

Researchers have discovered some fascinating gender differences in the use of home appliances and electronic equipment.[17] They distinguish between the "white goods" originating from the typical white refrigerator, stove, and oven—appliances more often used by women—and the "brown goods" based on the faux-wood veneers of television and stereo equipment popularized in the 1970s—typically more often used by men.

Studies show that women tend to make minimal use of multiple functions, whereas men tend to want the perception of being in control as "master of the machine." This pattern reflects some broad gender differences in relationships with technology. For women, technology tends to be an aid in accomplishing a task, whereas for men, technology itself is a source of entertainment.

When targeting the female market, manufacturers have often resorted to a traditional strategy of "shrink it and pink it." But many women find this approach offensive. It misses an important point: women have distinct physical needs from men and a lower tolerance for obtuse design. Women influence 80 percent of household purchases. Companies that ignore their needs risk doing so at their own peril.[18]

HAZARDOUS LAWN MOWERS

Although people of all ages use lawn care equipment such as lawn mowers, leaf blowers, and snow blowers, for some age groups the design of these machines can be especially dangerous. In a study published in *Pediatrics*, medical researchers at Ohio State University and Children's Hospital in Columbus, Ohio, reported on the epidemiology of lawn mower–related injuries to children in the United States.[19] According to their research, every year an estimated 9,400 people age twenty or younger are treated for lawn mower–related injuries. Older children and teenagers are most likely to be injured, although one-quarter of the injuries sustained are to children younger than age five, and 78 percent of those injured were boys. And although the *Pediatrics* study focused on children, no doubt lawn mowers injure many adults too.

The study called for safer product design and more rigorous voluntary safety standards from the American National Standards Institute/Outdoor Power Equipment Institute. These included measures to keep feet and toes from going under the mower and into the path of the blades, shielding of hot mower parts from access by young children, and equipping all ride-on lawn mowers with a no-mow-in-reverse default feature located behind the seating position of the ride-on mower operator, requiring the operator to look behind the mower before mowing in reverse.

With more women mowing the lawn, smaller yards, and greater environmental concerns about power mowers and the pollution they create, manual lawn mowers are making a comeback. With lighter metals and plastic, manual mowers are much lighter than the heavy steel mowers of the past. Compared with gas-powered mowers, manual mowers are much less expensive, quieter, easier to maintain and control, and far more energy-efficient.

PERILOUS SNOWBLOWERS

"My neighbor and I bought a snowblower together. He had an old one—I called it 'the beast.' And I'm not weak. I'm in good shape and I work out regularly . . . but the handgrips were way too big for my small hands. I have very small hands. I've got this big piece of machinery and I get really anxious. It really hurt whenever I was done. So we went in together on a new one. The new one is a sleek design, brand new. But it's definitely designed for someone way taller than me. The angle that I have to be on to do it is not right. I have to be all hunched up." (Female, white, age 56, 5′1″, 107 lb.)

Summertime isn't the only time of year that lawn care equipment can cause injuries. Every year about fifty-seven hundred people injure themselves while using a snowblower. According to the National Electronic Injury Surveillance System, a national probability sample of hospitals in the United States, since 2003 roughly nine thousand Americans have lost a finger (or two or three) to a snowblower-related injury. Overall about 15 percent of those who visit the emergency room due to a snowblower injury have fingers amputated. The average snowblower amputee is male, about fifty years of age. In addition to amputations, snowblowers can cause serious burns, hand fractures, lacerations, and aches and pains.[20]

Many accidents strike first-time users or people using snowblowers during the first snowfall of the year who try to clean out the machine's auger or discharge chute with their hands. Objects other than snow, when propelled from the discharge chute, are hurled farther and harder than the snow itself.

Snowblowers vary in weight, from sixty-pound single-stage versions to professional two-stage versions weighing one hundred pounds or more. For younger or petite people, the safest snow-removal equipment may still be the old-fashioned shovel—or just pay someone to do it for you.

POWER TOOLS FOR WEEKEND WARRIORS

Although some left-handed persons may find themselves more accident prone than their right-handed counterparts, the problem is not
their left-handedness but rather the design of the products they're
using. The design of many power tools disadvantages and endangers
left-handed persons. Researchers analyzed the records of patients
treated at the Philadelphia Hand Center during a three-year period
to identify cases of amputating hand trauma, an injury involving at
least one digital amputation near the nailplate.[21] The team reviewed
patients' charts for mechanism of injury, place of occurrence, side
of injury, and hand dominance. Researchers found that left-handed
patients were more likely to sustain an amputating injury of their left
side (70 percent, compared with 49 percent of right-handed patients).

Power saws were the most common source of injury in those
who suffered amputating hand injuries. When the nondominant
right hand is used for the task needing the greatest dexterity—for
example, guiding the wood to be cut while operating a table saw,
the dominant left hand is more exposed to injury. And when the
dominant left hand is used to guide the wood, operators must reach
across their bodies, cross their arms, and expose both hands, with an
increased risk of injury.

The research team stressed the important implications for the
design of tools, assembly lines, and workstations that are generally
designed for right-handed people. In these situations, left-handed
individuals must use their nondominant, less-skilled hand in a con-
trolling position.

RAPID "BOUNCE FIRE" NAIL GUNS

The design of rapid "bounce fire" nail guns has long been a dangerous problem for the male-dominated construction industry,
causing serious injuries to construction workers and professional carpenters. But in recent years, with the increased popularity of do-it-
yourself home improvement projects, easy access in hardware stores,

and the decline in prices of home tools, nail guns have become a serious problem for many "weekend warriors" and amateur carpenters as well. These users, who may naively purchase designs that lack safety triggers, don't receive any kind of training on how to safely use nail guns.

A team of researchers at Duke University Medical Center and the National Institute for Occupational Safety and Health, led by Hester Lipscomb, professor of occupational and environmental medicine, studied nail gun injuries among construction workers and consumers. Her research team collected data from emergency departments across the United States, the CPSC, and the CDC's National Institute for Occupational Safety and Health over a fifteen-year period. They found that the number treated each year for nail gun injuries in emergency rooms more than tripled during this period, increasing from 4,200 in 1991 to about 14,800 in 2005.[22] By 2014, the number of ER visits had climbed to an estimated 37,000 per year, with consumers accounting for 32 percent.[23]

Many nail guns are now manufactured with "sequential-trip trigger mechanisms" that allow nails to be fired from the gun only when its nose is firmly placed on the target. Researchers recommend that only nail guns with this safety feature be sold and that nail guns come with proper training and warnings for consumers.

LEFT-OUT LEFTIES AT SCHOOL

"Lately I have been noticing more that the things we use in our everyday lives are oriented around right-handed people. As a left-handed individual, I have had to adjust my lifestyle to fit into this right-handed world. Notebooks, certain chairs, and student desks are some examples, but lately the one that frustrates me the most are debit/credit card machines in the checkout lanes in stores. The signing pen isn't quite long enough [for me] to be able to sign my name comfortably or reach all the numbers when using the PIN pad; [on] some machines I can't even sign my full name because the cord doesn't reach long enough!" (Female, white, age 20, 5'1", 125 lb.)

From kindergarten classrooms to university lecture halls, seating design disadvantages left-handed students. Most side-biased tablet arm school desks are designed for right-handed writers, with an armrest for the right elbow but nothing on the left. In some cases, left-handed desks are available but tend to be placed in the back of the room, where it's harder for students to see and hear the teacher.

Trade-offs like these can affect students' behavior and even their grades. Because the left arm lacks support, left-handed students are forced to contort their entire bodies into an uncomfortable position, making them susceptible to back, neck, and shoulder pain. Such pain varies depending on the way students hold a pencil or pen, as well as on the width of the desk. Left-handed students forced to use right-handed desks may complain of muscle spasms, severe lower back pain, and carpal tunnel syndrome. They write more slowly than their right-handed counterparts, putting them at a disadvantage during timed examinations.

Policy makers and furniture buyers take infrastructure bias for granted. Yet better-informed parents, students, teachers, administrators, classroom designers, and furniture buyers must be on the alert. Proactive measures, such as purchasing long tables that allow left-handed and right-handed students to sit wherever they like, rather than using tablet seating, avoids infrastructure bias altogether.

CLASSROOM SEATING

"As students, we walk into a variety of classrooms on a daily basis, seminar rooms, studios, lecture halls, etc. Walking into a cramped auditorium at the movies or play is frustrating (especially when you need to use the restroom), but in a classroom it's just plain not functional for a lot of users. The chairs are too small for comfort, the arm rest is too low and short, and the folding desk—well, let's just say if everything else is too small, what makes you think this contraption is going to work?

"Now that the chairs are discussed, let's talk spacing. Auditorium design is meant to cram as many people as possible into one tiered room. If you are above 5 feet 3, your knees just may hit the seat in front of you, and really how much of the population is under 5 foot 3? Then you have the issue of egress . . . getting out of a row without disturbing everyone you pass is nearly impossible unless you have an aisle seat. . . .

"A friend of mine brought up all of these issues. His body width typically squeezes into the seat, the arm rests are equal to or lower than his legs, and finally the desk won't lay flat because of his legs (not his stomach, as many may think). How are we supposed to learn if we cannot be comfortable?" (Male, white, age 27, 6′, 300 lb.)

In addition to disadvantaging left-handed students, the mismatch of classroom furniture design with students' body dimensions can pose other, more serious problems.[24] Although we tend to associate back problems with adults, a surprising number of grade school children and teenagers report routine bouts of back pain, neck pain, and headache.

Much attention has been paid to seating in workplace design for adults, but relatively little interest has been given to seating in the largest workplace of all: schools. Children are at risk of suffering negative effects from poorly designed, ill-fitting furniture because they spend so much time in it every school day. Their fidgeting may result from musculoskeletal stress from their efforts to adapt to uncomfortable seating, a condition not conducive to focused learning. Negative effects of poor posture later in life may often be traced to the design of school furniture. About half of schoolchildren suffer from postural problems.[25]

One of the few studies to examine this issue was conducted by researchers in nursing at Michigan State University. As they note, classroom furniture is typically not designed to accommodate varying body dimensions. Although some desks offer overall height adjustment and some different size chairs are available, few schools offer individual adjustments for the seat, arm, and back, instead adopting a "one size fits all" philosophy. The researchers contacted the five major school furniture manufacturers in the United States to ask them what research they relied upon for their furniture designs, reporting: "The response was that they did not rely on any. Instead, each company based their designs on specifications from the American Furniture Manufacturers Association and the National Standards Board to decide 'seat width, belly room, and prohibited combustible materials.' Existing designs have basically been unaltered for years."[26]

Their results found a substantial mismatch between the body dimensions of sixth through eighth graders and their classroom furniture. Most students were sitting in chairs with seats either too high or too deep, and at desks that were too high. Girls were less likely to fit into the chairs, even after height effects had been accounted for. For many children, school furniture was simply too large.

In fact, children who develop early or later than their peers are disadvantaged by one-size-fits-all classroom seating design. Studies reveal that people working on unpadded chairs cannot sit still and concentrate for more than fifty minutes, yet classroom chairs are rarely upholstered or adjustable.

"BED WARS" IN THE HOSPITALITY INDUSTRY

The design of increasingly luxurious hotel rooms has taken a toll on the health of hotel workers, especially women.[27] Recent "bed wars" among the major hotel chains have introduced amenities such as extra pillows per bed, duvets, triple sheeting, thicker mattresses, and heavier linens—without reducing the number of rooms assigned to housekeepers per day.

During a typical eight-hour shift, housekeepers must clean about fifteen or more rooms. Their work has become more strenuous as they push heavier carts full of linens and amenities, lift heavier mattresses while making beds, and stuff multiple pillows and duvets.

Sprains and strains are the most common injuries among housekeepers. These health perils can lead to back injuries, housemaids' knee (bursitis), and shoulder pain. Among housekeepers, the rate of injury is almost double that of other service workers. Of the 1.3 million hotel workers in the United States and 280,000 in Canada, 25 percent are housekeepers, most of whom are women. Many are ethnic or racial minorities or immigrants with smaller-than-average body size.

INDUSTRIAL DESIGN AND THE WORKPLACE

Increasing numbers of women around the world have moved into industry. For industrial workers, manual handling injuries are a major source of back injuries and musculoskeletal disorders. In all occupations, mechanical equipment injuries account for a high proportion of work-related injuries.

Poor design of machinery and equipment is a major culprit. Manufacturing machinery and equipment is designed based on anthropometric data that doesn't always reflect the characteristics of the workers who will use them. To make matters worse, most personal protective equipment and tools used worldwide are based on male populations from Germany and the United States. This often endangers those who do not fit those norms, such as female workers and male Asian workers, who may not be as tall or heavy.[28]

Reproductive hazards in the workplace can pose problems for both men and women. For males, they can lead to sterility and genital defects. When pregnant women are exposed to sources of radioactivity, their fetuses can suffer permanent damage. Women in developing countries are often hired for low-paid, exploitative jobs in the microelectronics industry and the manufacturing of semiconductors, where they're often exposed to hazardous chemicals with carcinogenic and mutagenic effects.

Many electronic assembly processes require rapid, repetitive wrist, hand, and arm motions that can spark repetitive trauma disorders and other musculoskeletal health impairments.

One of the few studies on the health and safety concerns of female construction workers, who face special occupational safety challenges, was published in the *American Journal of Industrial Medicine* by Linda Goldenhar and Marie Haring Sweeney, of the National Institute for Occupational Safety and Health.[29] Goldenhar and Sweeney focused on tradeswomen such as carpenters, welders, electricians, plumbers, laborers, and mill workers. Among the tradeswomen's chief concerns were exposure to chemical and physical agents such as dust; back injuries from lifting, bending, twisting, falling from heights, or falling objects; eye injuries and lacerations of fingers and hands; lack of proper education and training; and health and safety risks specifically related to tradeswomen.

What were some of those health and safety risks? Due to negative attitudes of workers and supervisors, women are not always given opportunities to practice learning how to use dangerous equipment. As a result, women are more vulnerable to injuries than their male counterparts. Gender-specific issues of greatest concern were the lack of protective clothing and tools designed to fit women. Goldenhar and Sweeney urged contractors to convey to manufacturers the need for women's and non-average-sized men's clothing and tools.

Women are often underrepresented in critical decision-making agencies such as national safety councils, occupational health services, and health committees, according to Valentina Forastieri of the International Labour Office in Geneva, Switzerland, in a paper on women workers and gender issues on occupational safety and health.

In the United States, Australia, and Canada, national standards for manual handling are moving away from regulating weight limits for men and women and adopting a nondiscriminatory approach based on individual's risk assessment and control. As globalization and massive migration becomes more widespread, anthropometric standards need to be based on human variation and body size rather than on "model" populations.

LEFT-OUT LEFTIES AT WORK

The GMB union that currently serves one in every thirty-two people who work in the United Kingdom called for research into the health problems faced by left-handed people at work. The union claimed that equipment tends to be designed for right-handed people, forcing left-handed workers to engage in more damaging, unnatural, and awkward movements. A study analyzing death certificates revealed that significantly more left-handed people than right-handed people died in accidents.[30]

Psychologist Stanley Coren, author of *The Left-Hander Syndrome*, found that on average, the life expectancy for left-handed people is nine years less than the life expectancy for right-handed people. He cited several possible explanations, among them the increased health risks that left-handed people experience living and working in environments designed for right-handers.

His groundbreaking article (co-authored with his colleague, psychiatrist Diane Halpern) in the scientific journal *Nature* also noted that left-handers are six times as likely to die from accident-related injuries and approximately four times as likely to die in accidents while operating a car or truck.[31]

Coren's research proved highly controversial, and he was deluged with hate mail and threatening phone calls from left-handed people fearing increases in their insurance premiums. As Coren has stated, "Our environment eats left-handers" because it's "set up for the safety and convenience of right-handers."[32] He calls for engineers and politicians to legislate and design improvements in everything from industrial equipment to cars.

THE PODIUM PROBLEM[33]

A wide variety of podia can be found at colleges and universities, convention centers, city halls, houses of worship, and elsewhere—anywhere one gives a public address before an audience. No matter what their design, podia convey a position of power. Much of that sensation is from the speaker being in an elevated position, with height being a symbol of power, authority, and control.

Public venues feature a variety of podium styles. The podium may be mounted on wheels, making it easy to move. Yet the typical podium is a fixed height.

Many podia that house complex audio and video systems are mammoth in size and scale. Such behemoth multimedia consoles appear best when accompanied by an oversized body type; behind these, even a thin average-sized male may look frail and lost. Technology, rather than body-conscious design, has driven the size and shape of these podia.

How well does the typical podium work from the point of view of diversity—specifically gender, body type, and age? With increasing numbers of women in leadership positions, thousands of women across the globe who serve as schoolteachers, principals, superintendents, city officials, legislators, and experts in their profession are disadvantaged by the design of podia every day.

From a gender perspective, the podium is a socially constructed, gendered space. Although an unintended consequence, its design accentuates the speaker's gender and body size, often leading to disparate perceptions of men and women, with women being viewed in a less favorable light. It calls attention to speakers' gender in a way that would not occur had it been properly designed to match their proportions. Compared with tall or average-sized men, who look just fine behind the podium, many women behind the podium may both feel and be perceived as marginalized.

From an accessibility perspective, podia are dysfunctional. Speakers who use wheelchairs can neither see nor be seen from behind the podium. The same is true for young children.

When a female speaker of small stature is dwarfed behind a tall podium, her credibility is diminished. When speaking behind a laptop or in a dimly lit space, she becomes even less visible, and her appearance becomes much less flattering. With most of her body hidden behind the podium, and when her laptop is opened for her to review the screen, only the top of her face can be seen. When a disembodied head is all they see, audiences may find it difficult to take her seriously.

Visiting dignitaries, commencement speakers, and award recipients are photographed or videorecorded at the podium. Commemorative photos appear in print and digital media, far outlasting presentations themselves.

During religious services, members of the congregation often participate at the podium for special readings or announcements. It's similar at weddings, funerals, memorial services, confirmations, first communions, bar mitzvahs, and bat mitzvahs. Short women and children struggle on tiptoe to reach the microphone, and in many cases, they can't be heard. If they're nervous to begin with, their discomfort at the podium merely makes matters worse.

In situations like these when a mismatch occurs, the podium design calls attention to itself. It's almost as if the speaker is wearing a set of clothes that just don't fit, like a woman with size 5 feet wearing size 12 men's basketball shoes. The podium distracts from whatever message the speaker is trying to convey. Instead it sends a different message: "You don't belong here, this wasn't made to fit you, and we don't care."

Podium design in political debates can prove to be highly controversial. For the US presidential debates, televised before a live audience, political staffers spar over space to cast their candidates in the most favorable light. Presidential candidates have alternated among different formats: standing behind a podium, seated at the same table facing the moderator, and a more informal town hall or talk-show style in which each moves across the stage. Candidates of shorter stature often stand on hidden stepstools or phone books to match the height of their opponents. Candidates' perceived height is an important factor in how viewers perceive them; evidence shows that voters prefer their leaders to be tall. In about two-thirds of all US presidential elections, including the highly controversial contest between Hillary Clinton and Donald Trump, the taller candidate wins.[34] And after the election, winners are perceived as taller than before, while losers are perceived as shorter.[35]

PRODUCTS THAT ADVANTAGE BY DESIGN

Our Universal Design Podium[36]

From 2009 to 2011, professor Gale Summerfield and I served as co-chairs of the provost's Gender Equity Council on the University of Illinois at Urbana-Champaign campus. During that time, we initiated the design, development, production, installation, and use of a gender-friendly, universal design podium. Our goal was to produce a tangible accomplishment, a long-lasting contribution to campus that would outlast our committee and benefit a large number of people, especially women of small stature and those with physical challenges, a small step toward creating a more favorable physical environment for female speakers on campus. A team of women led the design, with an ample budget from our provost's office.

In addition to the unusual gender composition of the design team, another aspect that set this design process apart was that it wasn't client-driven. That is, the university hadn't initiated the project. Instead, our provost's Gender Equity Council, a university committee appointed by the provost, had recognized a glaring deficiency on campus and sought to address it with a design solution. We had a budget from the provost's office to use as we saw fit, and our committee saw this as one of its top priorities.

Our Gender Equity Council design team comprised our two co-chairs, our administrative assistant and program coordinator, Anita Kaiser, and our secretary, Kelly Sullivan, a graduate student from the School of Architecture. Together we worked closely with two staff members of the university's mill shop, Mark Barcus, mill foreman, and Brad Ward. They were enthusiastic about our proposal, and they contributed technical ideas about how to realize our goals.

The project took just a few months: the design work began in January, and the result was unveiled in March. We selected a simple design as a template and then adjusted it to meet our needs.

We discovered an existing operating mechanism to enable a podium to be adjusted with the push of a button. We just needed a design where that push-button mechanism could be installed.

Our design team made several visits to the chilly warehouse of the mill shop in mid-winter in order to oversee the design and construction process and to refine its design. During one of our more entertaining visits, a six-foot-eight employee from the mill shop and I (five-foot-two) tested out the podium and were pleased to find that it worked just fine for both of us.

Colleagues of ours who used wheelchairs suggested several refinements to its design. We also had an expert from our university's Disability Resources and Educational Services test the design to see how it would work for others with physical challenges. She too recommended a number of revisions to its design. Others who were involved in critiquing the preliminary design included an architecture faculty member with expertise in small-scale architecture and furniture design. Several women tried it out with several different styles of handbags in order to determine the ideal size for stowing their bags and purses inside the podium.

We also explored different kinds of materials. Many podia are constructed with dark stained oak and appear very heavy and imposing (as if they belong in an attorney's office or courtroom), a look we wanted to avoid. We chose a lighter wood finish, but one that could be easily stained to match the décor of the space where it would be used.

The final design included the following special features:

easy push-button operation allowing speakers to raise and lower the podium using two electronic activators
a microphone
flexible lights on both sides of the podium
slide-out for wheelchair access accommodating both left-handed and right-handed speakers
power provided on both sides
a slide-out cup holder
a space for bag/purse storage
heavy-duty wheels
a hidden stool for extra height
a modesty panel

The easy height-adjustment mechanism allows speakers ranging in height from four-foot-two to seven feet to speak comfortably and to be seen by a large audience. The podium is raised and lowered by an electric linear actuator, produced by the Linak Company out of Denmark. Two lifting columns are hidden inside the body of the podium, one on each side. A small power supply controls both columns. An up/down switch is attached to the power supply.[37]

The prototype was unveiled at the Krannert Center for the Performing Arts, the university's major performing arts venue, on March 10, 2011, at the same event at which several multimedia projects funded by the council were on display. The event was held in conjunction with Women's History Month. Hundreds of visitors, including students, faculty, administrators, staff, and community members saw the podium. Several people of varying shape, size, and physical ability tried it out. One of these visitors was University of Illinois alumna Jean Driscoll, a wheelchair racer who has won twelve medals at the Paralympic Games and won the women's wheelchair division of the Boston Marathon eight times. The podium received an enthusiastic reception from all who tried it.

Over the span of just a few months after its unveiling, the provost's Gender Equity Council funded the design, production, construction, and installation of ten of our podia at major venues and key lecture halls on the University of Illinois campus.

"We were actually contacted last summer by the University of Connecticut because they saw the podium here at a conference," Barcus said. "They [had] searched for an ADA-compliant podium that functioned like ours did but didn't have any luck. We were able to fabricate one and ship it to them, and they are interested in purchasing more! It just goes to show that our design is something that is needed to accommodate all genders, tall and short, left-handed or right-, even in a wheelchair."

Wasabi Smoke Alarms Raise a Stink

Conventional smoke alarms emit an ear-piercing wail. Because fires spread with lightning speed, every second counts. But what if you're hard of hearing or deaf, and the alarm sounds while you're sleeping? Chances are that you'll sleep right through it. According to professor Makoto Imai from Shiga University of Medical Science in Japan, this is a major problem. He adds that his research indicated, "The proportion of the elderly among fire victims was nearly 50 percent."[38]

In collaboration with Seems, a company that makes perfume, Professor Imai developed an innovative smoke detector that uses scent instead of sound. When it detects smoke, it sprays out a synthesized wasabi smell to wake up people who might have slept through a traditional fire alarm. A red LED on the alarm also begins flashing. The scent, a chemical compound called allyl isothiocyanate, is based on the pungent smell of Japan's spicy horseradish-like condiment typically tucked under sushi that causes noses to run and eyes to water.

During tests with sleepers with normal or no hearing at all, the device woke up nearly everyone within two and a half minutes after the odor hit their nostrils. The wasabi smoke alarm was launched in

2009. One hotel in Nagoya, Japan, offers it for its hearing-impaired guests. Developers are also targeting noisy gathering spots, such as karaoke parlors, where conventional fire alarms may not be heard.

The wasabi alarm earned its inventors one of ten Ig Nobel prizes awarded in 2011. The Ig Nobel prizes seek to "honor achievements that make people laugh and then think. The prizes are intended to celebrate the unusual, honor the imaginative—and spur people's interest in science, medicine, and technology." The awards are organized by the magazine *Annals of Improbable Research*, with an awards ceremony each year at Harvard University.[39]

The Walk Station: A Winning Workplace Design

Do you feel as if you don't have enough time to exercise? Do you sit in front of a computer screen at work for eight hours a day? So do millions of Americans, which is one reason why our nation's obesity rate is at an all-time high. The CDC reported the proportion of American adults who are obese at 37.9 percent, with resulting medical costs of $147 billion.[40] Many more Americans may not be technically obese (with a body mass index, or BMI, of 30 or more) but are seriously overweight (BMI of 25–29.9).

An innovative "walk station" design featured on NBC's *Today Show* and ABC's *Good Morning America* incorporates a computer into a treadmill so that workers can exercise on the job. Several companies are starting to install treadmills so that employees can burn off calories and stress while at work. Based on research from the Mayo Clinic, Mutual of Omaha Insurance is experimenting with treadmill walk stations, a healthy alternative for workers to escape from their cubicles.

Sixteen employees agreed to walk and work for about two hours a day. Among their responses were:

"I went down one dress size."
"I have less stress, feel very relaxed, more alert."
"I have a lot more energy."
"It feels great."

One male employee lost seventeen pounds in twelve weeks. "My wife likes it too," he said. Elsewhere, some employees' first response was cynical—"You're just trying to make me exercise"—but once they tried it, they were hooked.

In some companies, the demand for walk stations exceeds the supply. Why? While on the treadmill, employees can send e-mails, talk on the phone, and produce documents—they can do just about anything they would do while sitting at a desk. The hope is that the workforce will take fewer sick days, save on healthcare costs, and be happier.

Steelcase, one of the largest makers of office furniture, debuted its first height-adjustable desks in 2004. Sales of its adjustable desks and treadmill desks surged five times over to over $40 million in a five-year period. Chevron, Intel, Allstate, Boeing, Apple, and Google are among its biggest corporate customers.[41]

In addition to walk stations and adjustable desks, recent years have seen the introduction of designs that allow employees to stand, cycle, or sit on a giant rubber ball while working. Although there has been some criticism of these "alternative" workstations—some people type poorly while walking, others complain of back pain, and issues of hygiene, etiquette, and liability have also arisen[42]—even *Wired* Magazine chose "Get a Standing Desk" as one of its "18 Data-Driven Ways to Be Happier, Healthier and Even a Little Smarter."[43]

Let's Talk about Sex: Femme Den

Femme Den started as an underground international collective of women who worked at Smart Design. They were searching for answers in a world that was not designed for them, a world in which women make up just 20 percent of industrial designers but influence 80 percent of all household purchases.[44] Femme Den "is here to save good women from bad products."[45]

Femme Den was born in 2005 when Nike hired Smart Design to figure out why sales of its line of watches were flagging. The all-male team at Nike brought in two female colleagues, who discovered that female athletes were buying men's watches because they wanted added functionality, but they struggled with the chunky size on their smaller wrists. So Smart Design redesigned the watches to be both technically advanced and attractive, and sales soared.

Designers at Femme Den insist that women are not a niche market and that companies must be careful not to confuse equality with sameness.

What are some of their most important principles in designing products for women? Stress the benefits of each product, like how much time it can save or how it makes something that was once difficult much easier. Understand that women represent an extremely diverse clientele that differ by age, life stage, and body type, and that women's bone and muscle structure vary among each other and compared to men. Avoid hyperfeminized stereotypes. In other words, don't just "shrink it and pink it."

And recognize that just as designers pay attention to aesthetics, function, and ergonomics in every product they design, attention to gender is equally important. Its potential remains untapped, but for clients and consumers alike it can add enormous value.

As *Fast Company* writer Kate Rockwood argues, "When women are factored in, everyone—including businesses—can benefit."[46]

Chapter 5

TOO CLOSE FOR COMFORT: THE DESIGN OF PUBLIC TRANSPORTATION

"One of the most unusual incidents I recall during my thirty-five years as a flight attendant was when an extremely large woman used the lavatory while in flight and got stuck inside. She was trapped and couldn't get out. We tried to help her but to no avail. So she had to remain inside the bathroom for the remainder of the flight, even during landing. After we landed, a special crew was brought in to remove the door, and she was able to exit. It turned out that she worked as 'the fat lady' at the circus." (Female, African-American, age 63, retired flight attendant for a major commercial airline)

Many of us spend more than ten hours a week traveling to and from work on public transportation. Over a lifetime, this cumulative commute constitutes years of our lives, a substantial investment of our time and income. On buses, subways, trains, and airplanes, transportation costs keep increasing, but comfort levels keep decreasing. Trapped in our seats for hours, rubbing shoulders with strangers, we guard every inch of space we can. During long trips, we're keenly aware of our need for personal space. The design of buses, trains, planes, and taxicabs poses special gender, age, and body biases that affect both passengers and staff. For some, the impacts of these designs may lead to mild inconveniences or irritations for some; for others, they lead to major health problems.

Transportation companies and agencies have cut costs by

replacing customer service agents with self-service kiosks. Many of these kiosks are designed for the fast-track man on the go, with no place for a woman to stow her purse, a parent to attend to toddlers, or an older person to lean on. Turnstiles, stairways, and stations with no attendants pose special challenges for the elderly, people with physical disabilities, nonnative English speakers who require assistance, and parents with strollers. The message is clear: survival of the fittest.

PASSENGER SEATS AND THE OBESITY EPIDEMIC

Travelers who routinely rely on public transportation confront the effects of being disadvantaged by poorly designed facilities. The design of seats on public transportation has not kept pace with the nation's obesity epidemic, forcing passengers to sit uncomfortably close to one another, often for hours at a time.

Severely overweight airline passengers suffer when they squeeze into economy-class seats and ask for seat belt extenders, but when their arms and torsos overflow into adjacent seats, their neighbors suffer too. Some obese public transit riders fear that people make fun of them when they can't fit into an available seat.

Many of New York's subway cars were manufactured in Japan, by Kawasaki Heavy Industries. New Yorkers complain that subway seats were designed for smaller bodies and that they actually seat one-third fewer people than they were designed for. The typical American commuter occupies more bench space than a typical Japanese commuter, especially when wearing bulky winter clothing. And yet the typical seating in Japanese subways is a long bench along the sides of the train, a more efficient way of handling crowds than the American standard of rows of contoured seats in pairs.

Several high-profile cases of possible discrimination against obese people have ended up in court. With mixed results, they have sued bus lines (*Green v. Greyhound*), airlines (*Hollowich v. Southwest Airlines*), restaurants, and movie theaters for inadequate seating, charging for two seats instead of one, or refusing services. Social attitudes imply that obese people take up more space than they deserve.

When sharp increases in fuel prices occur and with surcharges for checked luggage and other extras, some have proposed that passengers pay a fee according to a combination of their body weight along with the weight of their luggage. Although such a policy would penalize the obese and privilege the petite, it would more accurately reflect the cost of fuel required to transport them.

According to the US Department of Health and Human Services, from 1960 to 2002 the weight of the average American increased by more than twenty-four pounds. By 2010, more than a third (36 percent) of adults and almost 17 percent of youth were considered obese, with a body mass index over 30.[1]

Yet the poor condition of American public transit facilities is contributing to the obesity epidemic. If our buses and trains were in better condition, ran more reliably, and offered diverse seat sizes to better meet the needs of a diverse population, people would be less likely to drive private vehicles. Those who walk even short distances to public transit stations tend to be much more fit, as seen in major European and Asian cities with enviable subway systems. As American waistlines have expanded, so has Americans' consumption of gasoline. A study at the University of Illinois showed that Americans are pumping 938 million more gallons of fuel a year than in 1960 because of the extra weight in vehicles. The added costs are linked directly to the impact of body weight on fuel economy. The researchers concluded that nearly one billion gallons of fuel are consumed yearly because of the weight gain of people living in the United States since 1960.[2]

FLYING THE UNFRIENDLY SKIES

The airline industry remains highly segregated by gender, and it's a workplace where women and men with smaller body types are highly disadvantaged by design. According to the US Bureau of Labor Statistics, about 87 percent of flight attendants and 7 percent of airline pilots and flight engineers are women.[3]

In 2005, the Association of Flight Attendants filed a complaint in district court against the secretary of labor and the Federal Aviation

Administration administrator for their failure to ensure the health and safety of flight attendants and other airline employees. Although the attendants lost the case,[4] data from the Bureau of Labor Statistics reveals that aircraft cabins are dangerous workplaces and that the injury and illness rates of flight attendants are four times those of employees in private industry and more than twice those of construction workers.

Occupational hazards that flight attendants encounter aboard commercial flights include turbulence, severe changes in cabin pressure, unwieldy service carts, exposure to toxic chemicals, unruly and sick passengers, threats of terrorism, and emergency evacuations. The design of service carts requires frequent bending, reaching, and pulling that can result in serious musculoskeletal disorders.

A study of flight attendants' injuries while working at the Canadian airline Air BC (British Columbia) found that an average of 12 percent of attendants were injured each year.[5] Primary risk factors were the handling of passenger baggage, the design of the galley, the design and maintenance of service trolleys, and flight attendant seating. The height of overhead bins also proved problematic. Shorter flight attendants are at greater risk for shoulder injuries, and taller flight attendants are at increased risk of lower back injuries.

"The report, citing design principles for human dimensions, said that aircraft design should allow enough space for flight attendants who are six feet tall and for 'easy reaches' by flight attendants who are 5 feet 2 inches tall."[6] According to the report, the aisle width in one model of jet was so narrow that flight attendants were forced to twist and rotate in order to serve passengers.

Among the most serious risk factors for musculoskeletal injuries reported in the study were handling heavy carry-on baggage; extra effort required to pull, push, and maneuver service trolleys; difficulties sliding drawers in and out; bending and squatting to access items in service trolleys and in the galley; reaching overhead for items in the galley and bins; and inadequate seating.

The study recommended that galleys and trolleys be redesigned. In galleys, frequently used items should be placed in areas that do not require frequent overhead lifting or bending, and input from flight attendants should determine the locations of items. Sliding drawers must move easily and be equipped with handles or grips that do not stress hands and fingers. When designing latch handles and grips, standard human measurements for fingers and hands should be used. Newer, lightweight service trolleys should be used, with larger wheel diameters and harder wheels, to reduce the force required to move them. Handle height of trolleys should be raised, to reduce bending.

The same study recommended that the design of flight attendant seating be evaluated to ensure adequate shock absorption. The study also called for handholds throughout the cabin to increase the safety of flight attendants and passengers during turbulence.

One retired commercial airline flight attendant with thirty-four years of experience indicated that she and her coworkers were most disadvantaged by design with cumulative daily exposure to extremely dry air. Pilots control the temperature and humidity levels in both the cockpit and the cabin, and she reported that although some pilots would respond to flight attendants' request for more moisture in the air, others would not. Another design flaw and source of irritation were the extremely narrow aisles that allowed only three inches on both sides to spare when the serving cart was in use. When squeezing in alongside the cart, she tried not to brush against passengers. Yet some male passengers, especially those who had had a few too many drinks, viewed this as an opportunity to take advantage of the situation, causing flight attendants to be more vulnerable to sexual harassment on the job.

A retired commercial pilot with thirty-five years of experience identified the biggest design disadvantage to be the high level of noise in the cockpit, which for him had resulted in a substantial hearing loss in one ear. According to him, the captain and the copilot wore alternate headsets such that one ear was more exposed to noise than the other. One had the left ear covered and the right ear exposed, while the other had the opposite, enabling them to converse while sitting next to each other. The exposed ear was more vulnerable to hearing loss.

In fact, hearing loss and industrial deafness in pilots has long been a problem.[7] Some lightweight active noise reduction headsets can cut ambient noise levels by up to half. While the accepted decibel level in Europe is 80, in the United States the noise level is unregulated.

According to a recent study in the *Archives of Ophthalmology*, airline pilots also have an increased risk of nuclear cataracts, a common type of cataract associated with aging, and the risk is associated with cumulative exposure to cosmic radiation.[8]

Petite female airline travelers struggle to store their carry-on luggage in overhead compartments. The larger the plane, the higher the overhead bins, the harder they are to reach. These women must rely for assistance on the kindness of strangers. One older friend of mine who is only about five feet tall has a foolproof strategy. She finds a young male passenger and, in a loud voice, asks him, "Are you strong?"

By contrast, men taller than about six feet two must crouch in order to avoid banging their heads in small commuter planes. Legroom is always an issue. When people lean back in their seats, tray tables often cannot be used. The increased popularity of budget airlines means even tighter seating than before, a special problem for taller and larger passengers. Airline seats have been shrinking, while passengers' waistlines have been expanding, making for increasingly uncomfortable travel, especially on long flights. Airbus, the company that builds jets for British Airways, Emirates Airline, and Virgin Airlines, has filed a patent for a "reconfigurable passenger bench seat" to accommodate both large passengers and small children.[9]

CLIMBING MOUNT EVEREST IN CHICAGO, TRAPPED BY A TURNSTILE IN NEW YORK

Short women traveling on subways and buses struggle to reach handgrips mounted at heights appropriate for tall men. Only during a trip to Hong Kong was I finally able to reach the handgrips while riding on the subway; they are mounted lower there to accommodate the local Chinese population. I loved it.

Crowded subways and buses with hard-to-reach handgrips force riders into uncomfortable positions, exposing them to possible sexual harassment and making pickpockets' job easier. For people who are uncomfortable in tight quarters, the lack of personal space on public transportation—especially during rush hours—can feel threatening.

In Chicago, only about 50 percent of the Transit Authority's train stations are accessible to those with physical disabilities. Many older "El" stations require passengers to climb up and down steep staircases with rusted-out risers and uneven treads.

During one of my visits to Chicago over a Labor Day weekend, some friends and I took a late-night ride on the El. It was a steamy night. Just as soon as we passed through the turnstiles, we heard the roar of the train approaching. While dashing up the steps to catch the train, I tripped and fell. I stubbed my big toe and shattered my toenail. I felt a sharp pain and looked down to assess the damage. I was bleeding, and soon my sandal was soaked with blood. When we reached our destination and I stopped to clean myself up at a nearby restaurant, I explained to the waitstaff what had just happened: "I feel terrible. I'm a mess. And I feel like a klutz." Much to my surprise, they replied: "Oh, don't feel bad. That happens all the time! People climbing those stairs on the El are always falling and getting scrapes and cuts, even breaking their arms. One woman even broke her nose."

For wheelchair users, access to the El is impossible except at those stations with elevators, which are few and far between. For many elderly people, access is nearly impossible. And for anyone just recovering from a respiratory illness, even a cold or flu, those stairways may feel like a climb up Mount Everest.

Such poorly designed and poorly maintained subway stations also disadvantage parents (usually mothers) with strollers, travelers with roller-bags, and bicyclists. Anyone with wheels who must travel up and down steep stairways is adversely affected. And the mobility of parents with young children is severely restricted.

In many cities like Chicago, the design of older turnstiles and rusted-out, revolving grated gates to enter and exit subway stations is dangerous for young children and almost impossible for parents with strollers. Rapidly rotating turnstiles can seriously injure young children and oversized individuals. They can also pose problems for those with backpacks.

During a visit to New York City a few years ago, I purchased a seven-day transit pass from one of the automated ticket machines. Once, I inserted in the slot next to a turnstile and waited for the rusted-out turnstile to unlock. But I had placed the ticket in the wrong way. I tried it again a few times, turning it in different directions. The turnstile still didn't open. Meanwhile, dozens of passengers scurried into the nearby turnstile. So I asked one of them what to do.

He explained: "You waited too long. It thinks you already went through the turnstile. You have to wait another eighteen and try again."

"Eighteen seconds?" I asked.

"No, eighteen minutes."

"You've got to be kidding!"

I darted up the steps and started walking. Several blocks later, drenched from oppressive heat and humidity, I hopped on an air-conditioned bus. I explained what had just happened to my seat-mate, an elderly woman.

"That happens all the time," she said. "It's crazy. I have many friends who never take the subway just because of that. That's why they take the bus."

And so it dawned on me that if this had happened to me, an able-bodied female in excellent physical condition, how often must the same experience befall elderly people who move slowly, visitors who speak no English, parents with children in strollers, and others who are new to the system? It wasn't my fault. It was a faulty design that no doubt frustrates hundreds of travelers every day.

Stroller design influences whether parents can travel on mass transit with small children. Double strollers are far better for use on public transport when they seat one child behind the other, rather than side by side.

Even in facilities that claim to be accessible, central poles in subway cars inhibit the movement of wheelchair passengers. Elevators that transport wheelchair users are often broken or in disrepair; many reek of urine, a sad commentary on American society and how little it values public transportation.

Passengers in wheelchairs or with strollers must contend with large gaps between the platform and the train. With a horizontal gap below, a wheelchair's front wheels can fall down and become trapped between the train car and the platform. With a vertical gap between the platform and the train entry door, it's impossible to enter without assistance. On New York's Long Island Railroad, these gaps have led to injuries—some of them fatal—even to able-bodied passengers.

"Mind the Gap" announcements are all over London's Tube—the world's oldest metro system, named best metro in Europe, and by far one of the fastest, most efficient in the world. If you miss a train at almost any station, in less than two minutes the next one appears. But even there, access to most underground stations from the street requires a trip up or down steps or extremely long escalators. On a recent trip from Heathrow Airport to London after a long overseas flight, my friend and I struggled to drag our luggage up a long flight of steps to the street from Knightsbridge station exit. On the way back, we took a ten-minute taxi ride to Earl's Court station to enjoy a stress-free lift to connect to the Piccadilly Line out to Heathrow. Although Jubilee Line trains are wheelchair accessible via elevators at all new stations east of Westminster, most other stations are not.

As of 2016, only around a quarter of Tube stations and half of above-ground stations in London had step-free access from street to platform.[10] The good news is that accessibility will increase with the planned renovation of thirty stations and construction of ten more stations along the new Elizabeth line, one of the largest public infrastructure projects in Europe.

SAFETY SHIELDS FOR TAXIS: UNSAFE FOR PASSENGERS, UNCOMFORTABLE FOR DRIVERS

Tens of thousands of taxicabs in New York, Los Angeles, London, Sydney, Shanghai, and elsewhere have safety shields, partitions separating drivers from passengers in order to protect drivers from holdups and assaults. In Chicago, a city ordinance went into effect at the start of 1993 requiring holders of more than one taxicab license to equip their vehicles with a safety shield, an emergency light, or a radio link to central dispatchers. The measure was a response to the demands of the 380-member Concerned Cab Drivers of Chicago, a group that staged horn-blowing demonstrations downtown to push for stronger safety measures after a rash of murdered cab drivers.[11] Since 1994, most taxis in New York City's fleet of approximately thirteen thousand yellow medallion cabs were required to install a partition. According to the Occupational Safety and Health Administration, taxi driving is a high-risk and dangerous occupation, ranking among the highest for homicides and assaults.[12]

Yet because the design of these partitions results in limited legroom in the back seats, elderly and tall passengers struggle to enter and exit the vehicles. Senior citizens may request to sit in the front with the driver, but most tourists don't even think to ask. The design of these taxis also makes for claustrophobic, uncomfortable rides for people of small stature, who can barely see out the window. And when heating or air conditioning is needed, hot or cold air rarely reaches past the partition and into the back seat.

The need for drivers to protect themselves must be balanced with the need for passenger safety. One should not jeopardize the other. Partitions raise a host of problems for passengers and drivers alike. Passengers slamming into bullet-resistant shields when a taxi decelerates sharply (such as in an accident) have suffered severe craniofacial injuries. Even those wearing seat belts are vulnerable. As Paul Lorenc, a New York City plastic surgeon, explained, "I see not just broken noses, but broken faces." Among the most serious injuries are crushed noses, fractured cheekbones and eye sockets, burst lacerations, and tears to soft tissue caused by the edge of the partition's sliding door or its metal track tearing the skin. Most severe cases involve "almost an avulsion" of the nose, according to Steven Pearlman, another facial plastic and reconstructive surgeon.[13]

According to Schaller Consulting, a firm that conducted New York City–commissioned studies on the subject, yellow cab passengers wearing seat belts were twice as likely to sustain serious or fatal injuries as riders wearing seat belts in other vehicles, and the gap is even wider for passengers not wearing seat belts. It could be "linked to the presence of partitions in most medallion cabs, which introduce a very hard surface in an otherwise cushioned environment."[14]

Many taxi cab drivers, too, are disadvantaged by the design of their cabs. They find the design of partitions uncomfortable and a drawback on the job. Whereas in a private car, drivers can adjust their seat to the appropriate distance for their feet to comfortably reach the pedals and for their back to sit comfortably upright, taxi drivers with safety shields cannot. The partition is fixed, making it impossible to adjust the front seat to the driver's body size. One Chicago cab driver described his plight and that of his fellow cabbies:

> It's a back problem, hip problem, leg problem, shoulder problem, and neck problem. Too many hours constantly sitting on the seat, with the typical shift ten to twelve hours. The city requires either a partition or a camera. Now they are changing to a camera so the seat can be adjusted. The partition was uncomfortable not only for the customer but also for the driver, because he could not adjust the front seat. And customers have a hard time getting in and out with that partition. Lots of taxi drivers are heavy or tall, and their legs touched the dashboard. When the taxi cab drivers complained, nobody listened. When the consumer and passengers complained, everybody's listening.[15]

According to the taxi driver, police cars also have partitions, but because police work more regular hours—typically eight hours a day, five days a week—and they get in and out of their cars, their situation is not as bad. By contrast, cab drivers must sit constantly inside the cab for longer hours, often for seven days a week.

In a growing number of cities, drivers are now permitted to have digital security cameras in their taxis instead of driver safety shields. In Chicago, for example, where taxis with driver safety shields were the norm until only recently, Taxicab Medallion Holders with security cameras must have decals posted on both the passenger- and the driver-side rear windows stating "This vehicle is equipped with a security camera." And the camera must be in plain sight, usually mounted near the rearview mirror,[16] as a deterrent to would-be criminals. The cameras have infrared capability and transmit images from the taxi to a central location so that even if a criminal attempts to destroy the equipment, his image is still captured. The cameras may prove to be a win for both taxicab drivers and passengers.

This is not the case everywhere, however. In Ireland, for example, after an extensive public consultation process, taxi drivers in 2016 expressed almost unanimous opposition to the National Transport Authority's proposal that security cameras be compulsory in all taxis. Taxi drivers preferred to be allowed to continue to exercise discretion about using such equipment. Most opposed it based on cost and potential financial impact, complaining that it would place a financial burden on them in an already difficult market environment. They also opposed installations of security screens, on the grounds that they could have a potentially negative effect on passengers' safety perception and enjoyment of the ride, reflecting poor customer service and ruining the reputation of the sociable Irish taxi driver. Taxi drivers issued a collective statement: "The proposal of a partition would create a bad representation of Ireland and give visitors the opinion that they were not in a safe environment both in the car and in our cities."[17]

If only Chicago taxi drivers had felt the same way two decades ago, what a different impression of Chicago would have been given to visitors from across the globe.

PARKING PREDATORS: PARKING LOTS AND GARAGES

The Bureau of Justice Statistics at the US Department of Justice's National Crime Victimization Survey found that, annually, more than four hundred thousand violent crimes (7 percent of all violent victimization crimes) and more than two million property crimes (11 percent of all property crimes) occurred in parking lots or garages.[18] In a parking lot, people are likely to be isolated and predators are likely to be unnoticed.

The design of many parking lots and garages makes them potentially unsafe for all users, but especially for women and children. Few lots have special paths for pedestrians to circulate separated from vehicular traffic, making them vulnerable to traffic accidents. Night lighting and security is often inadequate. Massive parking lots outside regional shopping centers and big-box stores attract criminals and teen gangs who target female shoppers. Female employees are often victimized while taking nighttime breaks or returning to their cars. Among the major themes featured in the 2005 documentary film

Walmart: The High Cost of Low Price were the dangerous parking lot designs.[19]

Purse snatchings and robberies are the most common violent crimes committed in urban parking lots. Less common but even more worrisome are carjackings and abductions. Women and the elderly are most vulnerable when they fumble for their keys or when they turn their backs and attention away from others nearby in order to load shopping bags, infants, or children into their cars. Most victims say that they never even saw the robber approach.[20]

Parking garages are typically designed to make it easier for cars than people to get around. They are often dark, cavernous spaces that feel especially unsafe at night. Large high-rise or underground parking structures have walls, columns, and elevation changes that reduce visibility. They offer fewer opportunities for natural surveillance than a single-level parking lot.

Parking garages have become symbols of danger, crime, and mystery in pop culture, featured in television and film. The shady parking garage in *All the President's Men* was the scene for clandestine meetings between secret informant Deep Throat and *Washington Post* reporter Bob Woodward, who uncovered the Watergate scandal that toppled President Richard Nixon. During the television show *The Sopranos,* scenes of fear and excitement took place in parking garages. In a 1991 episode of the popular television show *Seinfeld,* the gang got lost in a suburban mall's parking garage.

TRANSPORTATION SOLUTIONS THAT ADVANTAGE BY DESIGN

Opening Up to Obesity: Sao Paolo Subway, Airbus

Brazil's largest city, Sao Paolo, has introduced oversized seating into its forty-mile subway system that carries more than three million people each day.[21] In response to a law passed in 2006, plus-size seats for the obese were installed in its subway trains and stations as well as in cinemas, movie theaters, and concert venues. The San Paulo city metro started installing these seats in 2009, and other Brazilian states and cities followed suit.[22] The chairs are nearly twice as wide as normal seats and can support passengers weighing up to forty stone (560 pounds) without breaking.[23] Signs accompanying the seats picture a rotund passenger with the words "Priority chair for obese people." Transportation officials installed them in response to Brazil's growing obesity problem and to encourage oversized people to use public transport; however, they report that obese customers often shun the new chairs. According to one manager, "It may be that they don't want to think of themselves as fat or they resent being put in with pensioners and the disabled."[24]

Some transportation officials argue that rather than singling out fat passengers, a better solution is to provide seating without contours and divisions, allowing obese travelers to have as much space as they need without calling special attention to themselves.

But in Brazil, public transportation isn't the only venue where plus-size individuals are accommodated. The 2014 World Cup in Brazil, held at the Arena Castelao in Fortaleza, was the first to offer special seats for obese fans who submitted a medical certificate recognized by the Brazilian Ministry of Health and World Health Organization proving that they had a body mass index of 30 or more. The 2016 Rio Olympics also offered special seats for obese fans.[25]

The aircraft manufacturer Airbus has submitted a patent for the "Re-Configurable Passenger Bench Seat." The new design can fit two obese passengers, three slim adults, or a family of two adults and two children.[26]

An Enlightened Parking Garage Design

In 2009 and 2010, the National Building Museum in Washington, DC, featured "House of Cars: Innovation and the Parking Garage" as its first exhibit. One of those highlighted was the parking garage designed by architect Santiago Calatrava for the Milwaukee Art Museum. The garage features an unusual amount of natural light, and its bright white sculptural arches make an unusual design statement.[27] It feels unusually safe, clean, and comfortable, an anomaly for this building type.

The Crime Prevention through Environmental Design movement suggests specific design concepts that make parking facilities safer. These include well-designed lighting, natural surveillance, stair towers and elevators, access control, signs and graphics, and restrooms.[28]

Family-Friendly Subways in Stockholm and Seoul

With adequate funding for sensitive design and regular maintenance, and when government officials deem it a priority, public transit can be a pleasure.

But we must still look abroad for the best examples. Some public transportation stations in Stockholm's subway are designed to be especially child-friendly. Stations are almost entirely accessible for parents with baby carriages, and subway cars can easily hold two or three large strollers. Subway trains and platforms are designed with no dangerous gaps. At the central train station, a large, well-equipped play area for waiting children passengers overlooks the main concourse, with breast-feeding and diaper-changing facilities nearby. Works of art by 140 artists can be found in ninety of the one hundred stations.[29]

Seoul's subway system is another of the world's largest and most family friendly. It has been consistently voted one of the best subway systems in the world. All stations on the Airport Express are wheelchair and stroller accessible, as are almost all stations in Seoul Metropolitan Subway, often with two or more elevators at each station.[30] The stations without elevators have mechanical lifts to move people up and down stairways. The gap between subway platform and train is modified to allow for easy crossing by wheelchairs, scooters, and strollers.

Many of Seoul's subway stations have clean, safe, attractive public restrooms, making travel more pleasant for families with children and for individuals of all ages. Children age six or under ride free of charge. At nearly every station there are glass doors in front of the platforms, making it impossible for passengers to accidentally fall or intentionally jump onto the tracks. The doors only open when the train arrives. A few years ago, I had the pleasure of riding Seoul's subway almost every day while visiting there for about a week. It was an amazing experience, and as an American, I couldn't help but wonder, *Why, by comparison, is our public transit system almost back in the Dark Ages?*

Innovations in Cattle-Class Seating Design:
Air New Zealand's Skycouch

Typically only first-class passengers on lengthy overseas flights have the luxury of lying down; all others are cramped in seats that don't recline enough. The Skycouch is a way to entice passengers who dread the marathon trip overseas and allow them to travel more comfortably. Air New Zealand developed its Skycouch to enable two passengers to sprawl across three airplane seats: three adjacent seats extend forward toward the row in front of them, allowing them to turn into a romantic couch for two.

BUILDING DESIGN

Chapter 6

A TABOO TOPIC: RESTROOM REVOLUTION

"How much can you do one-handed with twenty-three pounds of a squirmy child? It's a mess! I'm trying to handle fourteen different things, removing his clothes, removing his shoes, and with no place to put them, they inevitably fall on the poor kid's head! You want to gripe about it, but there's no one to gripe to!" (Female, age 34, 5′10″, 150 lb.)

Although we're forced to use them whenever we're away from home, the standard designs of public restrooms raise a host of problems that people encounter almost everywhere. These issues adversely affect women and men, adults and children, people with visible and invisible disabilities, and those who are able-bodied. For people who live in poverty around the world, especially women and children, dangers posed by public restrooms can prove life-threatening.

If you're like most people, you use a toilet about six to eight times per day, as many as 2,920 times each year. By age eighty, you will have taken up to 233,600 trips to the toilet and spent two years of your life in a bathroom.[1] Many of those toilet visits occur outside the home. No matter what our stature in life, public restrooms affect us all.

Slowly, the design of public restrooms is changing. Yet because new laws and codes only apply to new construction and major renovations, the vast majority of the existing building stock remains untouched.

A TABOO TOPIC THAT TOUCHES US ALL

The availability and design of public restrooms has disparate impacts on men and women, posing special problems for both. Every day, men and boys are disadvantaged by urinals that force them, like it or not, to display their most private parts in public. Professor and student, manager and busboy are lined up only inches apart, within easy view of each other. Some boys become targets for bullying—not perceived as "manly" enough to stand up and show their equipment—merely by entering a toilet stall. Some suffer lifelong problems stemming from feelings of powerlessness.

Divorced or single fathers may have no choice but to bring their young daughters into the men's room. Outside, a single mother waits, fearing for the safety of her young son. An elderly woman worries about her husband who has Alzheimer's disease. Desperate parents with young children, grandparents with grandchildren, people with chronic health conditions, and adults on certain medications struggle to find restrooms in their time of need. When denied access, some have embarrassing accidents. Teenagers refuse to use their schools' filthy restrooms, rushing to the bathroom as soon as they return home.

Public restroom design deficiencies affect women and children even more adversely. Only women must attend to feminine hygiene needs and breast-feed babies. Women are more likely to accompany young children into restrooms. At the ladies' room, a mother changes her baby's diaper while eyeing her toddler, who's ready to charge out the door. Women—many of them pregnant—are trapped in long lines waiting to relieve themselves. Many suffer serious physiological consequences such as cystitis and other urinary tract infections when forced to wait. Urinary tract infections during pregnancy are associated with low birth weight and babies at risk for medical complications.

When mothers bring their preschool-age children into women's restrooms, they must lift them up to reach the toilet seat—no easy task. Yet in many men's rooms, at least one urinal is mounted several inches lower than the rest, allowing young boys to urinate without assistance from their dads. Such double standards are classic examples of disadvantaging by design—encouraging very young boys to be independent while forcing girls to be dependent on others.

When public restrooms are unfit or unavailable, we are all disadvantaged. The activities of people with invisible disabilities such as overactive bladder, enlarged prostate, urinary tract infections, irritable bowel syndrome, ulcerative colitis, and Crohn's disease, as well as those people on medications that compel them to make frequent restroom visits, are severely hampered. Young children, the elderly, and people with medical conditions who have to relieve themselves right away are forced to operate in emergency mode—and sometimes they just don't make it in time.

For millions facing conditions like these every day, public restrooms are no laughing matter. Some people are rebelling. A quiet restroom revolution is under way.

A BRIEF HISTORY OF PUBLIC TOILETS

Public toilets are important historic artifacts that reflect the psychological, social, and cultural values of society. For as long as humans have inhabited the earth, there have been public toilets. Hygiene facilities have always included a container for holding water for washing and a container for holding body wastes. The wastes were disposed of either by returning them to the soil or by washing them away with water. What distinguishes public from private hygiene facilities are considerations of sanitation, maintenance, vandalism, and physical safety.

The gender segregation in public restrooms that we take for granted today has not always been the norm. According to sociologist Sheila Cavanagh, the first separate toilet facilities for men and women were at a Parisian restaurant for a ball held in 1739.[2] Before that, they were either gender neutral or marked for men only. The public street urinal first appeared in Paris in the 1840s, but it wasn't until the 1860s that Paris constructed "pavilions pour dames," fully enclosed kiosks for women. By the 1880s, the "chalet de necessite" was available to both men and women, incorporating water closets as well as urinals for men.

In 1887, Massachusetts was the first state to pass a law requiring workplaces with female employees to have women's restrooms. By the 1920s, most states had passed similar laws.[3] Gender segregation in restrooms reflected that of other public spheres, such as ladies' reading rooms at libraries and parlors at department stores.

In America, public restrooms were often tied to modes of transportation. By the late nineteenth and early twentieth centuries they were included in railway terminals, and by the mid-twentieth century in airports and rest areas off interstate highways. The program to provide "comfort stations" along the interstate highways of New York began in 1968. By that time, public restroom facilities also had been constructed for hikers and campers in regional, state, and national parks.

Public restrooms historically have been settings for privileging one group and discriminating against another.[4] Not only have they embodied gender discrimination, favoring the needs of men over those of women, but also they have mirrored social discrimination among classes, races, levels of physical ability, and sexual orientation. Throughout much of the American South, African Americans were long forced to use separate restroom facilities from those of whites. This distinction was true not only during slavery but also after the Civil War, through the enactment of Jim Crow laws that persisted for decades. Such laws called for racially segregated places of public accommodation, including hotels, motels, restaurants, movie theaters, stadiums, concert halls, and transportation cars. In each of these environments, African Americans were either denied access to public restrooms altogether or forced to use racially segregated restrooms of their own, designated for "Blacks Only" and much more poorly maintained. These laws were not dismantled until the passage of Title II of the Civil Rights Act in 1964.

And it was not until 1990 that South Africa's Parliament repealed rigid apartheid laws forcing blacks and whites to use separate public restrooms. The laws also applied to taxis, ambulances, hearses, buses, trains, elevators, benches, parks, church halls, town halls, theaters, cinemas, cafes, restaurants, hotels, schools and universities, and even beaches and the seashore.[5]

Public restrooms in the United States were completely inaccessible to those with physical disabilities, especially those using wheelchairs, prior to the passage of the Architectural Barriers Act (ABA) of 1968. The ABA required that buildings constructed, altered by, or on behalf of the federal government; leased by the federal government; or financed by federal grants or loans be designed and constructed to be accessible by persons with disabilities. Yet it was poorly enforced. Subsequent congressional action linked this policy to civil rights by creating the Architectural and Transportation Barriers Compliance Board in 1973 under Section 502 of the Rehabilitation Act. However, public accommodations in the private sector were still not addressed, so that except for those in federally funded buildings, the vast majority of public restrooms remained inaccessible to people with disabilities. It wasn't until the passage of the Americans with Disabilities Act (ADA) in 1990 that public accommodations in the private sector—including public restrooms—were required to eliminate physical, communications, and procedural barriers to access. The new law covered a broad range of sales, rental, and service establishments, along with educational institutions, recreational facilities, and social service centers.[6]

The 1964 Civil Rights Act and the 1990 Americans with Disabilities Act provided equal access to public restrooms for African Americans and people with disabilities. Yet, no such federal legislation provides equal access to public restrooms for women.

Regarding sexual orientation, public restrooms have long provided a venue for derogatory graffiti as well as hate crimes toward gays and lesbians. In addition, today's transgender population must decide which public restrooms to use, because they do not fit neatly into either of the existing categories, men or women.

As Attorney General Loretta Lynch remarked in May 2016: "This action is about a great deal more than just bathrooms. This is about the dignity and respect we accord our fellow citizens and the laws that we, as a people and as a country, have enacted to protect them—indeed, to protect all of us. And it's about the founding ideals that have led this country—haltingly but inexorably—in the direction of fairness, inclusion and equality for all Americans."[7]

In 2016, President Barack Obama signed an executive order stating that all schools in the United States that would not allow transgender students to select the restroom of their choice would have their federal funding cut off. In North Carolina, which had passed a bill earlier in 2016 forcing transgender residents to use public bathrooms and locker rooms corresponding to their sex at birth, the economy lost $500 million as individuals across the nation abstained from or discouraged travel to North Carolina and major corporations withdrew their support.[8]

As architectural historian Barbara Penner argues in her 2013 book *Bathroom*: "Unless we recognize the part that bathrooms play in enforcing order and existing power relations, it is hard to make sense of why they are often such bitterly contested spaces."[9] Perhaps psychologist Nick Haslam put it best: "By focusing our basic fears and making the gender divide so conspicuous, bathrooms are lightning rods for the sorts of hysteria we are now witnessing. Freud wouldn't have been at all surprised."[10]

LINE UP FOR THE LADIES' ROOM: PAY TOILETS AND POTTY PARITY

> "I just recently spent some time in Europe, and the public restrooms there leave much to be desired, beyond having to pay up to two euros! It seemed that most of the toilets, no matter where I went, had no seat. So every time I went to go to the bathroom, I would feel like I was going to fall in. I just don't understand why there were no seats." (Female, white, age 21, 5′6″, 130 lb.)

> "It seems like there is always a line for the women's restroom. There is either one stall, or a few stalls but only one works. Usually, the toilet paper runs out, the toilet doesn't work, or the lock on the door is broken. There is never enough room inside the stall and usually nowhere to put your bags or purse." (Female, Asian American, age 24, 5′3″, 130 lb.)

After a commercial break at the first Democratic primary debates in Las Vegas in 2015, presidential candidate Hillary Clinton was the last to return to the podium. Moderator Anderson Cooper of CNN welcomed her back to the stage. "All the candidates are back, which I'm very happy to see. [Audience laughter] It's a long story. Let's continue, shall we? Secretary Clinton, welcome back."

Clinton: "Well, thank you. You know, it does take me a little longer. That's all I can say."[11]

At the third Democratic debate at Saint Anselm College in Manchester, New Hampshire, Secretary Clinton had exactly one minute and forty-five seconds to walk out of the gymnasium to the ladies' room and another one minute and forty-five seconds to return to the stage. Because the men's room was much closer to the debate stage, her male opponents, Senator Bernie Sanders and former governor of Maryland Martin O'Malley made it back more quickly. But this time, ABC News hosts stuck to the live TV schedule and proceeded with their questioning while Secretary Clinton's lectern sat empty. When she finally took her place, she simply said, "Sorry." Her aides had expressed concern about the long walk beforehand, even timing the distance to and from the lectern. But because no closer options were available, all they could do was advise her to be speedy.[12]

Her tardiness provoked sneers from her Republican opponent, Donald Trump. At a rally of seventy-five hundred supporters, he asked the crowd four times where Clinton had gone. "I know where she went—it's disgusting, I don't want to talk about it," as the crowd laughed and cheered. "No, it's too disgusting. Don't say it, it's disgusting."[13]

Clearly, Secretary Clinton was disadvantaged by design.

The prevalence of long lines for women's restrooms has raised public awareness about the need for equal access to public restrooms, a phenomenon now known as "potty parity." The lack of potty parity can be readily seen at places of assembly such as sports and entertainment arenas, amphitheaters, stadiums, airports, bus terminals, convention halls, amusement facilities, fairgrounds, zoos, institutions of higher education, and public parks hosting special events. Anywhere crowds of people need to use the restroom at the same time—such as when an airplane arrives or when a theater lets out for intermission—women are forced to wait in long lines while their male counterparts zip in and out.

Some women have given up waiting in lines altogether. When, out of desperation, they choose to enter the men's room, they can pay a hefty price. The most famous case is that of Denise Wells, a legal secretary. In 1990, Wells was arrested on entering the men's room after waiting in a long line at a concert at Houston's Summit, a seventeen-thousand-seat auditorium. The charge: violating a city ordinance. She had to plead her case in court. A police officer testified that twenty women were waiting to enter the ladies' room and that the line spilled out into a hallway, whereas the men's room line did not even extend past the restroom door. The jury, two men and four women, deliberated for twenty-three minutes and found Wells not guilty.[14]

Potty parity legislation first made national headlines in 1974, when California Secretary of State March Fong Eu smashed a toilet bowl on the steps of the state capitol in Sacramento as part of her successful campaign to ban pay toilets in her state.[15] They have since been outlawed throughout the United States. No longer can calls of nature be collect. However, pay toilets can still be found in many other countries. And if you don't have the correct cash, you're out of luck.

Decades later, potty parity laws requiring greater access to women's restrooms have passed in several states. At least twenty-one states and several municipalities now have statutes addressing potty parity. Although these laws have made great strides for women by increasing the *quantity* of available toilet stalls, they have not yet improved the *quality* of restrooms for women or for men.

Almost all potty parity laws apply only to new construction or major renovations of large public buildings where at least half the building is being remodeled. Despite the fact that these laws represent substantial progress, most older buildings remain unaffected.

In recent years, building codes have been revised to take potty parity into account, especially at major places of assembly such as new stadiums and theaters where significant improvements can be found. In fact, building codes are an even more effective way of making gains in potty parity than legislation. Once implemented, codes affect many states and municipalities, and they are updated regularly. Rather than requiring a vote of the state or municipal legislature, they require a vote of building-code officials. Still, women are rarities among building- and plumbing-code officials, and changes have been slow in coming.

The International Code Council publishes building safety, fire prevention, and energy efficiency codes used in constructing residential and commercial buildings. As part of a three-year effort, I had the privilege to be part of a fifteen-person committee working with the International Code Council to develop global guidelines for the design and installation of public toilet facilities. They're available for code officials in any country to easily adopt and follow. The guidelines call for a 2:1 ratio of women's fixtures to men's fixtures in bars, nightclubs, theaters, dance halls, stadiums, shopping centers, and other places. They also call for diaper-changing facilities in locations that families might use.[16] As Jay Peters, executive director with the Code Council's Plumbing, Mechanical and Fuel Gas Group, stated: "This is a relatively straightforward and practical concept. But it has not been undertaken before and will dramatically increase access to public sanitation in many nations around the world. We are so proud to be playing such an integral role in the development of these guidelines."[17]

Yet even in new construction, architects can still miss the mark. Despite meticulous planning, the Getty Center in Los Angeles, built at a cost of $1 billion, was plagued by restroom problems soon after it opened, infuriating visitors.[18] No restrooms had been included in the North and South Pavilions, causing long lines to form at a small set of women's restrooms in the West Pavilion. Since then, more restrooms have been added.

Potty parity laws differ by state. Most states require a ratio of two women's toilet stalls to one men's stall, while others require a 3:2 or simply a 1:1 ratio.[19] And which places are required to achieve potty parity may vary. A key question has been raised in the legal literature about exactly what equality in restrooms means: is it equal square footage, equal number of toilets, or equal waiting time? Wisconsin's law is a model because it defines potty parity in terms of equal speed of access for women and men:

> The owner of a facility where the public congregates shall equip and maintain the restrooms . . . with a sufficient number of permanent or temporary toilets to ensure that women have a speed of access to toilets . . . that equals the speed of access that men have to toilets and urinals . . . when the facility . . . is used to its maximum capacity.[20]

POTTY PARITY GOES TO WASHINGTON

In 2010, potty parity made national headlines when US Representative Edolphus Towns (D-NY), chair of the US House of Representatives Committee on Oversight and Government Reform, introduced H.R. 4869, the Restroom Gender Parity in Federal Buildings Act. The bill had bipartisan sponsorship.[21]

In his press release, Towns stated, "Due to biological and social distinctions, women often need to allow more time than men in restrooms, and limited restrooms impose undue hardship on women, especially those who are pregnant or suffer from other medical conditions." Towns said that "exasperating lines" at women's restrooms are "an inconvenience seen in almost every type of public building. . . . Our nation's history shows that the structure and accessibility of American public restrooms have served as manifestations of more deeply rooted problems of discrimination, among race, physical ability and gender."[22]

In fact, that was the second time that potty parity has been proposed at the federal level. Towns had introduced a similar bill three years before: H.R. 693, the Restroom Gender Parity in Federal Buildings Act of 2007, would have required buildings that receive at least $1.5 million in federal funds to have a 2:1 ratio of women's and men's restrooms.[23] It had sole Democratic co-sponsorship and died in committee.

By contrast, the bipartisan H.R. 4869 called for all new construction, major renovations, and buildings leased by the federal government to have facilities that meet or exceed the women's toilet to men's toilet (including urinals) ratio of 1:1.

I had the honor of being the only private citizen invited to testify in support of the bill during the congressional hearing on May 12, 2010. Others testifying included Representative Yvette Clarke from Brooklyn, New York, who, as a New York City councilwoman, spearheaded the passage of the Women's Restroom Equity Act in 2005; Representative Steve Cohen from Memphis, Tennessee, who served for twenty-four years in the Tennessee Senate, where he led legislative efforts in support of the Tennessee Equitable Restrooms Act, passed in 1994; former commissioner Robert Peck, Public Building Service, US General Service Administration, who oversaw more than eighty-six hundred government-owned or leased buildings; and Sharon Pratt, the District of Columbia's first female mayor.

Here's a short excerpt from Sharon Pratt's powerful testimony:

> I am a native Washingtonian and except for three years in New York, I have lived here all my life. Not surprisingly I have regularly patronized federal buildings for meetings, major events, and recreation. I can speak from personal observation and experience, as a woman resident, the former mayor of this city, and as a mother who reared two daughters in this city, that the disparity in restrooms is glaring, inconvenient, enormously inefficient, and downright unfair. . . .
>
> Our society has come a great distance in my lifetime. We certainly are a society that now genuinely supports equal rights for women. However, if the practical reality is a woman will be late for a meeting, miss much of a concert, because there are built-in impediments to equally navigating the world at large stemming from an absence of parity in restrooms—women are still not equal.[24]

And here's an excerpt from my testimony before Congress on one of the most exciting days of my career:

> I applaud the committee for addressing an issue near and dear to my heart, and near and dear to the hearts and bladders of women and children all across the United States—one that is long overdue. . . .
>
> I stand here today on behalf of your mothers, grandmothers, daughters, granddaughters, sisters, aunts, nieces, and countless female friends. No matter what our race, color, creed, age, size, shape, or political party—Democrat, Republican, Independent, or Green—we all share one frustrating experience. All too often we watch our male counterparts zip in and out of the restroom in a flash, while at the ladies' room, we are stuck waiting in long lines. And the men in our life have been stuck waiting for us. Why?
>
> Much of our built environment—including that owned by the federal government—was constructed in a different era, one where women were not as prevalent in the public realm and in the work-

force as we are today. Until recently, most architects, contractors, engineers, building code officials, and clients were not concerned about this issue. They rarely contacted women about their restroom needs, women were rarely employed in these male-dominated professions, nor were they in a position to effect change. But, finally, now we are! . . .

We may laugh, and we may joke, but for millions of people around the world—boys and girls, men and women of all ages, especially pregnant and menstruating women—using the restroom is no laughing matter. . . .

Forcing half the population to wait in line for restrooms is a subtle yet powerful form of gender discrimination. . . .

It is now time for our federal government to act. Today's proposed legislation is a small but significant step in the right direction, an achievement worth celebrating, one that you can all be proud of. It will have a positive impact on millions of women and children across the USA—and on the men who wait for them.[25]

Yet despite Towns's efforts and all the compelling testimony, H.R. 4869 never made it out of committee. Towns reintroduced the same bill again in 2011 as H.R. 1361, but it appears that it, too, met the same fate.[26] Nonetheless, for the first time, the issue of potty parity for women was brought before the US federal government, and in that sense, we all made history.

POTTY PARITY PROTESTS

What has been the impact of potty parity legislation in many US cities and states? In many cases, while women rejoiced, men protested.

As a result of the Tennessee Equitable Restrooms Act passed in 1994, Nashville's Adelphia Coliseum (now Nissan Stadium), built in 1999 for the Tennessee Titans football team, opened with 26 restrooms: 288 units for men (70 toilets and 218 urinals), compared with 40 restrooms with 580 toilets for women. It also included 12 family restrooms spread throughout its main concourse, upper concourse, and club levels.[27]

The result: according to a reporter for the *Tennessean*, a snake-like line of forty men formed at the top level, forcing some to wait fifteen to twenty minutes to use the restroom. Security officers had to station themselves at the exits to some men's rooms in order to stop those who tried to avoid the line by entering the wrong way. One police officer was quoted as saying, "We're just trying to keep fights down."

Among the comments from women visitors: "For years, I've had to sneak into the men's rooms at events. This is the first place there's no waiting." Yet a male visitor complained, "We hate it. If we had a tree, we'd be OK. This is not right. It's not funny, either."[28]

Even Tennessee's state architect acknowledged that its potty parity law needed more flexibility. So soon after it was built, and almost before the concrete had dried, Adelphia Coliseum was awarded an exemption from the state's new mandate of two women's toilets for every men's toilet (2:1 ratio). State lawmakers changed the ratio instead to 1.65 to 1.[29]

Yet State Senator Andy Womack argued against the bill, saying that lawmakers were "micro-managing. . . . The intent of the original bill is to give parity. Now we're carving out exceptions to parity." In a matter of months, a group of mostly male legislators had undermined a law whose intent was to undo decades of discomfort for women.

Restrooms at Soldier Field, the renovated stadium for the Chicago Bears reopened in 2003, also sparked heated controversy. The new stadium boasted about nine hundred toilets, and recent potty parity legislation proved detrimental to male football fans. As a result of the construction that improved wait times for women's restrooms, men were forced to wait for fifteen minutes or longer at some restrooms, especially in the end-zone sections. In response to complaints, five women's restrooms on the mezzanine and colonnade levels (seventy-one fixtures) were converted to men's rooms. After the change, the wait for men was reduced to one to two minutes; the wait time for women increased to twenty-one to thirty-two minutes.[30]

Controversy also beset the opening of Saint Louis University's Chaifetz Arena in 2008, According to the law, it had too many fixtures for women—120 compared with 103 for men—and, after much debate, the gender gap was allowed. Ironically, potty parity laws in other states and municipalities would have required an even greater majority of fixtures for women, creating no need for dispute.[31]

At one of Amazon's buildings in Seattle, where almost three hundred male workers were added in less than three years, one of employees' top complaints was potty-parity reverse discrimination. Workers complained to the Washington State Department of Labor and Industries at least once a year since 2012, although no complaint resulted in a citation. Certain floors are overwhelmingly male dominated, a symptom of diversity issues in the high-tech industry.[32] One male Amazonian wrote in his complaint filed with the state, "Due to a typical gender imbalance of our employees, we typically have long lines for using restroom stalls in most of the South Lake Union Amazon offices." Another wrote: "There are 150 males on the 8th floor with 2 urinals and 2 stalls. Even if I were to go to another floor, the situation is the same."[33] A former Amazonian posted in a widely read blog:

> Even more alarming was the bathroom culture. I can only speak to the men's room, most of which each had two urinals and two stalls. . . . At Amazon, the men's room is an extension of the office. People chitchat about work in the bathroom, as if it is just another meeting room where you can piss everywhere. . . . whenever I needed to go to the bathroom, I went to the floors occupied by the rare teams that had more women than men. Amazon Apparel, Amazon Mom, Amazon Baby—these were the places where you had a better shot of getting a free stall in the men's room. . . . It was a relief from the craziness of Amazon's corporate culture. These were the best floors. The worst floors were dominated by engineers. I regularly saw people bring their laptops into the bathroom, where they would sit on the toilet and write code.[34]

BIG SPLASH IN THE BIG APPLE

Two of New York City's legendary baseball venues, Yankee Stadium and Shea Stadium, home of the New York Mets, were replaced with new facilities that first opened for exhibition games on April 3, 2009. The new Yankee Stadium and Mets' Citi Field are the largest facilities to be constructed with the recent potty parity legislation in place.

Roughly fifteen hundred new toilet fixtures (water closets and urinals for men) greeted fans at the two ballparks, an increase of about 30 percent at Yankee Stadium and 10 percent at Citi Field.[35]

The increased number of toilets is a reflection of New York City's potty parity legislation passed in 2005, which required that all new or significantly renovated places of public assembly have two women's toilet fixtures for every one devoted to men. This includes concert halls, arenas, Broadway theaters, and stadiums. According to New York City's Department of Buildings, the new Yankees Stadium required a minimum of 358 women's toilets and 176 men's fixtures, of which no more than half could be urinals, for its large seating capacity of 52,325. As a result, the architectural firm Populous, formerly HOK Sport Venue Event, designed the stadium to have 369 women's toilets, 98 toilets and 298 urinals for men, along with 78 fixtures in unisex restrooms for families or in luxury suites.

The same architects designed Citi Field, which has a slightly smaller seating capacity of about 45,000. Although it was required to have 303 women's toilets and 152 men's fixtures, the final design included 374 women's toilets and 111 toilets and 240 urinals for men. Once minimum requirements are reached, the mix of toilets is tailored to specific needs of each building. Because baseball games bring in more men than women, stadium builders tend to first meet the requirements and then add in more urinals.

Sports reporter John Branch of the *New York Times* interviewed me shortly before the two New York City stadiums were about to open. I told him that this event was probably "the biggest splash ever for potty parity that we have seen, to have two big facilities open at the same time, and all these restrooms open at once." And I added, "Until relatively recently, most architects, contractors, engineers, building-code officials and clients were not concerned about this issue."[36]

You can imagine my surprise when, a few days later, I discovered my interview on the front page of the *New York Times,* even more so when my sister called me from afar to inform me that my words were featured as the *Times'* Quotation of the Day. Thanks to John Branch and his editors, potty parity was finally getting the attention it deserved.

BRIDES AND BATHROOMS

Have you ever tried to use a toilet while dressed in a bridal gown? It's no mean feat. Last-minute bridal-party preparations involve elaborate transformations of face, hair, and clothes. Many brides now hire specialists to prepare them on the spot. But no matter how well prepared they may be, just before the wedding begins—when all eyes will be upon them—nervous brides, bridesmaids, grooms, groomsmen, flower girls, ring bearers, and parents and grandparents of the bride may have just one last-minute thing they need to do—run to the restroom.

Whereas men's formal wear in the bridal party isn't all that different from what many men wear every day, women's formal wear is. Brides, bridesmaids, flower girls, and the mother of the bride are likely to be wearing long, cumbersome gowns. At many historic houses of worship, the trip to the restroom requires a set of steep turns down a narrow staircase. The only restroom may be a small one in the basement, hard to access while in formal wear and high heels.

Even the typical accessible toilet stall doesn't have enough room for the bride's gown and train. Some brides need to ask another member of the wedding party to assist them in the bathroom for fear of dropping the gown in the toilet—an embarrassing situation for all. At my niece's wedding in a historic church in San Diego, her twin sister had to help her maneuver her bridal gown around the toilet stall. Minutes later, the bride was walking down the aisle, arm in arm with her father.

BATTLING IT OUT WITH BABIES

"I think it is strange that women's restrooms have baby-changing tables, and so many men's restrooms do not. I am a woman, so I have not seen many men's restrooms, but the few I've seen did not have changing tables. Don't men change diapers?" (Female, white, age 24, 5′2″, 120 lb.)

The design of most public restrooms does not work well for infants and toddlers and the parents who accompany them. Although babies' voices can be loud, their concerns have not yet resonated with restroom designers and building-code officials. Diaper-changing stations installed in restrooms are a step in the right direction. Yet many parents find the location, design, and maintenance of these stations to be problematic.

Babies' diapers may need to be changed ten or more times a day. An infant needs to be changed about every two hours; a one- to three-year-old, about every three to four hours. If their diapers are not changed in a timely manner, children may develop diaper rash, infections, and other health problems.

Some diaper-changing stations are located in stalls designated for people with disabilities, while others are outside the stalls. When families occupy the accessible stall for purposes of changing diapers, it's inaccessible to people with disabilities who may need it. As one mother explained: "I feel guilty, so I leave the door open if I can. That way if someone needs it, I can see them and apologize."

Not all stalls for people with disabilities accommodate strollers or multiple users. As one mother put it, "I've had three of my kids in the stall with me at once."

Some changing stations work well for babies but not for toddlers. One mother complained of the changing station in the ladies' restroom at a local toy store. The surface was large enough only for a tiny baby, but her young son had already outgrown it. "His head was not supported," she explained. "If my husband were allowed inside, he could cradle the child's head while I was changing the diaper, but instead he had to wait outside."

Adequate space is rarely provided for all the accessories carried in bulky diaper bags, such as extra diapers, wipes, creams, changes of clothes, and a clean changing pad to spread out on the changing surface. So if the bag is hard to access, the process becomes a juggling act.

For parents of twins or triplets, all the above problems are compounded. Oversize strollers are even more awkward to maneuver in tight restroom designs. Changing diapers and getting toddlers and small children to "go potty" becomes a major ordeal.

While serving as chair of the Chancellor's Committee on the Status of Women (CCSW) at the University of Illinois at Urbana-

Champaign, I led an effort to document the numbers of diaper-changing stations and lactation spaces across campus. Our building operation service workers collected data for us during their shifts cleaning campus restrooms. At that time, in 2003, our campus had 1,875 restrooms, and we were able to study many of them, but not all. Our final report showed that of the 1,221 restrooms observed, only thirty-six had diaper-changing stations. Fifteen of these were men's rooms, and twenty-three were women's rooms.

Years later, as co-chair of our provost's Gender Equity Council, I led the effort to develop a checklist of gender- and family-friendly public restroom standards to be used by our campus's Facilities and Services Department during new construction and building renovations. We evaluated the extent to which restrooms in our campus's most public buildings, including those at the alumni center, the recreation centers, the student union, the museums, and the performing arts center, were gender- and family-friendly. We found that only about half these buildings had well-placed changing tables, if they had them at all, and none had retractable child protection seats to accommodate a second child. Even the newest facilities surveyed didn't meet the standards set out in our Gender Equity Council Design Checklist.[37]

One of my graduate students, Muhammad Taimur, a father of two young children, shared my interest in diaper-changing stations because he and his wife, Sana, were facing this problem every day. He worked with me to study this issue both on and off campus. We found that twelve years after the CCSW study, out of over 1,880 restrooms on campus, only forty (2 percent) had diaper-changing stations.

Muhammad, Sana, and I teamed up to study nearby restaurants, eateries, and coffee shops frequented by students and their families. They took turns photographing men's and women's restrooms and interviewed each store owner or manager. Of the sixty-eight dining establishments they visited, only nine (13 percent) had diaper-changing stations, of which four, representing national chains like McDonald's and Panera Bread, had changing stations in both men's and women's rooms. Three were in unisex restrooms, and two were only in women's rooms. Fifty-nine establishments (87 percent) had no changing station at all.[38]

In California, the state legislature with broad support approved two Potty Parity for Parents Acts bills that would have modified existing state laws to ensure that public places such as movie theaters and shopping malls installed diaper-changing tables in both men's and women's restrooms. But, in 2014, Governor Jerry Brown vetoed them both, stating, "At a time when so many have raised concerns about the number of regulations in California, I believe it would be more prudent to leave the matter of diaper changing stations to the private sector."[39]

In 2015, Ashton Kutcher, a new dad, and star of the sitcom *Two and a Half Men*, brought widespread attention to this issue when he launched a Change.org campaign and posted on his Facebook page: "There are NEVER diaper changing stations in men's public restrooms. The first men's room that I go into that has one gets a free shout out on my FB page! #BeTheChange," Two days later, nearly 215,000 people had liked his post.[40]

Just one month later, New York State Senator Brad Hoylman introduced a bill requiring public buildings and other places of public accommodation to include changing stations in men's restrooms if they exist in women's restrooms. Hoylman, who has a young daughter with his husband, David Sigal, believes the double standard is "an anachronism that reflects the bias toward women being the caregiver. . . . That's simply not the case today. In addition to same sex couples of men and men in heterosexual couples, there are also a lot of single male parents out there too."[41] Because of the lack of changing tables in men's rooms, the two dads were often forced to change their daughters' diapers on bathroom floors, in hallways, and even outside in parking lots. As of 2016, it appears the bill remained in committee and was not voted upon.[42]

In 2016, US Representative David Cicilline of Rhode Island introduced H.R. 5147 at the federal level "to amend title 40, United States Code, to require that male and female restrooms in public buildings be equipped with baby changing facilities"[43] what became known as the "Bathrooms Accessible in Every Situation (BABIES) Act." The term "baby changing facility" refers to a table or other device suitable for changing the diaper of a child age three or under. The bill, which passed the House and Senate in September and was signed into law by

President Obama on October 7, 2016, applies to restrooms in publicly accessible federal buildings, those constructed, altered, or acquired by the Public Building Service of the General Services Administration. It goes into effect in October 2017. Not covered by the law are public buildings in general, such as movie theaters, shopping malls, and restaurants. Exceptions are also made for public building restrooms that are not available or accessible for public use; restrooms in public buildings that have conspicuous signage indicating where a restroom with a diaper-changing station is located on the same floor; and if new construction would be required to install the diaper-changing station and the construction cost would be "unfeasible."

ACCESSIBILITY VS. AVAILABILITY

Public restrooms in the United States were completely inaccessible to those with physical disabilities, especially for those using wheelchairs, prior to the passage of the Architectural Barriers Act of 1968.

Yet it wasn't until the passage of the Americans with Disabilities Act (ADA) in 1990 that public accommodations in the private sector—including public restrooms—were required to eliminate physical, communications, and procedural barriers to access. The ADA covers a broad range of sales, rental, and service establishments, along with educational institutions, recreational facilities, and social service centers. Detailed accessibility guidelines are spelled out in the *Americans with Disabilities Act Guidelines for Buildings and Facilities*, which is updated and amended periodically.

Although the ADA succeeded in providing greater *accessibility* for people with disabilities in public restrooms, *availability* is still a problem. For many people with disabilities—for example, those with spinal cord injuries who have less control over urinary or digestive systems—finding a restroom in a hurry is essential. And although the ADA addresses a broad range of physical disabilities, it doesn't recognize the "restroom-challenged"—people with bodily issues requiring frequent restroom use—as a disability. Legal action or legislative lobbying action may be the most effective means of forcing the US Department of Justice to confront this issue.

Even though restrooms in public buildings must now comply with ADA requirements, people with disabilities still often find them problematic. Harold Kiewel, an architect who uses a wheelchair, wrote in an e-mail:

> Why are hand dryers and paper towel dispensers never near the sink? Here's the scene. You're in a public restroom. After using the facilities you go to wash your hands. Now your hands are wet and you reach for a towel. But, they're across the room behind you! Your hands are wet, your wheelchair wheels are on the floor of a public restroom, and you have to wheel around to get to the towels or hand dryer!! . . . Paper towels are never where you need them.[44]

Kiewel believes that "because the ADA (Standards for Accessible Design) are descended from a lineage of model building codes, the designer's questions are always, 'what do I have to do?' and 'how small can I make this?' I'm practically never asked, 'how do I make this work?'"

Individuals who are blind or who have poor vision find navigating public restrooms especially difficult. One such person is Beth Finke, author of *Long Time No See*: "I find myself always carrying a small container of antibacterial soap with me." She explained in an interview how difficult it is for a blind person to work out where the soap dispenser, the paper towels, and the garbage are located in public restrooms. "By the time I feel around for all that stuff, my hands are full of germs again!"[45] Finke's life would be easier if all public restrooms were set up the same way, because "then I could predict where the soap, the towels, the garbage can is . . . any chance of this happening one day?"

But even for those who are completely able-bodied, access in and out of toilet stalls can be challenging. Add a backpack or luggage to the mix—or worse, more than one piece of baggage—and the squeeze is even tighter.

STIGMAS AND TABOOS: A SENATOR AND A PRINCESS

Public restrooms can serve as settings for hidden, private lives. On June 11, 2007, Senator Larry E. Craig (R-ID), then age sixty-two, catapulted toilet stalls into national headlines. An undercover police officer at the Minneapolis–St. Paul International Airport investigating sexual activity in the men's room discovered the senator peering between gaps in toilet-stall partitions and engaging in foot tapping, a code used to solicit sex. He handed the arresting officer his business card and asked, "What do you think about that?"

The senator was arrested but denied any sexual intent. He explained to police that his foot had touched the undercover officer's foot in the adjacent stall because he had "a wide stance when going to the bathroom."[46] Nearly two months later, Craig pleaded guilty to disorderly conduct. A second charge of interference with privacy was dismissed. He was fined more than $500, given a suspended ten-day jail sentence, and placed on unsupervised probation for a year. He later regretted having pleaded guilty, arguing that his judgment had been clouded by a "witch hunt" by Idaho newspaper reporters.

Craig instantly became embroiled in a media frenzy. Fellow Republicans called for his resignation and party leaders ousted him from committee leadership posts. Several Republicans called for Craig to resign. One of them, Senator Norm Coleman of Minnesota, stated that Craig had pleaded guilty to "a crime involving conduct unbecoming a senator."

Strangely enough, the senator had been disadvantaged by the design of the Minneapolis airport restroom and that of most American restroom stalls. And so had the unsuspecting men in the restroom who were just going about their business. Our toilet-stall partitions are so high off the ground that our pants, legs, socks, and shoes are all too visible when we're trying to do our business. Gaping spaces between partitions allow predators and passersby to catch a fleeting glimpse of us while we're in our most vulnerable positions.

Had Craig used the airport restroom in London, Stockholm, or Tokyo, his career might not have ended up in ruins. Throughout much of Europe and Asia, restroom privacy is assured, because toilet-stall partitions are tightly sealed and extend all the way down to the floor. For this reason, many European and Asian visitors to the United States feel uncomfortable using American restrooms.

In fact, sex and drug trafficking are all too common in today's outmoded public restroom designs, particularly in men's rooms. And it's largely for this reason, sadly, that too many public restrooms are closed altogether, not available for those who truly need them.

But sex and drugs aren't the only secrets kept in public restrooms. Young women who share public restrooms in dormitories or sororities may be surprised to discover their girlfriends suffer from bulimia nervosa. Bulimia is an eating disorder in which a person uncontrollably consumes an excessive number of calories (1,500–3,000) in a short period of time (less than an hour). In order to get rid of all those calories, the individual vomits, takes laxatives or diuretics, fasts, or exercises excessively. Bulimia received international attention with the 1992 publication of Andrew Morton's book *Diana: Her True Story*, which revealed that Princess Diana of Wales suffered from the disorder.

Eating disorders have become a serious health problem for those obsessed with the need to maintain a perfect body image. According to Marcia Herrin of Dartmouth College's Eating Disorders Education, Prevention and Treatment Program, five million to ten million females and one million males suffer from eating disorders. Most tend to be young, from age fourteen to twenty-five.[47]

About 5 percent of college-age women suffer from bulimia. Those who live in apartments off-campus can keep their disorder hidden even from roommates, much more so than those who share communal bathrooms in group-living arrangements such as dorms and sororities. After meals, they disappear to the bathroom, where they attempt to camouflage their purging with running water or a loud exhaust fan.

At one sorority at a large northeastern university, hundreds of sandwich bags began mysteriously disappearing from the kitchen. The sorority president investigated and was shocked to find bags filled with vomit hidden in a basement bathroom. She later learned that the building's pipes had been eroded by gallons of stomach acid and would have to be replaced.[48]

SHY BLADDER SYNDROME

Although few discuss it publicly, some men worry about the lack of privacy in the standard men's room lineup of urinals, with users in full view of each other. A disorder called paruresis, which makes it impossible for someone to urinate in public if others are within seeing or hearing distance, affects more than twenty million Americans, or about 7 percent of the US population. This disorder is also known as shy bladder syndrome (SBS), bashful bladder syndrome (BBS), bashful kidneys, or pee-phobia.

According to Steven Soifer, co-author of the 2001 book *Shy Bladder Syndrome*, about two million people suffer so seriously from BBS that it interferes significantly with their work, social relationships, and other activities:

> The emotional pain associated with paruresis is severe and crippling. From the father who avoids taking his son to a ball game because he can't use the troughs at the stadium to the mother who doesn't take her daughter clothes shopping because she can't use a department store bathroom, to the executive who loses promotions because he or she cannot travel distances from home, to the applicant who loses a job opportunity because he or she can't provide a urine sample for pre-hire drug testing, paruresis destroys lives.[49]

Along with Robert Brubaker, program manager of the American Restroom Association, and the International Code Council, Soifer was instrumental in helping revise building codes in the United States to ensure that the partitions between men's urinal stalls are wider and taller than previously required.

"HOLDING IT IN" AT SCHOOL

Public school restrooms in America and around the world present myriad problems. As of 2013, the United States had almost 99,000 public schools and almost 31,000 private schools—about 130,000 schools in total. If one assumes each of these schools includes

The beautifully designed Acropolis Museum in Athens, Greece, features glass-floored galleries and stairway promenades for visitors to view ancient archeological treasures. But it also provides them with a peek up skirts and dresses. *Photo from Kathryn H. Anthony.*

Too much transparency in government? A glass stairway designed with clear risers posed problems for anyone wearing a dress or skirt at the $105 million Franklin County Courthouse in Columbus, Ohio. Judge Julie Lynch, who wore dresses under her robes every day, complained, "How can you open a brand-new building and not take in consideration half the population?" *Photo from Brad Feinknopf / OTTO. Quote from Elizabeth Johnson, "Glass Staircase Not Dress Friendly," CNN, This Just In, June 9, 2011, http://news.blogs.cnn.com/2011/06/09/glass-staircase-not-dress-friendly/.*

As part of the $88 million renovation of University of Iowa's Kinnick Stadium, the locker room for visiting football teams was designed to intimidate the opposing team and question players' masculinity when it was decorated in pink. *Republished with permission © 2016 The Gazette, Cedar Rapids, Iowa.*

The pink locker room design at the University of Iowa's Kinnick Stadium has attracted a great deal of publicity from fans and foes alike. *Republished with permission © 2016 The Gazette, Cedar Rapids, Iowa.*

They make women look taller, slimmer, and sexier, but the design of high heels can cause ankle sprains and breaks. Women who squeeze their feet into stylish pointed-toe high heels for years often develop painful degenerative diseases and may require surgery. Stiletto heels can interfere with driving and can damage hardwood floors. *Photo from Madhuri Shashidhar.*

The "size problem," returning clothes that don't fit, is a massive, expensive problem for both consumers and retailers, especially online. Just as touch ID revolutionized smartphone security, new technology provided by 3D body scanners captures hundreds of measurements around the body, providing a perfect fit for all shapes and sizes and revolutionizing the world of fashion design. This space-saving Fit3D ProScanner uses a single camera to capture a point cloud of roughly 500,000 vertices and 380 body measurements. *Images courtesy of Fit3D Inc. | www.fit3d.com | (650) 275–3483.*

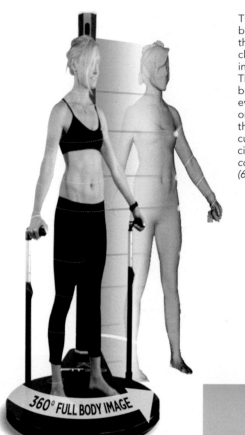

Through Fit3D.com, people can scan their bodies for a minimal fee, then upload their data to an e-commerce portal to buy clothes designed to fit them perfectly, saving buyers and retailers time and money. The company's aim is to democratize 3D body scanning and make it accessible to everyone. Fit3D ProScanners are placed once every two days at locations around the world to enable people to receive customized products and services specifically crafted for their bodies. *Images courtesy of Fit3D Inc. | www.fit3d.com | (650) 275–3483.*

Coaches, trainers, and wellness professionals find it heartbreaking to watch clients become discouraged, fade away, or disappear. Repeated measurements from affordable Fit3D ProScanners like these help clients measure subtle, positive changes in their bodies as they attempt to lose weight and reach their fitness goals. *Images courtesy of Fit3D Inc. | www.fit3d.com | (650) 275–3483.*

Child-safety seats come in many different designs, styles, and colors, and they are required by law throughout the United States. Yet they are not subject to the rigorous testing one might expect, which gives all parents cause for concern. Motor-vehicle accidents are the number one cause of death for young children. *Photo from Andrea Cecelia. Statistic regarding accidents from US Department of Transportation, "Children Injured in Motor Vehicle Traffic Crashes," National Highway Traffic Safety Administration, DOT HS 811 325, May 2010, http://www-nrd.nhtsa.dot.gov/Pubs/811325.pdf.*

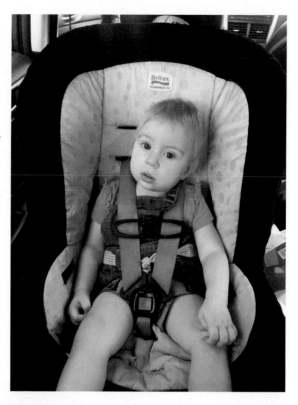

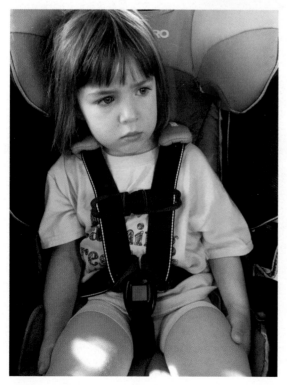

Federal regulators provide ratings for ease of use for child car seats, but not for their safety. Different kinds of tests for child-safety seats should be required for front-end collisions and side impacts, at varying speeds including freeway driving, and for children, toddlers, and infants, each of whom may be impacted differently in a crash. *Photo from Andrea Cecelia.*

Every two weeks, a child in the United States is killed when a piece of dangerously designed furniture or a TV tips over. In 2016, IKEA announced a recall of over 35 million chests and dressers in the United States and Canada after six children died from furniture tip-overs. The company reached a tentative settlement to pay $50 million to three families whose children, all around age two, were crushed to death. *Photo from Andrea Cecelia. Settlement information from Jonah Engel Bromwich,"Ikea Reaches $50 Million Settlement over Deadly Furniture Accidents," New York Times, December 22, 2016.*

No matter how many well-designed childproofing features you add to your home, children will find a way to outsmart you. These homeowners had no idea the design of this stairway was dangerous—until their daughter showed them. *Photo from Andrea Cecelia.*

Tall beds with tall mattresses and lots of pillows make fashion statements in furniture stores, hotels, and homes, yet their design can prove dangerous to those who sleep in them, especially the elderly and children. Housekeepers who earn their living laundering tall beds at hotels, often petite women, can face long-term injuries from handling oversize mattresses day after day. *Photo from Kathryn H. Anthony.*

Bunk beds are a great way to save space and are a popular design in children's bedrooms, in the military, and in dormitories. Yet, every year, many people are injured falling out of them either during their sleep or on their way up or down. *Photo from Kathryn H. Anthony.*

Short women and men are disadvantaged by the one-size-fits-all design of most podia, especially when you add a computer. People in wheelchairs can't even use them. *Photo from Kathryn H. Anthony.*

Every year, thousands of commencement speakers, award recipients, professors, and politicians are photographed behind poorly designed podia. Commemorative photos in print and digital media far outlast the events themselves and leave a lasting legacy that shortchanges many speakers. *Photo from Kathryn H. Anthony.*

As co-chair of the University of Illinois at Urbana-Champaign's Provost Gender Equity Council, I led the design, development, production, and installation of a gender-friendly universal-design podium, the first of its kind on our campus and one of the few available anywhere. It accommodates anyone from four feet two to seven feet tall, plus those who use wheelchairs, along with those who are left-handed. It was built in our university mill shop (shown here), and we now have several on campus. *Photo from Kathryn H. Anthony.*

My first chance to use the podium that we designed was at our university commencement ceremony, where I read the names of all the graduates. With the press of a button, I adjusted it to my height, and speakers before and after me did the same. *Photo from Kathryn H. Anthony.*

The design and construction team from the Provost's Gender Equity Council at the University of Illinois at Urbana-Champaign celebrates the unveiling of our universal-design podium at the performing arts center. *Photo from Kathryn H. Anthony.*

Segway personal transporters are designed for use by people 100–259 pounds. They work well for most adults, regardless of gender, age, or body size.

Steelcase Walkstations incorporate space for a laptop computer atop a treadmill, allowing workers to exercise on the job, burn off calories and stress, and eliminate a trip to the gym. They have come into great demand in the workplace and help combat the growing rate of obesity. *Photo from Steelcase.*

Whereas short passengers struggle to lift their baggage into overhead bins and often must ask others for assistance, tall passengers routinely bang their heads on luggage bins when entering and exiting aircraft, even on transatlantic jumbo jets like this one. Tall men hit their knees on the seats in front of them and are squeezed in like sardines throughout the flight. In smaller commuter planes, they hit their heads while entering, exiting, and walking throughout the aircraft. Today's airline passenger seats have not kept pace with the growing sizes of people's bodies. *Photo from Kathryn H. Anthony.*

In this crowded Tube car in London, short women hold on to vertical poles while tall men use high horizontal rails. Offering passengers choices like these is an example of good design. *Photo from Kathryn H. Anthony.*

Subways and buses designed with hard-to-reach handgrips often expose short passengers to pick-pockets. *Photo from Kathryn H. Anthony.*

"Mind the Gap" signage and loudspeaker announcements are ubiquitous throughout London's underground railway system, the Tube, one of the most efficient public-transportation systems in the world. Without a reminder in subways elsewhere, gaps between platforms and trains are dangerous to able-bodied people, persons with strollers, and persons in wheelchairs. *Photo from Kathryn H. Anthony.*

The design of the subway system in Seoul, Korea, with its glass partitions that prevent passengers from falling onto the tracks, is one of the best in the world. Several other cities elsewhere have them too, but except at airports, they are very rare in the United States. *Photo from Kathryn H. Anthony.*

Women and girls all over the world are forced to wait in long lines for ladies' rooms designed with an inadequate number of toilet stalls, a subtle yet persistent form of gender discrimination. The prevalence of long lines at ladies' rooms at theatres, airports, stadia, fairgrounds, and elsewhere has raised awareness of the need for equal access to public restrooms, or "potty parity." At this popular London theatre, no men were waiting for the men's room while a long line formed outside the ladies' room before and after the play, as well as during intermission. *Photo from Kathryn H. Anthony.*

Along with District of Columbia former mayor Sharon Pratt and other members of Congress, in 2010 I had the honor of testifying before the US House of Representatives Committee on Oversight and Government Reform on behalf of potty parity legislation. It was the first time a congressional hearing had been held on this issue. *Photo from Kathryn H. Anthony.*

Millions of parents around the world struggle each day, several times a day, to change their children's diapers, often in inconvenient or dangerous places and while handling more than one child. Diaper-changing stations are needed in all restrooms. *Photo from Anastasia Lewis.*

Diaper-changing stations are signs of progress, but most public restrooms around the world don't have them. Sometimes they can be found in women's but not men's restrooms, which is a form of gender discrimination. *Photo from Andrea Cecelia.*

Often those who design and install plumbing fixtures like this hotel shower fixture fail to think of anyone shorter than they are. At this European hotel, I could only either shower with one hand or risk injuring myself trying to put the showerhead back in place. *Photo from Kathryn H. Anthony.*

At this hotel, I could barely reach the hangers. The robes were totally out of my reach. Whoever designed and selected this wardrobe forgot about people like me. *Photo from Kathryn H. Anthony.*

Children struggle to reach faucets, while parents struggle to hold them in place every time they wash and dry their hands. The design of most public restrooms is not family-friendly. *Photo from Andrea Cecelia.*

Children struggle to reach hand dryers that are installed much too high. If they leave with wet hands, they're even more susceptible to germs. *Photo from Andrea Cecelia.*

Two sets of beautifully designed unisex restrooms at La Jolla Shores in San Diego opened in 2005 and 2014, replacing old gender-segregated restrooms that had fallen into disrepair and where women and children were forced to wait in long lines. Even on peak summer weekends, lines at the new unisex restrooms move quickly, and men, women, boys, and girls wait together in the same line. *Photo from Kathryn H. Anthony.*

Every year, more than two to three million swimmers, surfers, snorkelers, and scuba divers at La Jolla Shores use these unisex toilets and showers, which are open twenty-four hours a day. This open-air public-restroom design is a successful prototype that can and should be used elsewhere. *Photo from Kathryn H. Anthony.*

Millennium Park, opened in 2004, has transformed the city of Chicago. Special events and award-winning designs like the Pritzker Pavillion, Great Lawn, Crown Fountain, and Cloudgate draw thousands of visitors each day, with plenty of well-designed, easy-to-access public restrooms, a critical ingredient in the park's recipe for success. *Photo from Terry Evans.*

At Carlsbad Premium Outlets, an outdoor shopping mall in Southern California just east of Interstate 5, the women's toilet stalls are designed with a recessed shelf for keeping purses, handbags, and shopping bags off the floor, a rare treat. *Photo from Kathryn H. Anthony.*

Joi Sumpton, a mother, designed Step 'n Wash to allow kids to wash their hands without splashing themselves and their parents, grandparents, or caregivers. No more need to lift up and hold a thirty- or forty-pound child or two against a counter. *Photo from Step 'n Wash Inc. / Allison Shirreffs.*

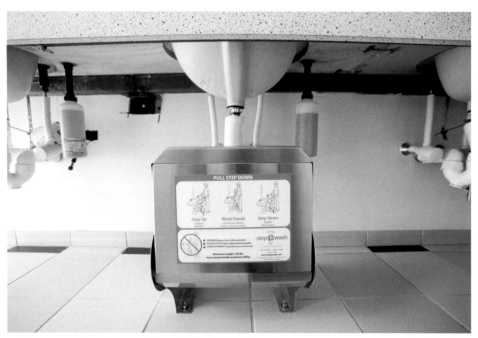

With Step 'n Wash, over 250 million children have safely reached the sink by themselves. *Photo from Step 'n Wash Inc. / Allison Shirreffs.*

More than forty million TOTO Washlets have been sold worldwide, and Washlets are now in almost half the homes in Japan. Their user-friendly, sustainable design eliminates the need for toilet paper and promotes independence for the very young to the very old. Here is mine. *Photo from Kathryn H. Anthony.*

Here is the basic model of the TOTO Washlet, the A100 with controls on the side of the toilet seat. Toilets like these are common in public restrooms throughout Japan as well as in private homes. Cleaning with water instead of paper is much more hygienic. *Courtesy of TOTO.*

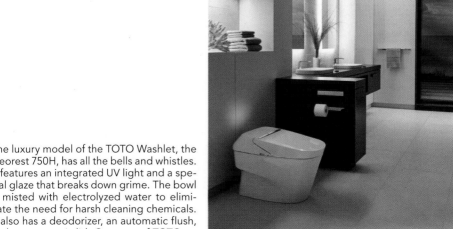

The luxury model of the TOTO Washlet, the Neorest 750H, has all the bells and whistles. It features an integrated UV light and a special glaze that breaks down grime. The bowl is misted with electrolyzed water to eliminate the need for harsh cleaning chemicals. It also has a deodorizer, an automatic flush, and an automatic lid. *Courtesy of TOTO.*

One reason for Google's success is its great attention to designing workplaces for a highly diverse group of employees from all across the globe. *Photo from Marco Zecchin, Google.*

Google's workplaces promote a healthy workforce by designing a diverse set of options where people can work as well as work out, accommodating employees of all shapes and sizes. *Photo from Marco Zecchin, Google.*

A wide variety of seating-design options at Google's workplaces provide people with different body sizes plenty of choices so they can work comfortably. *Photo from Marco Zecchin, Google.*

At Google's Chicago headquarters in the West Loop, opened in 2015, an open stairway design through a central atrium encourages exercise on the job and keeps Googlers in shape. Extra space at each landing encourages employees to stop and chat without blocking traffic. *Photo from John Musnicki, Google.*

The cuisine at Google is designed to appeal to tastes from all over the world. At microkitchens like this one in Google Chicago, healthy food is placed front and center, with less-healthy options harder to reach. *Photo from John Musnicki, Google.*

The design of this glowing glass mural of the Milky Way at Children's Hospital at Montefiore in the Bronx, New York, takes children on a journey to health, discovery, and possibility, which is part of the hospital's mission. Depending on the theme of each floor, patients' rooms are decorated with constellations, terrestrial animals, or aquatic creatures. *Courtesy of Montefiore Health System.*

This is one of a series of artwork installations at Montefiore Health System in the Bronx, New York, intended to inspire patients, visitors, and staff of all ages. Created with a full-color spectrum of art glass and partnered with a swirling galaxy-like design in stainless steel, *We Are Stardust* pays homage to the hospital's namesake, Albert Einstein, and his theory of relativity. The beauty of the glass reflects the diversity of humanity; the intricate overlay suggests our place in the cosmos; and together they speak to our human connections and the cycle of life. Art Credit: *Laurel Porcari We Are Stardust 2016. Fused art glass with brushed stainless-steel overlay. The Montefiore Fine Art Program and Collection. Photo credit: Ken Shung.*

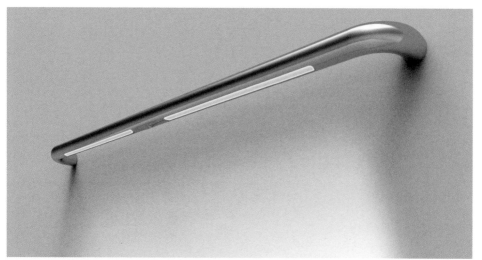

A team of healthcare designers and a design researcher developed the Balance Beam to improve safety for patients and for anyone who has to climb out of bed in the dark. A simple touch of the hand activates the LED bar, illuminating a path to your destination. When used at home, it can help elderly people live healthier, more independent lives. *Provided by HOK Product Design.*

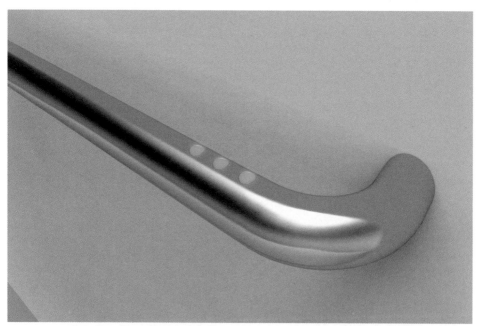

A close-up of light sensors on the Balance Beam. Three lit touch sensors at the top can be preprogrammed for any length of time, and are amber so they don't interfere with sleep patterns. The Balance Beam's integrated LEDs illuminate the path from the bed to the restroom, or any path where trips and falls are common. *Provided by HOK Product Design.*

approximately ten restrooms, this yields a total of about 1.3 million school restrooms.[50]

Estimates are that at least 20 percent of these restrooms suffer from poor upkeep and are in dire need of improvement. Among the problems are clogged toilets, poor ventilation, missing toilet paper or soap, clandestine cigarette smoking, drug trafficking, graffiti, vandalism, and violence. Such problems have attracted attention from national media such as *USA Today* and the *Wall Street Journal.* Poor-quality school restrooms have also been a pressing problem in the United Kingdom, where, according to Jenny Perez, director of education and resources for Improving Childhood Continence, legislation on school toilets is lacking, and the National Healthy Schools Programme omits school toilets, resulting in schools achieving healthy school status even if their toilets are unhealthy.[51]

Many children who face deplorable conditions in their school restrooms avoid them altogether and wait to use their bathrooms at home. This can lead to serious health problems for both boys and girls, but the long-term health risks such as cystitis and other urinary tract infections for girls are greater. If left untreated, such infections can cause renal damage.

The design of school restrooms and locker rooms can disadvantage school-age children, especially boys. Restrooms and locker rooms with heavy doors allow vandalism, graffiti, and bullying and gang behavior to occur unnoticed. Some bullies stop whenever the door is opened, then continue once the door is closed. An alternative to door entries is maze entries, walkways with turns that block views from outside but allow sounds from within to be more easily heard. Further, if a restroom or locker room has a maze entry, offenders can't count on the sound of the outer door opening to warn them that an authority figure is about to enter, and cigarette smoke is not masked. Students' right to privacy must be balanced with protection from entrapment while they're undressing and vulnerable to attack.

At Shasta Middle School in Eugene, Oregon, a troublesome bathroom was hidden beside a pass-through vestibule between buildings, making it the perfect spot for vandalism and other misbehavior. But when vestibule doors were locked in the open position, the problem evaporated.[52] Sometimes the simplest design solution can reduce or eliminate criminal behavior.

For two decades, educator and activist Tom Keating has worked with representatives in twenty states as well as India, Ireland, and Germany to advocate for cleaner school restrooms as part of his campaign for Project CLEAN—Citizens, Learners, and Educators Against Neglect.[53] His philosophy and tried-and-true method? "R.E.S.P.E.C.T. in the restroom begins with flushing, washing, stashing. Maintenance, repair and custodial care begin with adults and kids talking together. . . . Get kids to buy into better restrooms by taking some ownership because custodians and other instructional and administrative staff form relationships with students around restroom improvement."[54] As he says, real relationships among first users and first responders is key. In 2015, Keating's efforts spurred a task force in his own DeKalb County, Georgia, to update and strengthen its new clean restroom ordinance, giving code-enforcement officers the authority to issue warnings or fines to violators in schools, businesses, stores, offices, county buildings, and parks. Students and other restroom users can report deficiencies to code enforcement.[55] The ordinance provides an example for other communities to follow.

POTTY PARITY, SCHOOL RESTROOMS, AND SANITATION ON THE GLOBAL STAGE

As Sharon LaFraniere reported in a powerful piece in the *New York Times*, "Another School Barrier for African Girls: No Toilet," fourteen-year-old Fatimah Bamun was the only girl out of twenty-three students in her class in Ethiopia. In her school of 178 students, she was one of only three girls who made it past third grade. Why? "Fatimah is facing the onset of puberty, and with it the realities of menstruation in a school with no latrine, no water, no hope of privacy other than the shadow of a bush, and no girlfriends with whom to commiserate."

In a region where poverty, tradition, and ignorance deprive an estimated twenty-four million girls of even an elementary school education, the lack of school toilets and water is one of many obstacles to girls' attendance. In some rural communities in the region, menstruation itself is so taboo that girls are prohibited from cooking or even are banished to the countryside during their periods. Female teachers, too, struggle with the lack of sanitation. LaFraniere wrote: "But that impact is substantial. Researchers throughout sub-Saharan Africa have documented that lack of sanitary pads, a clean, girls-only latrine and water for washing hands drives a significant number of girls from school. The United Nations Children's Fund (UNICEF), for example, estimates that one in ten school-age African girls either skips school during menstruation or drops out entirely because of lack of sanitation."[56]

Girls in rural China, too, often avoid going to school during their menstrual periods, as schoolchildren are badly in need of sanitary latrines. A 2012 joint UNICEF and World Health Organization report documented that overall, 36 percent (and in rural areas, half) of the Chinese population lacks access to safe toilets.[57]

In 2012, Li Tingting, age twenty-two, a public management student in Shanxi Province, made headlines by turning into an activist for potty parity. She and half a dozen others commandeered the men's stalls at a busy public restroom near a park in the Chinese city of Guangzhou. They warded off men and invited women waiting in line to use the vacated men's stalls for three-minute intervals, after which they let the men back in. They called their operation "Occupy Men's Toilets," and it resulted in a new ratio of men's stalls to women in all new or renovated public restrooms being set at 1:1.5. But when Li and other activists tried to do the same in Beijing near the long-distance bus terminal, ten officers and three police vehicles confronted her. At yet another restroom she encountered more police officers, and she and her friend were forced to spend the next five hours sitting in a nearby restaurant, rather than trying to occupy another bathroom.

China's 1:1 ratio for men's to women's street toilets was set in national standards in 2005. Taiwan's recommended ratio is 1:3, and Hong Kong's is 2:3, a ratio that China adopts only in certain public structures such as shopping malls.[58]

International organizations are now rallying behind the notion of a "girl-friendly" school: closer to home, more secure, with enough women teachers and a clean toilet with a door and clean water for hand-washing.

Globally the issue of sexual equality and sanitation has reached epic proportions. And it means far more than mere discomfort. As Josie Delap reported in the *Economist*, about 330 million women in India lack access to toilets.[59] Many wait to relieve themselves until under cover of nighttime; when they do, they risk rape, kidnapping, and snakebites. Many school toilets in rural India remain locked, often for the exclusive use of teachers. Although the toilets were funded by the School Sanitation and Hygiene Education Program, it was schoolchildren's responsibility to clean them, and when this proved to be a struggle, the duty fell upon the teachers. Toilets that ultimately fell into disrepair were locked.

Indian prime minister Narendra Modi called for change in his first Independence Day speech in 2015, when he proclaimed: "Brothers and sisters, we are living in the twenty-first century. Has it ever pained us that our mothers and sisters have to defecate in the open? Whether dignity of women is not our collective responsibility? . . . All schools in the country should have toilets with separate toilets for girls. Only then our daughters will not be compelled to leave school midway." A study conducted by Anjali Adukia, assistant professor at the University of Chicago Harris School of Public Policy, showed that in India, regardless of children's social class and income, school latrines improved educational outcomes, attracted more female teachers, enrolled more children, and boasted higher pass rates for middle-school board exams.[60]

A TRIP AROUND THE WORLD: A QUIET RESTROOM REVOLUTION

> "World Toilet Day has the potential of becoming as popular as Valentine's Day. After all, both days are about celebrating intimate, personal relationships."
>   —Jack Sim, president, World Toilet Organization[61]

In some countries, safe, well-designed, and well-maintained public restrooms are considered an essential biological and social need. In others, the public relies primarily upon the private sector to provide good restroom facilities. In many impoverished countries, public restrooms are used only as a last resort.

Cultural differences play a major role in how public restrooms are used around the world. Special practices for urination, defecation, cleansing of the genital and rectal areas, and hand-washing behavior prohibit the development of international standards for toilet facilities. Religious differences play a role as well. Depending upon which part of the world you're from, to clean yourself you may use paper, water, sand, stone, or even sticks.

Western-style sit-down toilets, such as those in the United States, are the exception rather than the rule in Asian public restrooms. In Japan, China, and other parts of Asia, the squat toilet prevails, although the traveler may find a token Western-style toilet in a lineup of stalls available for tourists. Although Asians in urban areas are likely to have a sit-down toilet in their own homes, many have an aversion to sharing a toilet seat with strangers at a public restroom, considering it highly unsanitary. (Many women in Western countries also dread sitting on toilet seats and prefer to "hover" instead.) In China, women and girls must always carry toilet paper with them—just in case. Westerners are also often surprised by the lack of paper towels or hand dryers in many Asian restrooms. Even in Japan, which is known for its technological advances in toilet design, Japanese women typically carry small washcloths in their purses.

As any visitor to Japan can attest, compared with most anywhere else in the world, the quantity and quality of Japanese public restrooms are outstanding. Visitors can find a safe, clean, and well-designed restroom on almost on every street corner. As essential components of the urban, suburban, and rural landscape, public restrooms contribute to a healthy national lifestyle that allows people of all ages—and unusually large numbers of children and elderly pedestrians—to circulate freely in public spaces day and night. Travelers to Tokyo are surprised to see groups of elementary schoolchildren in uniform commuting long distances by train, darting in and out of subway-station restrooms with no adult in sight. A free app, Check a Toilet, lists over 53,000 restrooms in major cities and specifies whether they're wheelchair accessible and/or have ostomate-friendly functions.[62] An ostomate is anyone who has undergone an ostomy, or any operation, including a colostomy, that creates an artificial passage for bodily elimination.

In an effort to make Japanese restrooms more tourist-friendly for the 2020 Tokyo Olympics and Paralympics, the Japanese government has recognized the importance of improving restroom quality in improving quality of life. In 2015, it launched the Japan Toilet Prize. One of its goals: reducing lines outside ladies' loos. Haruko Arimura, the Japanese minister for women's empowerment, believes that restrooms are pivotal to women's advancement and is pleased to be known as "minister of toilets."[63] Recipients for Toilet Awards Japan were selected from among 378 applicants by six ministries. Eleven winners, including Tokyu Department Store Co. and the Sapporo Cultural Arts Foundation, received the women's empowerment minister award for making women's restrooms more attractive, including making space for breast-feeding and reducing waiting lines.[64]

According to the China National Tourism Administration, 14,320 new toilets were built in 2015 and an additional 7,689 were upgraded as part of a three-year campaign to build thousands of toilets at tourist sites in China. China's "toilet revolution" calls for greater propaganda efforts to encourage best practices. These efforts include the decals now frequently displayed on urinals, with the slogan, "One small step forward for you, one giant leap for civilised behavior."[65]

The Restroom Association of Singapore, Malaysia, was founded in 1998. In 2001, its founder, Jack Sim, a retired Singaporean construction and real estate entrepreneur, founded the nonprofit World Toilet Organization (WTO) and became its president.[66] Sim's efforts also sparked the formation of the American Restroom Association in 2004, a small nonprofit, all-volunteer organization devoted to clean, safe, and well-designed restrooms; its website provides a wealth of information on the current status of restrooms in the United States, including relevant laws and regulations.[67] Sim's vision is to provide clean urban public toilets and adequate rural sanitation worldwide, improving conditions for the estimated 2.6 billion people who do not have access to toilets and whose groundwater is often contaminated by fecal matter. Each year, more than two million people die from waterborne diarrheal diseases.

In 2011, Sim and the WTO received $270,000 in funding from the Bill & Melinda Gates Foundation to support its efforts for global advocacy on sanitation and to build new partnerships with the private sector. WTO's efforts tied in well with the Gates Foundation's goals for improving water, sanitation, and hygiene "to enable universal access to sustainable sanitation services by supporting the development of radically new sanitation technologies as well as markets for new sanitation products and services."[68] The foundation has funded groundbreaking improvements for toilet design, emptying pits, and treating sludge, along with new ways to reuse waste that can help governments and their partners meet the enormous challenge of providing quality public sanitation services. Most of its sanitation projects are in South Asia and sub-Saharan Africa, where sanitation problems are most acute.

One of the Gates Foundation's main initiatives is the Reinvent the Toilet Challenge (RTTC), funding research to develop aspirational "next-generation" toilets that don't require a sewer or water connection (or electricity), cost less than five cents per user per day, and are designed to meet people's needs. Since 2011, the foundation has awarded sixteen RTTC grants to research organizations worldwide, with two specific to India and China. It also supports private-sector providers to profit from by-products with market value, such as energy and fertilizer generated from fecal sludge. In Nairobi, Kenya, for example, toilets are distributed through local entrepreneurs who collect waste to use in generating electricity and producing fertilizer.

According to the WTO's press release about its grant from the Gates Foundation, "With its unique mix of humor and serious facts, WTO created a global movement awareness of the struggle of 2.6 billion people without access to proper and clean sanitation."[69]

Proclaiming November 19 "World Toilet Day," Sim initiated a series of World Toilet Summits, World Toilet Forums, and expositions that have taken place around the world. Sim's organization also hosts a World Toilet College (WTC) based in Singapore, a social enterprise that seeks to professionalize the sanitation and restroom industry. The WTC aims to ensure the dignity of sanitation workers, elevate their poor image and low pay, and train them in best practices in toilet design, cleanliness, and sanitation technologies, in the process ensuring that the needs, design, maintenance, and cleanliness of restrooms receive mainstream attention. Courses are offered in restroom specialist training, national skills recognition systems, sustainable sanitation, restroom design, school sanitation and hygiene education, and disaster and emergency sanitation. Since 2005, World Toilet Colleges have trained more than four thousand people in China, Indonesia, India, and Singapore.

Sim is promoting basic, ecologically sound latrines that can cost as little as $10. Yet he cautions against simply gifting toilets to residents of poor villages, because unless the residents receive proper education, the toilets often go unused. He's working to partner toilet manufacturers with fertilizer businesses so that human waste can be used to give crops a boost. He also promotes the emerging technology of transforming sewage into biogas that can be used as cooking fuel.

Time magazine recognized Sim, a one-man tour de force, as one of its "Heroes of the Environment 2008" who "is not afraid to talk about poop." In 2013, a joint initiative between the Government of Singapore and the World Toilet Organization led to Singapore's first United Nations resolution, titled "Sanitation for All." The resolution was cosponsored and adopted by 122 countries, and November 19 became an official United Nations day.[70] Starting in 2015, the World Toilet Organization brought together communities from around the world for a run or walk to raise funds for sanitation in the lead-up to World Toilet Day. Sim called it "The Global Urgent Run."

RESTROOMS, SINKS, AND TOILETS THAT ADVANTAGE BY DESIGN

An Award-Winning Restroom at the Beach

The award-winning unisex restrooms at the south end of Kellogg Park at La Jolla Shores in San Diego, California, came about only because a local citizen—Mary Coakley—cared enough to get involved. When she learned that the existing restrooms at the park were slated for replacement, Coakley, who lived in the neighborhood, decided to check out the plans. Although the building permit had already been issued, Coakley could see that the proposed design was no better than that of the existing facility, which for years had been plagued by vandalism, graffiti, drug use, and long lines for the ladies' room. Over three years, she intervened in the process by standing in front of the existing restroom, asking people to sign petitions protesting the proposed design, and working with talented neighborhood architect Dale Naegle and city officials to produce a design that worked for all.

Her aim in the redesign of the new restrooms was to produce maximum benefit in the minimum amount of space. So instead of separate men's and women's rooms, the restrooms have individual unisex toilet stalls that open directly to the outdoors. After its construction in 2005, the Kellogg Park "comfort station" received a Public Works of America Award for successfully addressing a wide variety of requirements: open-air trellis roof, minimizing odors; stalls opening directly to the outdoors, removing fear of crime; and vandal-proof amenities constructed from the same grade of material used in jail cells. Coakley then spearheaded improvements to the grounds adjacent to the new restroom, including an educational playground inspired by the nearby underwater canyon and sea life, creating a popular tourist attraction and an unusually child-friendly environment. As Coakley put it: "I didn't reinvent the wheel. It was a matter of taking the best pieces of the ones I saw and putting it together."[71]

Because La Jolla Shores is a popular Southern California beach for swimmers, surfers, scuba divers, and kayakers, the comfort station receives more than two million visitors annually. Its success led to the construction of a second set of restrooms at the north end of the park in 2014, replacing another gender-segregated restroom that had fallen into disrepair. According to a maintenance worker there, "Both these unisex restrooms are far easier to take care of than the usual men's and women's restrooms. I don't have to close the whole space down in order to clean, which is always a problem. It's much faster, and there's no need to wait till all is clear. It's way better for kids. I have no complaints, no problems!"

Winning Restrooms in the Windy City

Chicago's Millennium Park exemplifies how city officials and designers worked together to create a twenty-first-century, pedestrian- and family-friendly environment that provides adequate restrooms for thousands of visitors at a time. The 24.5-acre park, which includes an ice-skating rink, an outdoor theater, and tree-lined promenades, offers enormously successful works of architecture and public art such as Cloud Gate (otherwise known as The Bean), Crown Fountain— and restrooms.

Millennium Park features large underground public restroom facilities on the east and west sides of the new Jay Pritzker Pavilion. These facilities can be reached via a long ramp and are accessible to those in wheelchairs, people using canes or other mobility devices, and parents with strollers. In an attempt to prevent long lines from forming at the women's room, the restrooms offer more fixtures for women than for men.

At the east side of the pavilion are forty-six toilets in the women's restroom and twelve toilets and ten urinals in the men's restroom. At the west side are twenty-four toilets in the women's restroom and nine toilets and eight urinals in the men's. Each side also has one family restroom. The restrooms on the east side are heated so that they can be used all year in anticipation of future program requirements. All restrooms are designed to be easily maintained. They feature three-person sinks, high-velocity hand cleaners, and floor and wall surfaces that can be power washed. The restrooms work extremely well even under peak crowded conditions, allowing locals and visitors alike the chance to enjoy this park, one of Chicago's brightest gems.

Unisex or Gender-Neutral Restrooms

Call it a restroom revolution, as many have. The movement to incorporate gender-neutral or unisex restrooms is gaining momentum, in part as a response to the need to make transgender users feel more comfortable, and also as a response to the pressures of potty parity. In 2001, Ohio University designated about thirty restrooms across campus as unisex. In 2004, the Memorial Union Building at the University of New Hampshire reassigned the men's and women's restrooms on its first floor to gender-neutral. Other schools that have considered these changes include Brown University, San Diego State University, the University of California's multiple campuses, the University of Chicago, and the University of Pennsylvania. By 2014, more than 150 college campuses in the United States had gender-neutral bathrooms.[72]

In 2013, ten students who openly identified as transgender faced the possibility of dropping out of Grant High School in Portland, Oregon, because of a perceived lack of safety. In order to help them, administrators designated four student bathrooms and two staff bathrooms as gender-inclusive. Each is an individual room with a toilet, sink, and mirror. But that was just a first step. The school district then hired architecture firm Mahlum to provide equitable restroom facilities for all seventeen hundred students when it was time to renovate the 1920s-era school in 2016. All existing gang-style bathrooms will be replaced with individual toilet rooms with full doors opening to a shared space for washbasins and drinking fountains. No urinals will be installed. Two entrance and exit points increase safety and security. When renovation is completed in 2019, Grant High School will become one of the few schools in the nation to feature 100-percent inclusive bathrooms.[73]

A similar trend toward mixed-gender restrooms can be found at some upscale restaurants sprouting up across the country. Benefits appear to be shorter lines, as well as an easier and cheaper way to meet building codes, including accessible stalls required by the Americans with Disabilities Act.

The construction of more unisex restrooms can solve the problem of the forced binary gender choices that transgender individuals are all too often required to make. In Europe, unisex restrooms have long been commonplace; in many restaurants, men and women share the same sink for hand-washing. And all over the world, planes and trains have unisex restrooms too.

Family Restrooms

Due to updated building codes, family restrooms are slowly gaining popularity. Some codes now require unisex restrooms for all newly constructed or renovated—when restrooms are added—assembly and retail spaces such as malls, theaters, airports, and stadiums. The *2003 International Building Code*'s Section 1108.21 required such facilities with six or more male and female water closets to provide a unisex restroom. State potty parity requirements also boost the need for these types of restrooms, because they increase the number of toilets needed. An article in *Buildings*, titled "Facilities for Families," distinguishes unisex from family restrooms:

> Unisex restrooms are single-user toilet rooms that can be used by either men or women—the term is more universal for code purposes. Family restrooms can have multiple unisex toilet rooms within them, but may also have space allocated for other amenities and often share a common hand-washing and diaper-changing area. In addition, upscale family facilities may include family lounges, private nursing rooms, and baby changing areas.[74]

Some family restrooms double up with child- and adult-height toilets, lavatories, and hand dryers. Family restrooms serve as selling points for commercial establishments and are even touted on websites for places such as the Dollywood theme park (in Pigeon Forge, Tennessee) and Minnesota's Mall of America, the nation's largest shopping mall.

By 2005, Seattle's Sea-Tac Airport renovated thirty-two restrooms to include family restrooms with diaper-changing stations, touchless faucets, convenient bag shelves, attractive tile finishes, and Pacific Northwest artwork in glass and ceramic tiles. According to the Port of Seattle, "When travelers are asked what most shapes their impression of an airport, the answer is always the same: its restrooms."[75]

Yet one can still question: Why is it that family restrooms like these, sprouting up in airports catering to upper- and middle-class visitors, are still missing from most transportation venues that serve less well-heeled travelers, such as train and bus stations? Compared with airline travelers, parents traveling with children on buses and trains are far more vulnerable to crime and theft. Ironically, people who most desperately need family restrooms may never find them at all.

Shopping-Friendly Toilet-Stall Designs

Some state-of-the-art, family-friendly and women-friendly restrooms can now be found at regional shopping centers. For instance, the women's restrooms at Carlsbad Premium Outlets in Carlsbad, California, just north of San Diego, feature upscale amenities with louvered doors on all toilet stalls such as one might find at a luxury hotel. Inside each toilet stall is an attractive tile wall. Grab bars assist the elderly and people with disabilities.

But the most unusual feature can be found directly behind each toilet: a wide, recessed shelf with guardrail, for visitors to keep their purses and shopping bags off the floor. How logical, and yet how rare! Such features would be welcome in most restrooms—especially in shopping malls, transit stations, and college campuses, where people are encumbered by handbags, shopping bags, luggage, and backpacks.

"Wash Your Hands" with Step 'n Wash

An innovative product called Step 'n Wash was designed to take the hassle out of hand washing.[76]

Many parents struggle daily to keep their kids' hands clean. Because most businesses fail to provide sinks that are easy for children to reach, the only way young children can wash their hands is when parents lift them up to the sink.

Every day, parents and grandparents are forced to lift and hold fidgety thirty- or forty-pound kids. This daily weightlifting not only can injure backs, but also results in poor hand-washing—a major concern in light of the H1N1 (swine flu) virus and other health epidemics.[77] Kids splash water in all directions while squirming in their parents' arms, getting everyone wet.

One mother, Joi Sumpton, couldn't figure out why this problem hadn't already been solved. Why was there still no easy way for kids to wash their hands? She soon hired a patent attorney and an engineer. Although a simple step stool would be the most obvious solution, this posed problems with liability because step stools are prone to sliding. So the retractable step that she designed is firmly anchored to the floor.

Sumpton's invention, Step 'n Wash, is the first and only self-retracting step for public restrooms that enables children to safely and effectively wash their hands. Step 'n Wash facilities keep sink areas cleaner, promote independence for young children, and provide a respite for parents.

They can now be found at thousands of businesses in North America, including Dallas–Fort Worth International Airport, Orlando International Airport, Atlanta Hartsfield Jackson International Airport, Olive Garden, the Los Angeles Zoo, Whole Foods, Universal Studios, and elsewhere. They have been used more than 500 million times and have a perfect safety record.

After partnering with a leading manufacturer of diaper-changing stations, Step 'n Wash facilities have gone international. Products like these should be integrated into new code requirements to make restrooms more family-friendly. They would be welcome improvements to public restrooms worldwide.

Chapter 7

HELPFUL OR HARMFUL TO YOUR HEALTH? THE DESIGN OF YOUR HOME OR NEIGHBORHOOD

"I just moved into an apartment on a college campus, and the mirror in my bathroom is placed too high for me to see my full face. It is a small mirror that doubles as the door to a medicine cabinet. . . . The person who designed it did not consider how people of different statures would use the mirror/cabinet. It was not designed for everyone." (Female, age 21, 5′2″, 115 lb.)

With the possible exception of whomever we decide to live with or to marry, few decisions in life are as important as where we choose to live. For most of us, whether we rent or own, the financial investment we make in our home is our most substantial one ever. The choices about where we live and the designs of our homes and neighborhoods can have enormous impacts on our mental and physical health. They can be extremely harmful or helpful. Some residential and neighborhood designs privilege people of a certain gender, age, or body type. Knowing what design pitfalls and biases to look for can prevent you from moving to a housing environment that may disadvantage you or your family members.

Your early home environment leaves a permanent psychological imprint on you. Your residential autobiography—all the places you lived while you were growing up—often has a powerful impact on the homes you choose to live in as an adult. Being aware of your unique, unconscious biases can make you more careful in choosing the home that is right for you. You should also recognize some stereotypic gender differences in territoriality that may be found in your home that can have a huge impact on the dynamics of your household. Men are often relegated to the basement, garage, and yard, while women rule the kitchen. Maintaining some of these stereotypic patterns can disadvantage men, making them feel like outsiders in their own homes, or disadvantage women left to fend for themselves if they suddenly find themselves divorced or widowed. Ideally, men, women, and children should all feel like the home is their castle.

MIES-CONCEPTIONS

Some well-known projects of stellar historic architects disadvantaged women through their design. For example, many of Frank Lloyd Wright's housing designs featured spacious living areas, yet the kitchens were so dark and tiny that most women—whether the clients or their household help—would have found it unpleasant to cook in them. The traditional woman's domain was not Wright's top priority. Most of his homes were designed for people about his own height (he claimed to be 5 feet 8), causing tall visitors to feel uncomfortable in them. They encounter many spots where they can accidentally bang their heads against the ceiling.

As an apprentice at the firm Adler and Sullivan, Wright worked on the Charnley-Persky residence in Chicago's Gold Coast, built from 1891 to 1892. He designed space for two female live-in servants who did much of their work in the kitchen pantry. With its long, dark shape, the pantry was a challenging environment for washing and storing dishes. The servants' rooms were connected to the service areas of the house by a twisting, narrow stairway, at its widest point only three feet. This claustrophobic, spiral tube presented daily challenges. Servants carrying trays, linens, or cleaning supplies had to squeeze by each other or stop in one of the connecting rooms to let others pass. A lack of windows hindered navigation and disoriented the maids as they traveled in circles. A window was added in 1927 between the stair and the backyard.[1]

At Wright's famous Robie House, built in 1909 and 1910, maids laundering clothes were forced to use an outdoor, albeit artistically designed, stairway throughout Chicago's frigid winters and steamy summers. At Wright's masterpiece, Fallingwater in Bear Run, Pennsylvania, where construction began in 1936, the kitchen measures just 11.5 feet by 14 feet 9 inches, and the lack of space was likely a problem for cooking and meal preparation. Stone floors and steel cabinets created a cold environment where the cook and maids stood for many hours each day.

In some cases, well-known architects designed homes for wealthy female clients who downplayed or ignored their needs. Ever since it was built in 1950, the famous glass house that Ludwig Mies van der Rohe designed for his client Edith Farnsworth in Plano, Illinois, has been considered one of modernism's greatest masterpieces. Yet when Farnsworth moved into her showcase house, the roof leaked so badly and the heating system produced such an unsightly film on the windows that a local plumber suggested the house be called "My Mies-conception." When Farnsworth refused to accept delivery of the furniture that Mies had designed for her, she refused to pay any more bills and soon began legal proceedings, resulting in a lengthy legal battle. In a 1953 interview for *House Beautiful*, Farnsworth explained:

> The truth is that in this house with its four walls of glass I feel like a prowling animal, always on the alert. I am always restless. Even in the evening, I feel like a sentinel on guard day and night. I can rarely stretch out and relax. . . . What else? I don't keep a garbage can under my sink. Do you know why? Because you can see the whole 'kitchen' from the road on the way in here and the can would spoil the appearance of the whole house. So I hide it in the closet farther down from the sink. Mies talks about "free space" but his space is very fixed. I can't even put a clothes hanger in my house without considering how it affects everything from the outside. Any arrangement of furniture becomes a major problem, because the house is transparent, like an X-ray.[2]

As Alice Friedman argues in her 1998 book, *Women and the Making of the Modern House: A Social and Architectural History*, in the past century women often served as collaborators in housing design or as catalysts for architectural innovations.[3] Yet architectural publications and history texts generally disadvantaged women by giving full credit to male architects while minimizing the roles of female clients who commissioned the projects, hired the architects, fully engaged in the complex design process, and paid the bills.

SUBURBAN HOUSING AND THE CHAUFFEUR SYNDROME

Carrying a large laundry basket down a flight of steps can be dangerous for anyone. But it's especially unsafe for women, who are more likely to be doing the household laundry, and for older people, who are more likely to have vision and balance problems. Some newer homes feature upstairs laundry rooms closer to bedrooms and bathrooms, the source of most dirty clothes, linen, and towels. Such designs are much safer for all.

During the past quarter century, feminist scholars have argued that the planning and location of suburban housing disadvantages women in several ways. The primary reason is that most suburbs force residents to rely on cars. During the early development of suburbs, men usually drove their cars to work, leaving women at home with the children and without the car. Today most suburban residents have at least two cars. Yet dependence upon the automobile means that during the weekdays, even when both husband and wife work, the driving—shuttling children to and from daycare, school, after-school activities, and doctors' appointments; going to the grocery store; and doing other household-running tasks—often falls disproportionately on women. Suburban mothers have assumed the thankless role of chauffeur. The suburban model is an even greater hardship in single-parent households.

In her 2001 book, *Misconceptions: Truth, Lies, and the Unexpected on the Journey to Motherhood*, social critic Naomi Wolf harshly critiques the way the suburban landscape treats mothers and caregivers of young children:

Eventually the playground became the center of my world. This too was a shock. It seemed to me amazing that at the end of the twentieth century, playgrounds were still built in an open pattern, often with no gate around them, which required mothers and baby-sitters of toddlers to hover continually behind small children to keep them from darting into the street. It seemed obvious to me that no one who had designed a playground in our suburb had ever cared for a child. All around us, the neighborhood was a cornu-copia of consumer comfort. But out on the playground, for women, it was 1947: no shelter from the hot sun or from thunderstorms, no heated area for rainy or windy days, no food, no bathrooms, nowhere to get a cup of coffee or even a box of juice.

The message you receive from your work environment about how valuable your work is to society affects your well-being psy-chologically. Every day I was getting the message that the work the women I knew and I were doing had little value: the needs of people sitting in bus shelters and municipal lobbies, I saw with amazement as I began to hobble around into the stations of my new life, were more carefully met than were the needs of moms and kids in the places in which we gathered.[4]

The typical suburban housing development also disadvantages by age. People without a driver's license, whether children under driving age or elderly people who no longer drive, are dependent upon their chauffeur for a ride anywhere beyond walking or biking distance. In so many of today's suburbs, that sense of independence—so critical to children growing up and to elderly people facing the aging process—is chipped away.

The suburban lifestyle also disadvantages people by body type. Residents in neighborhoods where the nearest grocery store, transit stop, or school is miles away, where sidewalks abut busy streets or are absent altogether, and where intersections are far too wide have no choice but to drive almost anywhere they want to go. In places like these, walking can be both unpleasant and dangerous. Many older or heavier people, parents with young children or strollers, and those with physical disabilities can't make it all the way across an intersec-tion before the traffic light turns red. And at many suburban inter-sections, even the most physically fit pedestrians can barely step out onto the street before the "WALK" sign changes to "DON'T WALK." The message is clear: you're not supposed to walk here! Whereas generations ago children walked to school, in many parts of the United States, this is no longer possible due to such poor walking conditions. Without walkable neighborhoods, physical activity is drastically reduced, and children and adults who are overweight are likely to become even more so.

One study published in the *American Journal of Health Promotion* documented a clear link between the built environment and activity levels and people's weight and health, concluding that residents who live in the most "sprawling" counties in the United States weigh an average of six pounds more than residents of the most compact county.[5] Other studies show that land-use mix around an individual's residence has the strongest association with obesity, with each quartile increase associated with a 12.2 percent reduction in the likelihood of obesity across gender and ethnicity. Every additional hour spent in a car per day is associated with a 6 percent increase in the likelihood of obesity, while every additional kilometer walked per day is associated with a 4.8 percent reduction in the likelihood of obesity. Strategies to increase the mix of land use and distance pedestrians walk while reducing time spent in a car may be as effective as health interventions in combating the nation's obesity epidemic.[6]

THE SAVING GRACES OF SIDEWALKS

Time magazine identified James Sallis, of the University of California at San Diego, as an "obesity warrior."[7] According to his research, the biggest factor influencing physical activity around the world is accessibility to sidewalks.[8] City dwellers worldwide are healthier than their suburban counterparts and are twice as likely to get exercise. Researchers examined data from 11,541 survey participants in eleven countries, including the United States, Lithuania, Brazil, Sweden, and Japan. Respondents who live in city neighborhoods with easy access to sidewalks are 15 to 50 percent more likely to get moderate to vigorous activity for at least five days a week. Sallis and his colleagues also completed a long-term study of communities in the United States that discovered that residents of highly walkable communities got substantially more exercise and were less likely to be overweight than those living in less walkable areas. Sallis believes that incorporating sidewalks into neighborhoods would encourage residents to exercise and should be a public health priority around the world.

Sallis's work is part of Active Living Research, a national program of the Robert Wood Johnson Foundation that issued 260 grants to researchers from 31 disciplines to identify environmental factors and policies that can increase physical activity, and to share this evidence with policymakers to help them create more activity-friendly communities.[9]

The Robert Wood Johnson Foundation's report *F as in Fat: How Obesity Policies Are Failing in America: 2009* outlines many recommendations to battle the nation's obesity epidemic. Several involve radical changes to the design of our housing and neighborhood environments to remedy some of the ways in which they now disadvantage the obese by design. Among the report's recommendations: School districts should work with communities to make it easier for students to walk and bike to school. Local governments should encourage mixed-use commercial and residential areas, walkable neighborhoods, green-space development, more sidewalks, and building design that prompts the use of stairs and offers other spaces in commercial and public buildings that facilitate activity.[10]

A consequence of once-soaring gasoline prices is that even those who might never have done so before are questioning the long-held attraction of suburbia. With increased ridership on public transportation and more infill housing sprouting up around public-transit stations, not unlike what has been the norm throughout European and Asian cities, we may finally see a reduction of suburban sprawl and the chauffeur syndrome.

THE CITY: HOME OF "THE FREE-RANGE KID"?

Although children are plentiful in the suburbs, in many American cities, children are an endangered species. As Dan Iacofano and Susan Goltsman argue in their 2007 book, *The Inclusive City*, children's urban habitat is endangered.[11] Cars are treated as first-class citizens, while people—especially children—are relegated to second class. And even with the recent emphasis on attractive housing developments constructed under the principles of the New Urbanism, children often get left out. According to Iacofano and Goltsman, free gathering spaces and parks are needed more than outdoor malls. Children need a place to play within three hundred feet of their home, and traffic calming is needed to slow down cars and create more kid-friendly urban neighborhoods. Children need high-quality schools near where they live, and they need safe forms of public transit so that the United States can be more like Japan, where six-year-olds routinely ride the subway to school by themselves. As Iacofano and Goltsman believe, a child-friendly environment is a healthy environment, and cities should be touted as "home of the free-range kid."

Many poor children who live in American cities are disadvantaged by the environmental quality of their housing and neighborhoods. According to psychologist Gary Evans, high levels of noise, street traffic, polluted air and water, crowding, and poor-quality housing design can harm children's social and emotional development, cognitive development, and self-esteem. Although each of these individual stressors in isolation can result in chaotic effects for children, the combined effects of multiple environmental risks are even more powerful.[12]

Children's exposure to nature around their housing environment can also have significant positive effects. Stephen and Rachel Kaplan have conducted research on the effects of nature for decades. Their research has concluded that many buildings are constructed with little or no attention paid to the view out the window, yet that view can have an enormous effect on people's competence and civility. Views of nature provide cheap remedies to many social problems, and the nature of the view from home can result in many psychological benefits.

Environment-behavior researchers Frances Kuo, William Sullivan, and Andrea Faber Taylor have discovered that children who grow up in low-income housing projects without views of nature have very different experiences from children who grow up in similar surroundings but *with* views of nature. Simply having trees and grass outside a child's apartment building is linked to superior attention, effectiveness, and effectiveness-related outcomes. In a sample of urban public housing children randomly assigned to architecturally identical apartment buildings—some with relatively barren views and others with relatively green views—children who lived in units with views of nature performed better on objective tests of impulse control.[13]

THE GREEN ADVANTAGE:
THE IMPACT OF NATURE ON CHILDREN WITH ADHD

Kuo and Taylor conducted a national study examining the impact of natural settings on attention-deficit/hyperactivity disorder (ADHD) symptoms across diverse populations of children. ADHD is the most common neurobehavioral disorder in children, consisting of an unusually high, chronic level of inattention and/or impulsive, hyperactive behavior. It may affect more than two million school-age children, about 7 percent of all children ages six to eleven. The Centers for Disease Control and Prevention (CDC) has labeled it "a serious public health problem." Kuo and Taylor's research is based on the results of 452 participants.[14] They concluded that spending time in green outdoor settings appears to reduce ADHD symptoms across a wide range of individual, residential, and case characteristics. They refer to this as the "green advantage" and suggest that daily doses of "green time" can supplement medications and treatments for ADHD. This could include doing homework at a window with a relatively green view, playing in a green yard, or even choosing a greener route for the walk to school. A green dose or series of green doses could even reduce the need for children's ADHD medication by one dose per day.[15]

HOUSING DESIGN ISSUES FOR SENIORS

Certain design features in our homes both disadvantage and endanger elderly people. Every year, thousands of elderly men and women suffer falls in the home. Many are seriously injured, and some become permanently disabled. The CDC reports that in 2014, more than 2.7 million people over age sixty-five were treated in hospital emergency rooms because of falls.[16]

Hazards in the design and maintenance of homes are often to blame, yet they can be easily remedied. Design hazards include throw rugs on the floor, missing lights over stairways, only one light switch at the top or at the bottom of stairways, handrails only on one side of stairways, lack of support getting in and out of the bathtub or up from the toilet, no lighting near a bed, dark paths from bed to bathroom, and dim lightbulbs. Home-maintenance hazards include clutter; excess furniture; wires from lamps, phones, or extension cords; loose or uneven steps; loose or torn carpet; loose or broken handrails; items on high shelves; and chairs used as step stools.

Certain floor surfaces in the home may disadvantage elderly people, who are especially vulnerable to falls and fractures. The number of hip fractures occurring worldwide is estimated at 1.6 million, and it is predicted to rise to 6.3 million by 2050.[17] The vast majority of these hip fractures are a result of simple falls and the impact of the femoral trochanter with the floor. Women are more likely to fall than men, as women's sense of balance is less stable as they age.

While most studies have addressed the problems from the patient's side of the impact, little research has examined on the floor itself. One of the few studies to do so examined thirty-four residential care homes in the United Kingdom, analyzing data about the number and location of falls and fractures on various floor surfaces over a two-year period.[18] Overall, 6,641 falls and 222 fractures were noted. Wood subfloor with carpet was associated with the lowest number of fractures per 100 falls, with a significantly lower risk of fracture compared with all other floor types (wood subfloor with no carpet, concrete subfloor with no carpet, and concrete subfloor with carpet). This study has implications for safer designs of housing environments for seniors, whether in their own individual residences or specially designed housing for the elderly.

Although household stairs can be dangerous for older people, they can also lead to health benefits. Climbing stairs significantly contributes to attaining the recommended amount of daily physical activity.[19]

People who climb stairs daily have stronger legs and more

aerobic capacity, allowing them to participate more fully in more activities. Climbing stairs every day can add years to your life, and studies show that the risk of heart disease and death is lower among people who regularly climb stairs. Stair-climbing increases leg power and may be important in helping elderly people reduce their risk of injury from falls.

My parents lived in their split-level home for more than forty-five years, well into their nineties. Their house had seven to eight steps between levels, making the stairways less daunting than a full flight of steps. In their later years, climbing up and down the steps was about the only exercise they did, but they did it every day, several times a day.

Ironically, because they fear falling, many senior citizens feel compelled to move into one-story homes or apartments. And they often face peer pressure to do so from friends and family. Yet if they're still in good health, they may be moving prematurely. After living in a one-story residence for a while, and if they maintain a sedentary lifestyle, their stair-climbing muscles will deteriorate, they may not even be able to handle steps, and they'll become even more vulnerable to accidental falls.

HOMES AND NEIGHBORHOODS THAT ADVANTAGE BY DESIGN

Cohousing

How can housing be designed to avoid disadvantaging by gender and age? One way is to share some of the common, time-consuming tasks of running a typical suburban household: not just mowing the lawn and taking care of the garden (in which case a condominium or townhouse would suffice) but chores such as grocery shopping, cooking, cleaning, and babysitting—all of which tend to disproportionately fall upon women.

Cohousing neighborhoods do just that and provide a sense of community lacking in most suburban neighborhoods. They encourage diversity among age groups, ethnic, political and spiritual viewpoints, and lifestyles. Cohousing communities combine the advantages of private homes with the benefits of more sustainable living, including shared facilities and meaningful connections with neighbors. Originating in Denmark as a "living community," cohousing was promoted in the United States by architects Kathryn McCamant and Charles Durrett in the early 1980s. Cohousing communities can be urban, suburban, or rural. They're typically a compact development of low-rise apartments, townhouses, or clustered detached houses. Each typically features a common house that serves as the social center of the community. The common house contains a large dining room and kitchen, a lounge, recreational facilities, spaces for children, and often a guest room, a workshop, and a laundry room. Optional group meals for cohousing communities are served in the common house at least twice a week.

At least thirty-six states in the United States have cohousing communities as of 2016; according to self-reports, 162 in the United States were established communities, twenty-five are building or expanding, and several new ones are forming.[20] Hundreds of communities can now be found around the world, especially in northern Europe, Denmark, the Netherlands, and the United Kingdom, as well as Australia and Canada, and the number of communities is growing. They can especially benefit single-parent families or elderly people who may need emergency childcare, shared outdoor maintenance, a ride to the airport, or meals prepared by their neighbors. They can also be a good place for newcomers to a city to meet neighbors and gain a sense of community.

Ecovillages

Eco-neighborhoods and ecovillages are designed to minimize ecological impact and maximize human well-being. They stress the connections among housing, local community facilities, open space, higher densities, and mixed-use developments. These are combined with a strong emphasis on public transportation and walking or bicycling to local services as a way of reducing environmental pollution.[21] They're designed and built using ecological construction methods and local autonomy for food, energy, and water supplies. They call for a mix of incomes, owners and renters, household sizes, special needs, ages, and family statuses. This deliberate social mix avoids what some have called the "syndrome of the social wave," in which almost all initial residents are of a similar family status—such as young parents with babies and toddlers—which leads to an uneven demand for daycare facilities, elementary schools, and high schools that ebbs and flows.

Ecovillages can be in urban, suburban, or rural areas and can range in size from a few to hundreds of residents. Some are newly created, while others attempt to infuse existing neighborhoods or towns with more sustainable living and a greater sense of community. One of the first ecovillages to be built is in Ithaca, New York. As of 2016, it had two thirty-home cohousing neighborhoods and one forty-home neighborhood, all on 175 acres.[22] In Los Angeles, a demonstration ecovillage neighborhood is developing in a two-block central city area.[23] Ecological townships where the entire town or city is targeted for sustainability include Delft, the Netherlands; Freiburg, Germany; and Bamberton, Vancouver Island, Canada.

Unlike in typical suburban developments, in ecovillages children can become "free-range kids," walking wherever they need to go, fostering their own independence, and freeing parents from the dreaded chauffeur syndrome. Sidewalks promote exercise and good health for residents of all ages.

Gender-Friendly Neighborhoods in Vienna and Seoul

In the Austrian capital, planners and designers have been melding mainstreaming and neighborhood design for over two decades. Before a project gets underway, data is collected to determine how different kinds of people use public space. One of the first projects to be built was an apartment complex designed for and by women in Vienna's twenty-first district, held as a design competition in 1993 called Frauen-Werk-Stadt (Women-Work-City). It was built in response to surveys compiled by the Austrian national statistics office showing that women spent more time each day on household chores and childcare than men did. Women-Work-City consists of a series of apartment buildings surrounded by courtyards for nearby children's play, and the site has a kindergarten, a pharmacy, and a doctor's office. Nearby public transit makes running errands and getting to school and work much easier.

In 1999, two parks dominated by boys in Vienna's fifth district were redesigned. Among the new additions were footpaths, volleyball courts, and badminton courts. Almost right away, city officials noticed a change: girls and boys began to use the parks without each overrunning the other. In 2008, the United Nations Human Settlements Programme listed Vienna's city-planning strategy in its registry of best practices in improving the living environment, and Vienna's parks-redesign project was nominated for the United Nations Public Service Award. In recent years, in order to avoid reinforcing stereotypes, Vienna officials have shied away from the term "gender mainstreaming," instead calling it "Fair Shared City."[24]

In Seoul, an Internet survey of local citizens showed that more women than men—three out of four—experienced daily inconveniences related to public restrooms, public transportation, parking lots, childcare facilities, and pedestrian walkways. The Seoul Metropolitan Government started the Women Friendly City Project (WFCP) initiative in 2007 to minimize these inconveniences. More than 4,000 citizens were involved to ensure that women's perspectives and experiences were reflected in new policies, programs, and designs.[25] By 2009, ninety programs were in operation, and guidelines had been developed for women-friendly restrooms, parking spaces, walking environments, parks, and apartment complexes.

When the WFCP began its work in 2007, there were only 87 public restrooms in Seoul. By 2009, there were 1,049. Over the same period, the WFCP installed 594 emergency bells, 1,264 closed-circuit TVs, and more than 2,500 lights to make parking lots brighter and safer, bringing the number of women-friendly parking lots from 68 to 23,324.

Refreshing Your Restroom with the TOTO Washlet

"Paper doesn't do the job. It just distributes the problem." So claims a TOTO toilet executive about the drawbacks of toilet paper. And no matter how soft, no matter how absorbent, and no matter what brand, most of us would have to agree. But what's the alternative to this daily routine that lasts a lifetime, all the way from toilet training to old age? TOTO's high-tech Washlet toilet seat cleans genital areas with pure water and dries them with fresh air, a practice much more hygienic than the use of toilet paper.

Assisting others with toileting is one of life's nastiest duties, yet with the Washlet, assistance is no longer needed. Its unusual design promotes independence for all, from the very young to the very old. Users control the temperature of the seat, the water, and the air. Because it reduces the need for toilet paper, the Washlet is more sustainable and better for the environment.

TOTO, the world's largest maker of luxury bathroom fixtures, introduced the Washlet in 1980, and more than 40 million have been sold.[26] Washlets are now in almost half the homes in Japan. According to TOTO representatives, more Japanese homes have TOTO Washlets than have microwave ovens or personal computers.[27] At Gallery TOTO, opened in 2015 at Narita's International Airport, an engaging space is designed to offer international travelers the opportunity to experience TOTO's state-of-the-art high-tech toilets, promoting the culture and technology of Japanese toilets to the world. With 25,700 employees in 69 offices around the world, including over 1,500 engineers on staff and three centers focusing on research and development, TOTO "is dedicated to engineering products that respect the environment while meeting people's needs for comfort, beauty and performance. . . . TOTO believes a high-quality bathroom is an experience and everyday luxury people value and appreciate."[28] TOTO's corporate philosophy, its People-First Innovation guiding principle, has led to numerous international awards and recognitions.[29]

Those who might especially enjoy the refreshing feeling of a TOTO Washlet include new mothers sore from childbirth; menstruating women; anyone who has ever suffered the pain of constipation, diarrhea, hemorrhoids, or surgery; and anyone age fifty or over who has endured the highly dreaded 100 percent cleanout required for colonoscopies. Because no bending, twisting, or turning motions are needed to grab paper from the dispenser, the Washlet design is a plus for elderly people, people with disabilities and their caregivers, and parents helping out young children.

TOTO Washlet seats are just beginning to sail their way across the Pacific. Most Americans have never even heard of them. Although they're standard fare in many hotels throughout Asia, only a few luxury hotels in the United States, such as San Francisco's historic Palace Hotel, are featuring them on their recently renovated floors and suites. Honolulu's upscale Halekulani Hotel showcases its TOTO Washlet seats in public restrooms located adjacent to its lovely tropical-themed lobby. Yet they're still definitely the exception to the rule.[30]

Another notable exception to the rule can be found at Google headquarters in Mountain View, California. After visiting Japan, Google's founders were so impressed with Washlets that they installed top-of-the-line versions in all their public restrooms. Mountain View Googlers are treated royally, from top to bottom.

I have been the proud owner of a TOTO toilet and Washlet for the past decade. Inspired by my travels to Japan and by my participation at World Toilet Organization expositions in China and Thailand, I decided to take the plunge during a major remodel and kitchen and bath addition to my home. My TOTO has become a popular attraction with visitors, and they can comment on their experiences in my bathroom guest book. I also purchased two new TOTO toilets and Washlet seats for my elderly parents to use in their home. My mother says that it's the best gift she has ever received. And she thinks of me every day.

Chapter 8

HIDDEN POWER: CLASSROOM, WORKPLACE, COURTROOM AND CORPORATE DESIGNS

"My employer suggested that I pump in the women's restroom. I replied that I would be happy to do that if the CEO would like to prepare his lunch there as well. It's ridiculous for a nursing mom to go through the process of sterilizing every part of the pumping apparatus and then have to finish the process in a public bathroom."

—"Content Mom" in Virginia[1]

W e grow up in school and we grow old at work. We spend a good portion of our lives there. Most of us are unaware of the powerful ways in which our classrooms and our workplaces shape us. The health impacts of hidden gender, age, and body biases in school and workplace design may last a lifetime.

When new working mothers are forced to hide out in restrooms or broom closets to pump milk, they feel like outcasts on the job. The design of our workplaces reflects powerful messages about who in the social hierarchy is important and who is not. Whether we're conscious of them or not, these messages can have profound influences on our daily lives. The design of work environments for traditionally male- or female-dominated professions such as firefighting and nursing has not kept pace with changing demographics, disadvantaging those who dare to break out of the norm. The same is true in

175

the civic realm, where secret biases in the design of courtrooms and capitols empower some while disempowering others. In such high-stress environments, disadvantaging by design can be all the more demoralizing.

SCHOOL DAYS

"In my school, my classroom is the only one with air conditioning, yet we can't even use it because all the other students are jealous." (Male, Puerto Rican, age 14, 5′9″, 115 lb.)

Many designs disadvantage both those of a certain gender and those of a certain age in the largest workplace environment of all: schools, where students spend more than one thousand hours per year and teachers spend even more. Women far outnumber men as preschool, kindergarten, elementary, and middle school teachers. As of 2012, 2.8 million women were employed as elementary or middle school teachers, the third most prevalent occupation for women in the United States.[2] Lighting, noise, heating, cooling, ventilation, furniture, and even backpacks can all affect the well-being of those in the classroom, as well as students' motivation to learn.

In order to reduce vandalism and improve security, many school administrators have removed student lockers. Yet this sweeping change in school design disadvantages children by requiring them to cart all their belongings back and forth from home to school every day. With seven to nine classes a day and textbooks for each class, students are dragging around a heavy load.

Most students now carry their books, school supplies, and other personal items in large, heavy backpacks, causing serious back problems even for young children and raising a major public health concern. The issue took a tragic turn in Hong Kong, where a nine-year-old boy fell twenty floors to his death after his heavy backpack pulled him over the building's safety rail; officials suspected that his backpack shifted as he leaned to look at something and it pulled him over the edge.[3]

Although the long-term effects have not been assessed, at least one study revealed that adults who experienced nonspecific back pain as adolescents—such as those caused by carrying heavy backpacks—have more long-term disability and chronic pain later in life.[4] One of the largest studies examined a sample of almost thirty-five hundred middle school students from two Southern California counties, measuring each student's weight and backpack load.[5] Students ranged in age from eleven to fifteen. The average backpack weighed 10.6 pounds, with a range of 0.5 to 37 pounds. Results showed a high prevalence of nonspecific mechanical back pain along with high levels of severe and chronic pain.

Almost two-thirds (64 percent) of the students reported having back pain at some time, and 41 percent felt back pain while carrying their backpack. Of those who reported back pain, 87 percent reported that their pain was "bad" or "very bad"; 16 percent said that it had caused them to miss school, gym class, or after-school sports. About 17 percent had been to a doctor for back pain.

Backpack weight, measured as a percentage of body weight, was effective in predicting back pain, and children who walk to and from school were more likely to report back pain. Middle-school-age girls may be more susceptible to back pain than boys, as their growth rate peaks at about age twelve to thirteen, two years earlier than boys.

Some school administrators have suggested a return to lockers constructed of clear acrylic materials to address safety issues, along with the use of rolling backpacks, lighter textbooks, use of digital resources, and two sets of books—one for home and one for school. Nonetheless, research has shown that even in schools where students have two sets of books, most students still prefer to carry their texts back and forth. With severe budget cutbacks in K-12 education, many school districts can't afford to issue even one book per student, much less two. The American Chiropractic Association offers guidelines for parents and students to prevent needless pain from backpack misuse.[6]

Ironically, the Occupational Safety and Health Administration (OSHA) has strict health and safety regulations that protect adults in the workplace, but no such regulations protect schoolchildren whose bodies and future health are in peril.

A generation of schools constructed during the 1970s reflected the belief that children must be protected from disturbances and distractions in order to concentrate. Yet studies soon demonstrated that this assumption was incorrect and that natural lighting has a positive effect on performance, well-being, and social behavior. Compared with white fluorescent light, natural lighting results in better attention, reading performance, and processing of basic information.[7] One study found that "cold" light has a negative influence on women's mood but a positive influence on men's mood.[8] Some researchers have found a gender difference on how light influences well-being.[9] Poor lighting can lead to increased fatigue, headaches, and damaged eyesight. Researchers call for additional lamps in classrooms with dimmers to regulate light intensity of selected zones rather than flooding the classroom with the same lighting levels throughout.[10]

According to a study conducted by the University of Southern California's Keck School of Medicine, traffic-related pollution near schools contributes to the development of childhood asthma, the most common chronic childhood illness in developed countries.[11] Children who attend schools located in high-traffic environments had a 45 percent higher risk of developing asthma. Researchers examined a group of 2,497 kindergarten and first-grade children included in the Children's Health Study who were initially asthma-free. They examined the relationship of local traffic around schools and homes in thirteen study communities, compared them with the diagnosis of new-onset asthma during three years of follow-up, and identified 120 cases of new asthma. Although children spend less time at school than at home, exercising outdoors during physical education classes may increase ventilation rates and the dose of pollutants entering the lungs. Traffic-related pollutants may also be greater during morning hours when children arrive at school.

High levels of noise from street traffic, trains, and airplanes that plague many school environments can cause high levels of stress for students and teachers, resulting in aggravation, irritability, fatigue, and throat and voice problems. Poor hearing conditions lead to reduced capacities for short-term memory and mental processing of information. Almost 15 percent of children ages 6–19 have some degree of hearing loss.[12]

According to a national study published in the *Journal of the American Medical Association,* researchers at Brigham and Women's Hospital discovered that in recent decades the prevalence of hearing loss has increased sharply among American teenagers. After analyzing data from nearly three thousand adolescents tested between 1998 and 1994, and nearly eighteen hundred teens tested between 2005 and 2006, researchers found a 30 percent increase. Teenagers from families below the federal poverty threshold had significantly higher risks of hearing loss. One of the investigators of the study, Sharon Curhan, MD, explained: "Teens typically underestimate their noise exposure, the symptoms that result from exposure to excessive noise and the importance of protecting their hearing. . . . Excessive noise exposure is a key environmental and lifestyle risk factor that can be modified to help preserve hearing. . . . Even mild degrees of hearing loss in children can have an impact on their educational performance, their social interactions and their social-emotional development. . . . Recognizing when hearing loss is present and making appropriate accommodations is essential."[13]

More children than ever are suffering from hearing problems, some of which may be congenital, some of which may be worsened by blaring music under earbuds, and some of which can be traced to noisy school environments.[14] Studies reveal that occupants of schools situated near roads with heavy traffic have significantly increased blood pressure. In elementary schools exposed to noisy traffic, children suffer from concentration problems, with a higher rate of mistakes when doing difficult tasks and a higher rate of giving up on tasks before time was up. Girls' performance is more impaired by traffic noise than boys', and autistic children are more affected than hyperactive children.[15]

Acoustic aspects are rarely given enough attention in school design. For teachers and students alike, poor acoustics can cause minor annoyance or major frustration, interfering with abilities to teach and learn. Even squeaky desks, chairs, and door hinges can get on people's nerves when they're forced to hear them all day long. And though it's for shorter periods of time, so can the roar of excessively noisy lunchrooms and school cafeterias.

Odors from nearby sewage treatment plants, agriculture, traffic, or restrooms adjacent to classrooms can have negative effects on the well-being of teachers and students.[16] Unpleasant odors negatively affect cognitive abilities, reducing motivation for work and increasing the time required for visual search tasks, perhaps even influencing mood and contributing to aggressive behavior.

NEW SPACES FOR NEW MOTHERS: LACTATION ROOMS IN THE WORKPLACE

Why do certain professions remain male-dominated? Why do so many female college students enter the pipeline to become future architects, engineers, and computer scientists but eventually drop out? This issue has been researched extensively, especially in professions in which women are underrepresented. Among the scores of possible explanations: gender pay discrepancies that worsen the longer women remain in these professions, minimal mentoring, few networks of support, and the lack of a powerful critical mass that can transform the corporate culture into a more family-friendly environment. Yet few researchers have examined the role that the physical environment plays in contributing to women's disenchantment with the workplace. Some of the women most acutely disadvantaged by design are new mothers.

New mothers face awkward situations in the workplace every day. Just as parents need public restrooms that better suit families and children, mothers of young children need private lactation spaces in the workplace. According to the Bureau of Labor Statistics, more than half (54 percent) of American mothers with children younger than a year old are employed. Of those, 73 percent work full time.[17]

Although breastfeeding in public has become more socially acceptable, pumping and storing milk has not. Pumping milk, which involves hooking a contraption up to the mother, is still a private activity.

Working nursing mothers have three important needs: time, privacy, and refrigeration.[18] They generally need two or three fifteen-minute sessions during an eight-hour workday, about every three to four hours, to express milk. Pumping throughout the day allows mothers to maintain their milk supply, enabling them to save and take home their nutrient-rich milk. Failure to do so can result in painfully swollen breasts and disruption of the lactation process. Mothers need a clean and comfortable place to pump in peace, not a restroom or a broom closet. Ideally the space should be near a sink and an electrical outlet. Pumping can be a messy process that requires washing up, and the pump needs to be plugged in. Refrigeration is ideal but not required; although it is not nearly as convenient, expressed milk can be stored in a cooler or an insulated lunch box. It can be safely stored at room temperature for about eight hours.

Prior to the passage of the federal Patient Protection and Affordable Care Act in 2010, several states had passed legislation to protect a working woman's rights to provide milk for her baby at work. New York was the first state in the nation to pass a law protecting a mother's right to breast-feed in public, a civil-rights law passed in 1994, but it wasn't until 2007 that New York passed legislation that protects nursing mothers who return to the workplace, requiring employers to provide uncompensated breaks for women to express their milk or nurse their children for a period of up to three years, and barring employers from discriminating against an employee exercising this right, and requiring employers to make reasonable efforts to provide a space where employees can express breast milk privately.[19]

Under federal law, employers are now required to provide "reasonable break time for an employee to express breast milk for her nursing child for one year after the child's birth" and to provide "a place, other than a bathroom, that is shielded from view and free from intrusion from coworkers and the public, which may be used by an employee to express breast milk. . . . A bathroom, even if private, is not a permissible location under the Act."[20] The LaLeche League website is an excellent resource for nursing mothers and has links to legislation in other countries, which varies widely.[21] An up-to-date list of legislation in various states can be found at the website of the National Conference of State Legislators.[22]

Nevertheless, the 2010 federal law generally only applies to workplaces with more than fifty employees, and it lacks clear provisions for enforcement.[23] As Jake Marcus, JD, notes in his 2011 article, "Lactation and the Law Revisited," "It is unclear what penalty violation of this new law carries, and no actions by the Department of Labor (DOL) against an employer have been reported." He argues that stronger legislation, with "adequate legal procedures to enable all lactating women to use the courts and regulatory agencies to enforce the rights that they have so long been denied," is needed.[24]

Furthermore, while the 2010 federal law addresses employers and employees, it does not protect nursing mothers from harassment and discrimination when breast-feeding in public places. In 2013, that dilemma prompted art students at the University of North Texas to create their "When Nurture Calls" campaign to drum up support for HB 1706, a bill in the Texas state legislature that would protect breast-feeding mothers from harassment and discrimination. Their campaign featured photos of women—a realistic but sharp contrast to typical mother-child photos of maternal bliss—nursing their babies on toilet stalls with such compelling captions as "Table for two," "Private dining," and "Would you eat here?"

The photos went viral.

So is it legal to force breast-feeding mothers out of public places—or to send them to toilet stalls or other unsanitary locations to nurse their babies? According to Carol Garvan, an attorney specializing in employment and civil rights, the answer is:

> It depends. Federal law permits women to breastfeed in federal buildings, but that only protects moms who happen to be breast-feeding on federal property. For the average restaurant-goer or traveler, it all depends on what state you're in. Some states, like Vermont, have progressive laws permitting mothers to breastfeed in places of public accommodations and giving mothers the right to file suit to enforce the law.
>
> But the laws in most other states . . . simply state that mothers can breastfeed their babies in any location where they are otherwise authorized to be, but don't provide any mechanism for enforcement. That means that although mothers technically have the right to breastfeed in public . . . there's little they can do if they're denied that right. A woman kicked out of a restaurant or movie theater for nursing cannot go to court to seek damages, and the offending restaurant or theater can't be held liable for penalties.[25]

HAIR SALONS

How does the quality of workspaces for female-dominated professions (such as librarian, bank teller, and hairdresser) compare with workspaces for male-dominated professions of similar income and status? According to Irene Padavic and Barbara Reskin in their 2002 book, *Women and Men at Work*, women worldwide still have fewer occupational choices than men, and three-quarters of women are crowded into just seven occupational groups: nurses, secretaries/typists, housekeepers, bookkeepers and cashiers, building caretakers and cleaners, and seamstresses and tailors.[26] Yet in some countries, a large percentage of men are nurses (in the West, nurses are traditionally women).

Because women dominate the hairstyling profession, one might assume that the typical design of a hair salon would suit women's needs. Yet the design of the most critical component of their work environment—the chairs in which clients sit while having their hair cut, styled, and blown dry—can pose serious problems. Although the chairs are adjustable in height, many don't go low enough. The problem is most acute when a short hairdresser is working on a tall client. Drying the crown of the head is one of the toughest tasks; so is any motion that raises the elbow above the shoulder.

Some hairstylists also find the design of the sinks uncomfortable. Because most sinks are wall-mounted, stylists must stand on one side or the other while washing their clients' hair. This puts a strain on stylists' arms and lower backs as they bend and twist to reach the far side of the head. Shorter stylists must reach up and over the edge of the sink, lifting their shoulders and elbows away from the body, making it difficult to apply enough force to wash, rinse, and massage the hair. Few salons have state-of-the-art freestanding sinks whose plumbing comes up directly from the floor, taking up more floor space than conventional wall-mounted sinks, but those that do may have happier, healthier stylists.

From the client's perspective, leaning your head back in a hair-salon sink can worsen pain in the neck caused by an injury or arthritis, and it may even trigger a stroke. According to *Stroke Smart Magazine*,

"Beauty Parlor Stroke Syndrome" is caused when the neck is bent backward in a sink for a long period of time. Although it's a rare form of stroke, people at high risk or who have carotid artery disease (a buildup of plaque inside the arteries that can slow down or block blood flow to the brain) should avoid having their hair washed this way, because it can cause arteries in the neck to rupture. Ask to pad the edge of the sink with towels in order to protect your neck, lean forward instead of backward into the shampoo bowl, or wash your hair before your appointment.[27] Some new salon-sink designs include a head support with a U-shaped frame with bendable supports.

Hair salons with inadequate ventilation systems can also prove hazardous. Researchers in Sweden found that, compared with the general female population, female hairdressers were at increased risk of three respiratory symptoms: wheeze, dry cough, and nasal blockage.[28] They were also more likely to have asthma. Hairdressers who performed bleaching treatments, exposing themselves to persulfates while mixing powders, had a slightly greater incidence of asthma. Exposure to hair spray was moderately associated with higher levels of asthma.[29] The Swedish research team surveyed more than seven thousand hairdressers over a twenty-five-year period, thirty-seven hundred of whom had children and worked while pregnant. They found that hairdressers' exposure to chemicals on the job influenced the health of their babies at birth. Hairdressers were one-third more likely to give birth to babies with major physical defects (most commonly heart defects) and more likely to give birth to smaller babies. Researchers advise pregnant hairdressers to always use gloves and to ensure that their salons are properly ventilated.[30]

SERVICE WORKERS AND SICK BUILDING SYNDROME

Increasing numbers of women worldwide have moved into the service sector, where they mainly engage in office work, teaching, healthcare, banking, commerce, hospitality, and domestic work. A serious health issue for service workers is sick building syndrome (SBS). Symptoms of SBS include headaches, nausea, dizziness, short-term memory loss, itchy eyes and throat, and possible damage to the nervous and respiratory systems. Asthma rates have increased substantially, largely due to poor indoor air quality.[31] In one shocking case, a woman's attorney claimed, "Her desk killed her." Investigators who scoured the deceased's office found formaldehyde levels in desk drawers up to five times the OSHA standard for short-term exposure. The woman had developed multiple myeloma and died at age fifty-one.[32]

SBS strikes more women than men. One recent study showed that women seem to be more sensitive to the indoor environment, as well as to work-related and psychosocial factors. Researchers concluded that the design of women's workplaces and the assessment of complaints should take their heightened sensitivity into account.[33]

The culprit is often a combination of undetected dangers such as carbon monoxide and other contaminants sucked into buildings when air-intake vents overhang exhaust-filled loading docks and parking garages; volatile organic chemicals seeping out of building materials, furniture, office equipment, carpet, paint, and pesticides; and molds and bacteria funneled through filthy ventilation systems.

COURTROOMS AND CAPITOLS

How does the design of courtrooms and capitols reflect traditional male dominance in the workforce, and what changes, if any, have been made to accommodate the increase in female attorneys, judges, and legislators? Does the design of courtrooms disadvantage those of a certain gender, a certain age, or a certain body size?

In her book *Why Women Should Rule the World*, former White House Press Secretary Dee Dee Myers, the youngest person and first woman to serve in this high-profile position, admits that she was disadvantaged on the job even before it began. Compared with the space in the press secretary suite assigned to her predecessors and to her male colleagues in the office of the White House communications director, hers was the smallest. Near the end of her two-year tenure, she was reassigned to the larger office typically given to the press secretary—but only if she agreed to resign soon. Her office-space quandary was emblematic of the classic woman's double bind. She was given responsibility without authority; furthermore, she was left out of key decisions and then taken to task by the press for with-holding information.[34]

In their oral histories deposited in the Manuscript Room of the Library of Congress, several former congresswomen discussed their exclusion from the House gym. Paula Hawkins, a senator from Florida, did an interview about gaining access to the Senate health club. Until the 1990s, both the gym and the health club had been the exclusive province of male legislators.[35]

In the second floor of the US Capitol is a "Senators Only" bath-room behind the Senate chamber. Until the 1992 election, which saw a spike in the number of female senators, it was a men's room, and female senators had to make a lengthy walk to the restroom that placed them in danger of missing crucial votes. On the House side is a "Members Only" bathroom behind the chamber; it still is a men's room. Off Statuary Hall is the "Lindy Boggs" room, named after the US representative from Louisiana who, in the 1960s, corralled a suite with a restroom and sitting area for women members. Before then, congresswomen lacked these basic necessities. And only in 2011 was plumbing added to Room H211, the House parliamentarian's office, to convert it into a restroom for congresswomen, providing them even more convenient access near the floor of the House.[36]

And what about courtrooms? The US Supreme Court justice robing room lacked a women's restroom until 1993, twelve years after Sandra Day O'Connor, the Court's first female justice, was named to the bench. As Justice Ruth Bader Ginsburg explained, "To mark my 1993 appointment to the Supreme Court, my colleagues ordered the installation of a women's bathroom in the Justices' robing room, its size precisely the same as the men's."[37]

In the United States, women who are victims of sexual assault or abuse are forced to confront their perpetrators in open court. Face-to-face confrontation with abusers and criminals can prove highly stressful and traumatic. In some countries, such as Taiwan, closed-circuit television is used as an alternative.

Child victims or witnesses, as well as children who accompany parents or guardians who are litigants, witnesses, or defendants in court proceedings, are disadvantaged by the design of many court-houses where their needs are ignored. As intimidating as courtrooms are to most adults, they're even more intimidating to children. Critics have raised the specter of reluctant children in custody cases enduring cross-examination in open court, arguing that participation in adversarial proceedings is harmful to them.[38]

Worries about presumed harm to children testifying in sexual-abuse prosecutions has resulted in some procedural reforms, such as videotaped testimony and special arrangements to testify outside the courtroom. Yet some courts have held that the judge must allow a competent child to be called to testify in custody cases.

Concerns have been raised about the widespread reluctance to interview children in open court and the preference for interviewing them in a different, less intimidating setting, such as the judge's chambers. Although the setting is less stressful for the child because fear of adverse parental reaction is reduced, a private interview may preclude parents from hearing all the relevant evidence the judge will consider when making his or her decision. Sometimes children may discuss parental behavior not known to the court, such as drug or alcohol use, physical abuse, or sexual activities. As a result, some states require in-chambers interviews to be recorded and made available to parties and their attorneys. Yet if an attorney insists on a child's testimony in open court, most judges would allow it.

Perched on the highest seat in the courtroom, and positioned at the end of the courtroom, the judge in the eyes of a child may appear to be the Wizard of Oz. The jury box, too, with its tiered seating and twelve sets of watchful eyes from above, can appear daunting. This loss of perspective in the courtroom can evoke fear. Some children can also cause distractions and disorderly conduct during courtroom proceedings. They need a place to go during court recesses and protection from potentially traumatic courtroom scenes.

Some parents—more often than not, mothers—fail to appear in court as litigants or witnesses because they're unable to find childcare. According to the National Center for State Courts (NCSC), as of 2016, only seventeen states plus the District of Columbia provided children's waiting rooms in at least some of their courtrooms.[39] Some states have several such state court facilities, while others have very few or none at all.[40]

As of 2016, sixty-seven California courthouses had children's waiting rooms. California Government Code 26826.3 called for each court to endeavor to provide a supervised waiting room for children under age sixteen who are present as participants or who accompany parents or guardians who are participants in court proceedings. If the court currently lacks space in the courthouse, the court should create the necessary space when court facilities are reorganized or remodeled or when new facilities are built.[41]

California's work on gender fairness has served as a model for other state and federal courts, in large part because it built upon the early work of its Advisory Committee on Gender Bias in the Courts, first appointed in 1987. Based on the work of this committee, in 1990 the Judicial Council unanimously adopted a comprehensive set of recommendations designed to ensure gender fairness throughout the California state courts. In 1995, the subcommittee launched new implementation efforts in several focus areas, including children's waiting rooms, childcare for court employees, and court security in domestic violence and family law. The Advisory Committee stressed that:

> a children's waiting room is not a daycare center, but rather it serves to reduce stress on children whose parents are attending to legal matters; provide child victim-witnesses with a place to go during court recesses; protect children from the potential trauma of courtroom scenes; reduce courtroom noise and disruption in public areas; allow parents full access to the court system; and reduce the incidence of failure to appear by the inability of litigants or witnesses to find child care.[42]

One of the oldest and most successful children's courthouse facilities is Kids' Korner at Lake County Courthouse in Waukegan, Illinois. Since 1994, it has provided a safe haven to nearly twenty-five thousand children involved in the court system. Kids' Korner received a 2007 Justice Achievement Award from the National Association for Court Management. Founded by a group of concerned judges, lawyers, and private citizens, Kids' Korner's mission "is to provide a safe and fun waiting area to children who are in the courthouse to testify in court or whose parents or guardians are conducting court business."[43] The first-floor waiting room houses toys, blocks, puzzles, art supplies, books, and other material appropriate for children ages two to twelve. It includes a diaper-changing station and can hold a maximum of nine children.

SPACE FOR THE SECRETARIAL POOL

"I have been working now for a little over a year at an office job, and I am about to leave. One reason is that the building is not for me. I work for a large insurance company with a huge campus. Since there are so many people that work there, they were able to save money by making every section and every department the same. So between the carpet, walls, desks, chairs, cubicles, tables, nothing is unique. This makes it hard for every day not to seem to be the same, which in turn makes it a very unpleasant working environment. I have only been working there for over a year, but it is already hard for me not to dread the building I walk into." (Female, white, age 23, 5′2″, 120 lb.)

As Ellen Lupton argued in *Mechanical Brides: Women and Machines from Home to Office*, throughout the twentieth century women dominated modern clerical occupations, although this was not always the case.[44] Before the 1880s, clerical work was primarily a male occupation that involved writing and filing letters, invoices, and other documents. The term "secretary," with the same root as "secret," was originally a sign of prestige, referring to the confidant and deputy of a powerful figure. Men who assumed this role could often look forward to upward mobility in a firm.

At the turn of the century, the male-dominated secretarial profession underwent a radical gender transformation. By 1890, 60 percent of all typists and stenographers in the United States were women; by 1920, the percentage had risen to 90. Both the typewriter and the switchboard became associated with women. Companies such as Remington that sold typewriters envisioned them being used for transcribing dictation rather than composing text. As is often the case, the introduction of this new technology lowered the status of those whose job it was to operate it.

With the digital revolution and the full-scale introduction of word-processing software on personal computers by the late 1980s, typewriters soon became obsolete and typing skills became a necessity for both men and women. But by a wide margin, women continue to dominate the secretarial field.

AT&T recruited the first telephone operators from the boys who delivered telegrams but soon replaced them with young women after customers complained boys were rude and played pranks. AT&T did not hire male operators again until the Equal Employment Opportunity Commission charged it with sex discrimination in 1970, but as of 2000, women still comprised 85 percent of telephone operators.

More often than not, today's secretarial pool is located in less desirable office space than that of the professional staff. In high-rise offices, clerical staff can usually be found in interior spaces, relegated to open-office designs with minimal natural light and views. Officials and managers tend to be given prime locations along the building's perimeter. This is despite the fact that clerical staff is usually in-house forty hours a week, while managerial staff is more mobile and more likely to be away on business for days at a time.

LAB SPACE AND WOMEN'S PLACE

Nancy Hopkins, a microbiology professor at Massachusetts Institute of Technology (MIT), sparked a widely publicized national movement to improve gender equity for scientists and engineers by comparing the amount of laboratory space assigned to men to the amount of space assigned to women. She had become aware of the problem firsthand when she needed an additional two hundred square feet for her own lab. Even as a full professor, she realized that she had far less lab space than her male counterparts and that she lacked the power to get what she needed to work efficiently.

Not only was Hopkins working on an unlevel playing field, but so were most of her female colleagues. During the summer of 1994, three tenured female faculty members in the School of Science started to compare notes about the quality of their professional lives at the university. They wondered whether their cases were part of a pattern, so they decided to poll their female colleagues. At the time, the School of Science had only 15 tenured women compared with 194 men, and the percentage of women faculty (8 percent) had remained virtually unchanged for at least ten years.

In 1995, after the women requested that a committee be established to address their concerns, Hopkins was appointed chair of the first Committee on Women Faculty at MIT's School of Science. She spearheaded a five-year investigation, the results of which revealed marginalized lab spaces that female scientists occupied were part of a pattern of excluding them from the power structure of their campus and of their profession.[45]

Although junior female faculty members tended to feel well taken care of and untouched by discrimination, senior female faculty tended to leave jobs even after achieving tenure because they felt they were not part of the system in the same way that their male colleagues had been. Marginalization increased as women progressed through their careers at MIT, making their jobs increasingly difficult and less satisfying. They tended to work alone, were not included in group grants, and were not given administrative positions. About half the female faculty members were unmarried without children, whereas nearly all their male counterparts had families.

The committee concluded that the atmosphere at MIT—including the allocation of space, resources, and equipment—was creating unintentional gender bias. Ironically, most women didn't complain, and many didn't even realize that they were victims of gender discrimination.

Robert Birgeneau, the dean of the School of Science, recognized that MIT was unique in making the document public. He stated: "I believe that in no case was this discrimination conscious or deliberate. Indeed, it was usually totally unconscious and unknowing. Nevertheless, the effects were real."[46]

MIT administrators responded swiftly. Within six years, the number of female science faculty members nearly doubled, the number of female faculty members in engineering increased almost fivefold, and MIT became a model for recognizing, acknowledging, and rectifying gender bias.[47]

FIGHTING FOR FIREFIGHTERS' SPACE

"After looking at some fire stations in and around Chicago, it became apparent that the designers are placing a higher emphasis on resting areas and the kitchen than on workout rooms or places to get up and exercise. As firefighters, one must be fit and in fairly good physical shape to be able to complete the tasks the job demands of you, but once you're on as a firefighter you no longer have to pass any tests to show you are still in good physical condition. By placing more emphasis on the kitchen and on resting, it is easy to gain weight and get out of shape, which can then lead to medical concerns for firefighters just to complete the demands of the job they were hired to do." (Male, white, age 23, 6'2", 180 lb.)

The design of work environments for traditionally male- or female-dominated professions such as firefighting has not kept pace with changing demographics. According to a female paramedic in charge in the Chicago Fire Department, although as of 2010 women made up nearly 6 percent of Chicago's firefighters, only about ten new firehouses (out of about 92 total firehouses) in the city provided dedicated space for women.[48] At most firehouses, women firefighters sleep in the same quarters as the men, and women sleep in their clothes while men walk around in their underwear. Because only communal showers are available, accessed from a communal locker room, women often feel uncomfortable taking a shower on the job.

Because of the rigorous physical requirements of the job, firefighting remains a profession dominated by men. According to the US Bureau of Labor Statistics, the percentage of female firefighters was only 5.7 in 2014.[49]

Firefighters are placed in harm's way every time a fire breaks out. They wear protective clothing and equipment to minimize their exposure to toxic fumes and dangerous situations. Such measures are not failsafe: firefighters have high rates of Parkinson's disease, heart disease, cancer, and other serious illnesses. Yet the exposure to fumes during fires is not the only culprit for these health hazards. So is the design of the firehouse.

When the protective clothing is off and all is calm, many firefighters are disadvantaged by the design of antiquated firehouses constructed without proper ventilation systems. In these environments, fire trucks entering and exiting the garage emit heavy fumes, which spread into the adjacent firehouse, where firefighters spend most of their time. In between alarms, firefighters work in confined indoor spaces with little access to fresh air. Because many firefighters work twenty-four-hour shifts, their exposure to diesel exhaust, when compared with industry workers who work an eight-hour day, is far worse.

Because firefighting is physically demanding, firefighters need to remain in top physical condition. Dashing into a burning building and racing up six flights of stairs lugging sixty pounds of gear tests even the youngest and fittest firefighters. But for older firefighters who are out of shape and haven't visited their doctors in years, that routine can be fatal.

As Maggie Wilson, health and safety coordinator for the National Volunteer Fire Council, a Washington, DC, lobbying group, points out: "For a firefighter, there is enormous stress on the heart. . . . It's 2:30 in the morning and the firefighter is fast asleep when the alarm goes off. He goes from being in a deep sleep to rushing off to fight a fire. That requires a tremendous surge of adrenaline. If a firefighter's blood pressure is 200 over 120 and he doesn't know it, he's in deep trouble." This repeated adrenalin rush places an intense strain on the body. Every year, up to half of firefighter deaths are the result of sudden cardiac issues.[50]

In fact, the number of firefighter deaths due to cardiac problems is triple that of the US population.[51] A ten-year study by the National Fire Protection Association discovered that about half of American firefighters who died of sudden cardiac arrest or suffered heart attacks had known heart conditions; about 75 percent had heart conditions that could have been detected by simple medical testing. Compared with workers in other hazardous occupations, including police officers and construction workers, firefighters have a lower physical-fitness level.[52]

Surviving family members pay a huge emotional price, and taxpayers pay a high price as well. When a forty-five-year-old firefighter with two children drops dead from a heart attack while on the job, his widow can expect to collect almost $2 million in benefits via worker's compensation and federal programs.[53]

Yet many older firehouses are designed with more space devoted to eating and lounging around than space for physical recreation or exercise. Such facilities both reflect and promote unhealthy lifestyles, where firefighters fill long hours by eating and watching television. Fire stations in densely populated urban areas and where space is at a premium offer few opportunities for firefighters to exercise. As a result, many firefighters are overweight, compounding the health risks of this treacherous job.

Although female firefighters are still in the minority, their presence has shone a new light on the dangers of poor air quality in fire stations, as pregnant firefighters and their unborn fetuses and nursing mothers and their infants, are especially vulnerable. Nursing mothers exposed to certain toxins may pass these chemicals on to their infants.[54]

Most fire stations today were designed for a men-only workforce, yet both women and men now use many of these buildings that serve as combination family, house, and work settings. Resulting inadequacies are a source of inconvenience, discomfort, embarrassment, and friction for all concerned. Inexpensive short-term solutions concerning personal privacy are usually the first to be implemented— for example, a "men/women" or "occupied/unoccupied" flip sign on the door of the station's only restroom or shower, or a lock on the door. Makeshift partitions can be placed between beds if bunkroom separation is desired.

Yet the underlying question is: should women and men firefighters on the job be provided with separate facilities? Local building or health codes generally require employers to provide restrooms for each gender in the workplace, but because fire stations are the property of municipal or county government, they're usually exempt from these codes. Some fire departments only assign women to stations that "have facilities for women," yet this restricts female firefighters and can draw resentment from their male counterparts, who often must rove from one station to another.

Some communities are finding out that separate not only does not mean equal, it may mean a big lawsuit. Female firefighters in

Long Beach, California, filed both federal and state lawsuits in 2013 to get the city to move faster on improving the fire station houses. As the federal suit's filing stated: "The disparities in facilities . . . discourage other women firefighters from applying to work as Long Beach firefighters. The city has singled out women to be a problem because of their sex, created an environment that fosters hostility, and does not place men and women on equal footing."[55]

Examples the women provided of the discrimination included female firefighters having to change clothes in the hallways and use portable toilets outside the station or having to wait, "sometimes covered in grime or chemicals from a call," for the men to finish their showers first before they could clean up.[56]

Some progress has been made. A number of new fire stations have been built to accommodate gender equity with unisex facilities.

When firefighters in a newly integrated workforce are forced to occupy inadequate facilities, two reactions usually occur. The first is that women are blamed for "causing" the problem, even though the real culprit is poor station design. Men may feel that "there wasn't a problem until she got here."[57] Solutions such as bumping an officer from his private room to give it to a woman firefighter can create resentment. A second reaction is the tendency to adapt and accommodate to less than ideal conditions. Lacking private shower facilities on the job, many female firefighters do not routinely shower at work, or they may rise an extra hour earlier in the morning so that they can shower before the men need the facilities. Some women have been forced to use broom closets as changing rooms, and firefighters of both genders routinely check for feet under the restroom-stall partitions. A lack of privacy can also lead to sexual harassment.

As the authors from a FEMA publication point out in *The Changing Face of the Fire Service: A Handbook on Women in Firefighting,* while "accommodation" provisions in the Americans with Disabilities Act have long been institutionalized to afford people with physical disabilities equal access and opportunities in the workplace, altering facilities to better accommodate female workers is often viewed as giving women "special treatment."[58] Modifying access for those with disabilities implies differences, yet "special treatment" implies inferiority.

Greater attention to design can make fire stations safer places for both men and women. Installing negative-pressure exhaust fans triggered when the apparatus bay doors close, along with ventilation systems providing fresh air to the bay, would help expel truck exhaust. Placing carbon-monoxide detectors and monitors in sleeping quarters and adding weather stripping to all doors between the bay and living areas can help reduce and warn of toxic fumes.

In 2012, the International Association of Women in Fire and Emergency Services issued a position statement regarding firehouses. The paper acknowledged that trying to provide identical facilities for men and women ignores the number and percentage of each gender, saying that "proportionality of those facilities will always be a commonsense consideration until the number of women in the fire service increases dramatically." The group advocates a more flexible approach, providing facilities that are described as "unisex"—"designed for use by only one individual at a time . . . to be truly open to all personnel equally."[59]

The best long-term solution for bunkrooms is to provide privacy for all. Some new firehouses are designed with cubicles holding a bed, a desk, a lamp, and three or four lockers that can be used by one person on each shift, along with a curtain across the doorway. These features provide privacy and reduced sound and light from others nearby. Partitions that are open to the ceiling provide air circulation and allow firefighters to hear emergency tones and information. These design solutions don't pit the women against the men, they avoid controversies over the size of the women's bunkroom versus the men's, and they respect the privacy and individuality of all firefighters.

WORKPLACES THAT ADVANTAGE BY DESIGN

Cologne's Waldorf School

Because inadequate ventilation in schools can reduce students' performance and lead to drowsiness, some new schools are being designed with innovative air handling systems that can keep students and teachers more awake, alert, and attentive. One novel solution can be found in the Cologne Waldorf School in Cologne, Germany.

There, a sophisticated ventilation system relies on subterranean air ducts that supply the school with air maintained at an appropriate temperature for each season, without the use of mechanical technology. This saves energy and circulates high-quality air throughout the school.[60]

A glass roof supported by a tree-like column admits sunlight, and the vertical meeting hall serves as the main ventilation shaft. Warm air is exhausted through vents at the top, and fresh air is sucked in at the bottom. Peripheral intakes admit air through a series of large underground pipes. Air exchanges heat with the mass of the earth underneath the building, cooled in summer and warmed in winter to reduce the heating load.

Architect Peter Hubner designed the school around Rudolf Steiner's holistic philosophy of anthroposophy, symbolism, and color. His design concept incorporated the views of school users, a centrally planned main building drawn symbolically as a rose with five petals along with the numerical progression 5/10/20, the growth principle of the rose and the generative geometry of the building. These are reflected in the types of rooms, the spatial layout, the way the school building interacts with the elements, and the fitting-out craftwork by staff and students.

Archipod's Pod: An Energy-Efficient, Eco-Friendly Garden Office

Today's workforce has access to cell phones, e-mail, videoconferencing, and the Internet. Yet many still waste time and energy with long commutes, rush-hour traffic, and road rage. And people who work at home often find it difficult to separate their work and family lives. Archipod, a UK architectural firm, designed an innovative, energy-efficient, eco-friendly small office that resembles a shed-sized coconut and can be installed in your backyard.[61] They now come in different sizes, constructed of timber from Forest Stewardship Council–registered suppliers or from reused lumber. The building is also highly insulated, with encapsulated fiberglass insulation made from recycled glass. Its heat source is an electric panel radiator. The Archipod features double-glazed stainless-steel porthole windows and a double-skinned carbonate roof dome that harnesses natural light and ventilation. It's clad with attractive Western Red Cedar shingles.

Inside the Pod is an ergonomic semicircular desk with cables below, and optional custom-made drawer units and hardwood desktops. A timber floor has fiberglass insulation. Concrete or steel posts form the foundation. The Archipod is prefabricated in sections, so if necessary you can carry the sections through your house to assemble them in your backyard, garden, or courtyard.

Kudos for Google

Throughout the United States and abroad, offices of the search-engine giant Google have become icons for cutting-edge designs that advantage their employees, a diverse group of people who hail from all over the world. Google's designs are intended to foster healthy, happy, and productive employees and to spark creativity on the job. Employee retention is a priority, because Google invests a tremendous amount of time and money in each new employee.

Google's new Chicago headquarters, in the West Loop, opened in late 2015 with more than 300,000 square feet on six floors of a ten-story building. Chicago architectural design firm VOA served as the interior architect on the project, an adaptive reuse of a ninety-two-year-old former meatpacking freezer. More than 650 employees work there, and depending on their mood, they may choose to work at a beanbag chair, a swinging chair, a sit/stand desk that can easily be adjusted for different body types, or even a treadmill desk (see chapter 4). Each floor has its own design theme, and employees helped choose the graphics.[62]

An open stairway through a central atrium promotes exercise and vertical communication across floors, and it was intentionally designed with extra space at the landings to encourage Googlers (as Google employees are called) to stop and chat without obstructing traffic. An attractive outdoor patio shared with other tenants in the building provides comfortable seating with sweeping city views, encouraging employees to refresh themselves with a breath of fresh air. A tech stop near the elevator on each floor provides quick and easy IT support. Micro-kitchens scattered throughout the complex allow workers to snack throughout the day, and healthy choices, such as fruit juices and water, are placed at eye level. Less healthy choices, such as sodas, are behind frosted glass and are harder to reach.

Great attention to specific design details has been based on feedback from Googlers at Chicago's prior headquarters. Colors, textures, materials, and artwork are all carefully chosen for a reason. The height of partitions between office areas was purposely reduced to fifty-five inches, lower than the standard height, in order to enhance communication, networking, and teamwork. Tapered meeting tables allow workers to see presenters and screens without obstructing anyone's view, as well as allow everyone present to be seen by a webcam. Informal, well-lit collaborative spaces are located at the prime viewpoint on every floor, allowing every employee to work in an area with the feel of a highly coveted corner office.[63]

At Google's office in Zurich, Switzerland, architectural firm Camezind Evolution teamed up with Google clients in the design of a twelve-thousand-square-meter, seven-story space for up to eight hundred staff that was completed in 2008. The site, Hurlimann Areal, was originally a local brewery within a short walk of Zurich's city center that was converted into a lively development of apartments, shops, offices, and a spa hotel.

A core philosophy of Google's office designs is "celebrating individuality, creativity, and innovative business practice within a high-energy environment and [emphasizing] the importance of the individual and maintaining a small-company ambience throughout the company growth."[64] Googlers participate in the design process to create their own local or regional identity.

Googlers in Zurich, referred to as Zooglers, worked under the guidance of Google's director of international real estate in Mountain View, California. They collaborated with the architects to conduct a survey of all Zooglers, along with a series of workshops and interviews guided by a psychologist. Their aim was to understand the opportunities and challenges posed by the building as well as the emotional and practical requirements of Zooglers.

Based on survey results, Zooglers chose to reduce their personal workspaces in order to have larger communal and meeting areas.

Since on average a Zoogler moves twice a year within the building, the design also had to accommodate frequent staff rotation, adaptability, and growth.

Open-plan workspaces for six to ten people and enclosed offices for four to six people are organized along a central core. Offices are constructed with a glass partition system, maintaining transparency and optimizing daylight, reducing noise, and achieving required degrees of privacy for work teams. For easy orientation, each floor is color-coded and themed. On the blue floor, with its water and snow themes, informal meeting areas incorporate Igloo Satellite Cabins with penguins and ski gondolas in a snowscape.

Because Googlers believe that relaxation and play are critical to innovation, the designers developed themed communal areas associated with sport and leisure. These include an aquarium water lounge; a room with billiards, table football, and video games; an antique-themes library; and a massage spa. Most spaces also contain micro-kitchens offering drinks and snacks throughout the day. A staffed gym offers yoga, Pilates, and fitness classes. The Milliways cafeteria offers free breakfast, lunch, and dinner, allowing Zooglers to meet new colleagues—and potential new collaborators—every day.

Chapter 9

SHOPPING, SPENDING, AND REACHING FOR THE STARS: RETAIL AND COMMERCIAL DESIGN

"I worked as a bartender for a couple years, and speed is the name of the game on a busy night. All of our 'top shelf' liquors were just that, on the top shelf, and if one of our shorter lady bartenders needed to get to a bottle quickly, there was no way she could reach it and [she] would have to ask a taller gentleman to get it . . . which obviously slows service down, cost[ing] the bar money. Although I never sensed this, it could also lead to other inadequate feelings for them." (Male, white, age 24, 6′3″, 165 lb.)

Over a lifetime, we spend vast sums of money and vast amounts of time in them, yet we may never realize the powerful ways in which the design of retail and commercial environments shape our lives. For those of us who patronize them, they provide the backdrop for recreation, relaxation, and romance, some of life's most special moments. For those of us who work there, the glitzy public façade may be in stark contrast with the dismal scene behind it. These designs can empower some of us and disempower others. They can maneuver, manipulate, and exploit us. And they can even make some of us healthy and make others sick.

PLUS-SIZE SECTIONS ARE SEPARATE AND UNEQUAL

"It's embarrassing to walk into a department store knowing that the plus-size section is on the third floor in the back corner, away from most customers. When I finally get there, people walk by and sneer at me." (Female, white, age 61, 4′11″, 200 lb.)

According to the *Los Angeles Times,* the average American woman weighs 162.9 pounds and wears a size 14, yet retailers treat her like an anomaly. Almost two-thirds (62 percent) of American females are considered overweight.[1] Many plus-size women shop online rather than face the unpleasant experience of shopping in a store, yet when they do so they lose the ability to see, touch, or try on merchandise in advance—and often have to return whatever they buy. As Ginia Bellafante wrote in her article "Plus-Size Wars" in the *New York Times Magazine,* "Given the fit challenges a plus-size customer faces, the shift to a virtual space where nothing can be tried on can seem alienating to her—a directive to wear a muumuu."[2]

Just as African Americans in the South had separate, "Colored" building entrances, a not-so-subtle form of discrimination occurs in the design of many retail establishments that place plus-size clothing in hidden, hard-to-find locations, out of sight from the rest of us.

Full-figured women can shop at plus-size chains such as Lane Bryant and Fashion Bug or big-box stores such as Kohl's and Target. Walmart is the top seller of plus-size apparel in the United States. Yet women who seek more style and fashion at mainstream department stores often feel like second-class citizens. And many retail stores don't even sell plus-size clothes at all, although they may have them available online. The message sent to plus-size customers: "You're not good enough to shop here."

As a result, large women face a catch-22: they purchase less than they might otherwise because they don't find enough appealing merchandise in stores, hence retailers point to poor sales figures as evidence of low demand and fail to provide the supply.[3]

Many blogs, websites like *A Curvy Cupcake,* and Instagram hashtags like #ThisIsPlus have helped plus-size women band together to show the world what a plus-size looks like and how it differs from the simplistic depiction in the fashion world, to share their experiences with each other, and to accept and celebrate their bodies as they are.

By contrast, the men's sector of plus-size clothing is called "Big & Tall," a less derogatory term that typically covers men with waist sizes 40 or greater, or over 6′2″ tall.

My student Joanne Muniz and I spent the past year studying "the plus-size displacement," or how retail-store design affects plus-size consumers' experience.[4] We discovered several previous studies focusing on "fat stigma" and "fat talk" and how these concepts affected shoppers' self-images and level of satisfaction with their shopping experience. Yet we found relatively little information about the impact of the layout and design of the retail environment.

So we visited several stores at our regional shopping mall, where we documented in-store signage, mannequins, target images, merchandise displays, fitting rooms, and proximity of store entrances, all of which can influence plus-size shoppers' experience.

Among our most striking observations were that at department stores, the plus-sized clothing aisles were often just as cramped and crowded as those in the rest of the store, an uncomfortable situation that also led to circulation problems. In several instances, we found a conspicuous lack of mirrors and very few mannequins, and those mannequins we did find often looked about the same size as everywhere else in the store.

By comparison, in a store exclusively for plus-size shoppers, we observed mannequins prominently displayed near the entrance. Warm, bright colors were used to make customers feel welcome, plus-sized people were used in store images, and aisles were spacious. According to the store manager, "the approach is to make the plus-size shopper feel comfortable, cared for, and most of all, worthy."

We developed an online survey to find out more about plus-size respondents and their typical shopping experiences, and we received 80 responses, including both women (84%) and men (16%), ranging in age from 15 to over 50. Most had a waist size from 40 to 52 inches, a shirt size from XL to 4X, and pant sizes between 16 and 52.

Their responses to our questions about the layout and design of plus-size sections were striking:

- Only a quarter (25%) said they typically found the plus-size area accessible and unobstructed.
- Only 18 percent said the plus-size section was welcoming.
- Only 18 percent said they could locate plus-size mannequins in the store.
- Only 15 percent of the respondents said they could easily locate the plus-size area once they entered a store.
- Only 14 percent said they could easily locate images of people who looked like them in the store.
- Only 13 percent said the plus-size section was easy to navigate.
- Only 13 percent said they could see the store entrances from the plus-size section.
- Only 11 percent said they could easily find the fitting rooms from the plus-size section.
- Only 9 percent said the plus-size section aisles were spacious.

In a nutshell, the respondents found the layout and design of plus-size sections to be inadequate for their needs.

And their customer experiences revealed a great deal of dissatisfaction. Just over a quarter (26 percent) said they felt comfortable purchasing plus-size apparel in mainstream apparel stores, only 23 percent said they felt comfortable with the store atmosphere in the plus-size section, only 20 percent said they were able to find apparel variety in the plus-size section, 19 percent said the clothing displays in plus-sized sections invited them to make purchases, 19 percent said sales associates motivated them to purchase apparel, 14 percent said sales associates were attentive, and only 10 percent said their overall shopping experience was agreeable.

When asked to elaborate on their experiences purchasing plus-size apparel, and how the location, layout, and design of the plus-size section in the store makes them feel, many stated that they felt ostracized and treated like "second-class citizens," uncomfortable, stressed out, frustrated, and unmotivated to return. Among the worst experiences: "I felt a bit asphyxiated." By contrast, several had their best experiences when shopping in plus-size-only stores, where they found plenty of clothing variety, as well as sales associates with a similar body type to their own, and where they could relate to the images portrayed. Still others could not even describe a "best experience" shopping for plus-size apparel in a store at all.

What changes did they want to see in the design of retail environments for plus-size shoppers? They called for larger plus-size sections, more clothing variety, more plus-size mannequins, better signage, more spacious aisles, and larger fitting rooms. But the following comment said it all: "Make the plus-size section more roomy, attractive, near the entrance of your store! Forcing fat people to retreat to the rear of a store speaks volumes: store owners don't want to wait on fat people!"

DEPARTMENT STORES, BIG-BOX STORES, SEASONAL AFFECTIVE DISORDER, AND VITAMIN D

"The design of box retail stores is very uncomfortable for employees. The stores are built to be cheap, so including comforts for employees does not seem to be of importance to these companies. In the particular retailer I worked for, the support areas, such as lounges and offices, are in the warehouse area of the store. Because of this placement, there were no windows in any of these spaces. Imagine escaping [from] customers only to have to sit in a beige room with fluorescent lighting and no windows. Also, since I have left that job, the smoking ban in Illinois was put into place. The smokers' lounge was removed, and the store created an outdoor space for the smokers, in the parking lot! The smokers sit in a roped-off space in the middle of parked cars. This is not only a safety issue, but the employees are baking sitting at tables on asphalt. Some employees who do not smoke still use the area to get 'fresh' air. It seems that an outdoor space would be valuable if done well. A parking lot is not an ideal outdoor retreat. It gives you a little insight as to what this company [that] wants people to 'Live better' thinks of its employees." (Female, age 24, 5′2″, 120 lb.)

"I spent nearly ten years working retail, and I noticed that a lot of the older women that I worked with suffered from hip, knee, ankle, and foot problems, largely owing to long hours standing at a register. I found out later that older women were especially prone to these problems due to lower bone density in comparison to white males of a comparable age." (Male, white, age 39, 5′11″, 230 lb.)

In *Discrimination by Design: A Feminist Critique of the Man-Made Environment,* Leslie Weisman refers to the department store as the "palace of consumption" and the shopping mall as "the signature building of our age." In shopping malls across the world, corporate branding of retail establishments conveys powerful gender stereotypes.[5]

Large numbers of women, men, and ethnic minorities work in department stores, indoor shopping malls, and big-box stores. Millions of these employees occupy windowless spaces, removed from natural daylight. Unable to see changing weather conditions, many find themselves feeling disoriented, disconnected from nature and time. Working solely under artificial lighting, along with indoor air pollution, poor acoustics, and other sick building factors, can decrease productivity and increase absenteeism. But the long-term psychological and physiological health consequences of working in such light-deprived conditions can be far more dangerous.

Every day, the amount of daylight that we receive influences the amount of energy we feel we have. Daylight controls the brain's secretion of the hormones serotonin and melatonin. In bright daylight, the brain secretes serotonin, making us feel more active, alert, and energetic. In low light or in darkness, the brain secretes melatonin, the "natural nightcap," making us feel drowsy. People who work under artificial lighting at large department stores, indoor shopping malls, and big-box stores risk having their internal clocks disturbed.[6]

Lack of serotonin has been implicated in many psychiatric disorders, such as depression, obsessive-compulsive disorder, social anxiety, and anorexia and bulimia, two eating disorders that plague women more than men. Melatonin is a key antioxidant that can neutralize hydroxyl radical agents that damage cells and DNA, which may be contributors to certain internal cancers.[7]

Increased evidence shows that daylight is essential for health and productivity. Extensive research indicates that we need at least two hours of natural light each day to function normally. Sunlight promotes the production of vitamin D, which is critical for metabolizing calcium and phosphorus to strengthen bones and teeth. Sunlight can also have a therapeutic effect on many diseases, even eating disorders. Employees in department stores, indoor shopping malls, and big-box stores are prone to vitamin D deficiency, also known as hypovitaminosis D. Among the most serious potential consequences of vitamin D deficiency are bone frailty, especially hip fractures; heart disease; multiple sclerosis (which afflicts two to three times as many women as men); and various internal cancers.[8] Although too much sunlight can lead to skin cancer, the most rapidly increasing form of cancer in the United States, too little sunlight and insufficient vitamin D can increase the risk of cancers that can be far more deadly. These include cancers of the colon, the breast, the prostate, and epithelial cancers of the digestive and reproductive systems.[9] Oliver Gillie, a British health journalist, has referred to this as "sunlight robbery."[10]

Lack of sunlight, or "daylight deprivation," can lead to seasonal affective disorder (SAD), commonly known as winter depression. SAD affects as many as 2 percent of Americans and 4 percent of Canadians. The exact prevalence is unknown but increases with geographic latitude. In the northern hemisphere, the higher the latitude, the higher the incidence of SAD; the opposite is true in the southern hemisphere. An additional 10 percent suffer from subsyndromal SAD ("winter blues") triggered by reduced exposure to sunlight. Symptoms include depression, fatigue, irritability, lethargy, changes in sleep patterns and appetite, headaches, joint and stomach pain, and low resistance to infection. Numerous studies show that women are four times as likely as men to have SAD.[11]

An added benefit of increased natural light is that it enhances the way we view products in a store. Studies show that sales in retail outlets significantly improve after natural light is introduced, improving the aesthetic appeal of merchandise.

MEN BUY, WOMEN SHOP

One major retail chain, Victoria's Secret, broke the mold by creating a design that catered to the way men shop for their wives and girl-friends, instead of catering only to women. And the rest is history. Roy Raymond, a Stanford Graduate School of Business alumnus, founded Victoria's Secret in 1977 because he was embarrassed to shop for his wife's lingerie in a department store. He opened his first store in the Stanford Shopping Center with a $40,000 bank loan and $40,000 borrowed from relatives. The original stores were designed to create a comfortable environment for men, with wood-paneled walls, Victorian details, and a helpful sales staff. Instead of racks of bras and panties lined up in rows, single styles of lingerie were displayed in pairs mounted on the wall and hung in frames, and sales staff pulled them out from the inventory in the back. The company earned $500,000 in its first year; its five stores and forty-two-page mail-order catalog grossed $6 million per year when Raymond sold them to The Limited for $1 million in 1982. By the early 1990s, Victoria's Secret had become the largest lingerie retailer in the United States, topping $1 billion in sales.[12]

At shopping malls around the world, senior citizens, teens, and even toddlers in strollers parade by risqué window displays of women's panties, bras, and bustiers. But displays of men's underwear tend to be far less conspicuous, lost amid a sea of merchandise in mammoth department stores.

The design of department stores reflects different attitudes toward the shopping behavior of men versus women, encouraging women to spend more money. Designers are aware of these behavioral differences and use both subtle and not-so-subtle strategies to accentuate them. Men's clothing is often located nearest the entrances and exits, allowing men to get in and out quickly. That location also allows women to pick up items for their husbands, sons, fathers, or boyfriends easily on their way into or out of the store. By contrast, women must travel past tempting aisles of cosmetics and perfumes and up and down escalators to search for women's clothes, encouraging costly impulse shopping along the way. Women's dressing rooms are full of mirrors and comfortable seating, encouraging shoppers to take their time and buy more, whereas men's dressing rooms tend to be more utilitarian.

A 2007 study by the Wharton School of the University of Pennsylvania and the Verde Group, a Toronto consulting firm, identified sharp gender differences in shopping behavior, namely that men buy and women shop.[13] Researchers discovered that women enjoy meandering through sprawling clothing and accessory collections, gliding up and down glass escalators past a grand piano, making detours to sample spray perfumes or view shoes along the way. Men are out to buy a specific item and flee the store as fast as possible. Women are more focused on the buying experience, looking for eye contact, support, and collaboration with the sales associate. Men are on a mission. The study was based on telephone interviews with a random national sample of 1,250 shoppers who were asked about a recent shopping experience.

According to WomenCertified, a women's consumer advocacy and retail training organization headquartered in Hollywood, Florida, that also worked on the study, women spend $4 trillion each year and account for 83 percent of American consumer spending, or two-thirds of the gross national product. Delia Passi, founder of WomenCertified, says: "It goes back to gatherers and hunters. Women are gatherers. Men are hunters. Women walk into a store and scan. Men look for a specific aisle." Passi admitted that not all men and women fit into these generalities, and some even behave in the opposite manner. Age, ethnicity, sexual orientation, and regional differences may also weigh in. In fact, we must question simplistic invocations of evolutionary psychology that would have us believe that psychological differences between the sexes are innate and not shaped by other forces.

And what about the design of retail venues aimed toward men, such as the auto parts department at Sears or the power-tools section of the Home Depot? Do men "shop" here the way women do for clothes?

With more female heads of households than ever before, more women owning their own homes, and more TV shows and websites about home improvement, many hardware-store chains are now targeting women customers. Old-fashioned stores with dark, narrow aisles filled with boxes of bolts and pipe fittings can seem intimidating to customers who may be unsure of exactly what they want. Hardware-store chains now feature more of a grocery-store experience, with well-lit aisles, clear signs, and instructions about how to use materials and products. One survey of Ace Hardware's smaller franchise stores shows that women spend 30 percent to 40 percent more than men per visit. A study of Lowe's Home Improvement

Warehouse customers found that women initiate 80 percent of all home-improvement projects and represent half of its customer base. Design changes made to appeal to women benefit men as well.[14]

Because women influence 80 percent of car-buying decisions, as well as buy 50 percent of new cars and 48 percent of used cars, auto dealerships too are now reaching out to women more than ever.[15] Although most auto dealerships are still owned and operated by men, by incorporating information and educational resources into their designs, along with attractive play areas for children, many dealerships are becoming more women- and family-friendly. As with hardware stores, the design of auto showrooms must communicate that women are welcome, not that they're entering a black box.

WATCH YOUR STEP: HAZARDOUS ESCALATORS FOR CHILDREN AND THE ELDERLY

Shopping malls feature escalators to ease travel from one level to another and to remove the hassle of climbing stairs, but if not used with care, escalators can be especially dangerous for children and the elderly. The design and maintenance of escalators is partially to blame. When there are missing teeth in the comb plates, people's shoes can get caught in the gaps, leading to severe foot injuries. Contact with the side of the escalator can cause injury when feet, legs, hair, fingers, or other body parts get caught. Sudden stops caused by machinery failure can hurl riders down the metal stairs, as can sudden acceleration or slowing down. Shoes, shoelaces, and backpacks can become entangled. Children wearing rubber clogs have been increasingly prone to escalator injuries.[16]

Escalator injuries to children have increased in recent years, according to a study published in *Pediatrics*. Between 1990 and 2002, escalators injured an estimated twenty-six thousand children per year. More than half of children injured on escalators were boys, and twelve thousand of these injuries were to children under age five. Design changes have made escalators safer, including narrowing the space between the moving stairs and the stairway wall to prevent entrapment.[17]

Although escalators' dangers to children have long been known, the dangers to the elderly have been uncovered only recently. A study by researchers at the Indiana University School of Medicine documented escalator-related injuries among adults age sixty-five and older in the United States from 1991 to 2005, analyzing data from the National Electronic Injury Surveillance System of the US Consumer Product Safety Commission. The study documented an estimated 39,850 escalator-related injuries, but no fatalities; 8 percent of victims were admitted to the hospital. The rate of escalator-related injuries to older adults doubled during the period studied. The mean age of those injured was eighty years, with almost three-quarters (73 percent) female. Older adults, especially women, have problems with balance and should not walk up or down a moving escalator, carry large objects, or wear loose shoes or clothing while riding, because all of these actions are associated with an increased risk of falling.[18]

STAIRWAYS PROMOTE HEALTHY LIVING AND COMBAT OBESITY

Most retail buildings in the United States are designed with the assumption that visitors will take escalators and elevators rather than stairways. The same is true for most large office buildings and high-rise apartments. Depending upon the building size, building codes require specific numbers of stairways within a specified distance of each other as fire exits. Yet stairways are often unattractive spaces that are hard to find, not climate controlled, and inconvenient to use. This is especially the case in the interior spaces of department stores and shopping malls. Many stairways feel like fire exits, guarded by heavy spring doors. Such designs disadvantage oversize individuals who would benefit from increased stairway use.

Studies have found that, when it comes to maintaining a healthy body weight, incorporating small amounts of exercise into your everyday routines can be just as effective as routine amounts of structured exercise. Slow but steady forms of exercise can be far less intimidating and less expensive than joining a gym.

At the Centers for Disease Control and Prevention's Rhodes Building in Atlanta, Georgia, researchers employed four passive environmental interventions over three years to see which methods were most effective at increasing stair use: (1) installing new carpeting, painting the walls, and painting large numbers on doors to identify building floors; (2) decorating stairway landings with framed artwork; (3) displaying motivational signs throughout the building as well as on a kiosk in the lobby; and (4) playing music in the stairwell.[19]

Results showed that motivational signs and music increased stairwell use among the building's 554 permanent and 110 temporary employees by about 9 percent. Additional studies have shown that the number of steps to the next higher floor and the number of floors in a building are significant predictors of stair usage and that interventions that increase stairway use include playing music, displaying artwork, offering incentives such as fruits and games, and displaying signs at decision points between the stairs and escalators or elevators.[20] Closing the elevator for a day is also effective, but this is not a viable option because it prohibits people with disabilities from using anything but the ground floor.

Health-promotion activists have called upon architects and building owners to design more buildings that feature attractive, safe, and readily accessible stairs. Such building designs could include more ample stairways with shorter steps, making them easier and more pleasant to climb. Adding lighting, music, and air conditioning that can be shut off automatically in case of fire would also make stairways more likely to be used. Incorporating stairways into light-filled atrium spaces, along with or instead of escalators, would also promote increased physical activity. Building owners could be provided with financial incentives to help defray the added costs of designs that promote exercise, and building codes could be altered to incorporate health concerns and support active living.[21]

As mentioned earlier, more than one-third (37.8 percent) of adults in the United States are obese. Individuals who are obese are more likely to suffer from heart disease, stroke, type 2 diabetes, and certain types of cancer, most of which are preventable. The more our buildings can be designed to encourage movement and activity, the healthier a society we will be.

DISADVANTAGED PAR EXCELLENCE:
THE WEDDING INDUSTRIAL COMPLEX

Stores selling bridal wear and formal attire are among the most notorious examples of gender privileging, epitomizing what some have dubbed "the wedding industrial complex." Merchandise in bridal departments is designed and marketed with the assumption that brides and bridesmaids purchase expensive, elaborately adorned gowns, while the groom and ushers rent their tuxedos, shirts, cummerbunds, and shoes just for the day. Ironically, the average bride wears her gown for a total of about seven hours but stores it in her closet for decades.

Far greater choices are available in bridal wear than in formal wear for grooms. Bridal gowns are usually available in a wide variety of styles and are tailored to fit each bride perfectly, whereas tuxedos come in a relatively limited range of sizes and styles. However, not only bridal gowns but also women's formal wear for debutante balls, senior proms, and quinceañeras are often far more expensive than men's tuxedo rentals, a reflection of gender-related design differences with deep-seated social, psychological, and cultural roots.

The cost discrepancy in the wedding industry isn't just for adults. Elaborate dresses for flower girls are designed to resemble styles of bridal wear and can even cost more than bridesmaids' dresses and young ring-bearers' tuxedos.

A TISKET, A TASKET: AND WHAT ABOUT THE CASKET?

Another retail environment whose designs shape us in ways we might not recognize is one that we don't like to discuss: the funeral business. And, here, body biases abound.

I was exposed to this recently when an elderly longtime friend and neighbor of mine passed away unexpectedly. His sister was visiting him at the time, and she knew few people in town. I was the first person she called after discovering that he had passed away in his sleep. Because she had no family members nearby, I was thrown headfirst into the whirlwind of planning a funeral.

My neighbor was a small man, probably no more than five feet five in his better days, but by the end he had downsized to about my height, five feet two. Upon visiting the funeral home with his sister and shopping for a coffin, I noticed that they were all the same size. So I naively asked the funeral director about this.

"Don't you have anything for smaller people? Why should a family have to pay the same price for a person who was five feet two and probably no more than 110 pounds as for someone who was six feet two and 320 pounds? This doesn't seem fair. Is there a smaller size that's less expensive?"

"Sorry, no, there really isn't," he replied. "Child-size coffins usually stop at three feet six in height, so after that you're up to adult sizes."

So my neighbor's sister ended up paying for a very attractive solid walnut coffin that provided about twice as much space as her brother required.

In fact, the funeral industry has responded in the opposite direction by catering to the increasing number of obese people. A 2011 ABC News story titled "Obesity Grows alongside Oversized Caskets" highlighted this trend: "The fatter Americans get, the more businesses stretch to accommodate them; even funeral homes, and casket and mortuary lift retailers."[22] As Leslie Bonci, director of sports nutrition at the University of Pittsburgh Medical Center said, "We're seeing the widening of seats, the widening of cup holders and, now, the widening of caskets." One company, Goliath Caskets of Lynn, Indiana, serves the oversize-casket needs of bigger people. During the past two decades, its business has grown. Its caskets start at twenty-nine inches wide and can run up to fifty-two inches wide and eight feet long.

Standard casket widths have grown from twenty-four inches to about twenty-seven inches as people became increasingly overweight. According to Keith Davis, owner of Goliath Caskets, "When we first started in 1990, thirty-six inches was the widest casket out there . . . Now we're up to fifty-two inches wide, which can hold someone who weighs eight hundred to one thousand pounds." As of 2011, he was selling about three to four oversize caskets per week.

THEATERS AND CINEMAS

"At a concert at the Rosemont Theatre in Chicago, the handicapped seating was behind a section of regular seating on the first floor. Because of the nature of the concert, we were standing and dancing, but a handicapped person behind us asked us to sit so she could see. Either way, someone's experience was compromised. The people in front of us were still standing, so we couldn't see when we sat either." (Female, white, age 22, 5'5", 120 lb.)

In another type of retail environment, theater and cinema design, people with certain body types are disadvantaged. In older theaters, tall men are squeezed into seats without enough legroom, and oversize men and women fit all-too-snugly in between armrests. When someone seated in the middle of the row needs to enter or exit, theatergoers in the same row must rise to let them pass. Theaters are designed to maximize the number of seats and sell the most tickets, yet the comfort and visibility of theatergoers has often been shortchanged.

Seating with minimal or no slope severely disadvantages children and short adults. When a taller theatergoer or one with a voluminous hairdo sits in front of them, even people in staggered seating may have obstructed sightlines. Sometimes even leaning to the right or left to peer between people's heads proves insufficient to help them gain a view. Stadium seating in multiplex cinemas has been an excellent solution to many of these sightline issues for children and short adults. For this reason, films with subtitles—where it's crucial to have an unobstructed view of the bottom of the screen—should only be shown in cinemas with stadium seating. Ironically, although seeing a movie at a theater costs far less than seeing a live performance, cinema seating options are usually far superior. At concerts and plays, orchestra sections (where seats are most expensive) often pose the greatest sightline problems.

Yet stadium seating may pose problems for elderly people or others who have difficulty climbing steps. And people using wheelchairs can't sit with their companions in stadium seating. The Americans with Disabilities Act guidelines require that wheelchair spaces be an integral part of the fixed-seating plan and that they be located to provide comparable lines of sight to all viewing areas.

Nonetheless, the comfort of theatrical seating design has improved, especially in cinemas. Seating design in movie theaters has undergone extensive changes over the past decade, with many state-of-the-art cinema seats featuring high backs, armrests that can rise, generous legroom, a side table or holder for drinks, and comfortable reclining seats. Movable armrests accommodate larger theatergoers.

RESTAURANTS

> "In many restaurant booths, I find the tables too high and the bench seats too low. I am not comfortable eating there. So I usually avoid booths if I can help it." (Female, white, age 53, 5′2″, 108 lb.)

> "My biggest problem eating out is finding a booth I can fit in. Usually I can't." (Male, white, age 32, 5′11″, 300 lb.)

> "In certain restaurants, the bar stools or chairs are very annoying. They're way too high. Every time I attempt to get onto the stool, I can't do it. Someone has to help me getting up and getting down. I'm afraid I'm going to fall off. They should make adjustable bar stools/chairs for shorter people." (Female, white, age 61, 4′11″, 200 lb.)

Have you ever gone on a dinner date or out for a job interview over lunch only to find that you were disadvantaged by the design of the restaurant table, seat, or booth? A few inches can make a huge difference in how comfortable or uncomfortable we feel at the table. And they can have subtle influences on how we feel and how we act. Tables that are too low can make petite people feel much shorter than they really are. Booths that are too narrow can make a slightly overweight person feel obese.

Many restaurants and bars have hard floors, ceilings, and walls. These surfaces cause sounds to reverberate, increasing noise levels. Moving chairs and barstools on hard floors can make screeching, irritating noises. Sometimes in order to be heard, you must shout across the table. And if you or someone you're with is even slightly hard of hearing or soft-spoken, the problem is even worse. As a result, many customers leave with hoarse voices and unnecessary stress, vowing never to return again. Behind the scenes, the design of restaurant kitchens can disadvantage workers who are short or who have small reaches. Narrow passageways within the kitchen and between the kitchen and dining room can disadvantage oversize servers, causing traffic jams, near-misses, or accidents when people collide while carrying heavy plates of food.

GRUELING GROCERY STORES

"The other day when I was shopping at the grocery store, I saw someone clearly 'disadvantaged by design.' It was a 'little person' about three feet six inches tall, using a small basket that grocery stores provide to shop. The basket was full of items, and the woman seemed to be struggling under the weight of all of her items. Then it dawned on me, *Why don't grocery stores provide a few 'half-size' grocery carts that little people are able to use for their shopping convenience?* It doesn't seem right that they have to carry around all of their items when people of average height are able to use a cart. Little people are severely disadvantaged! Grocery stores need to have smaller carts available for people of all heights." (Female, white, age 23, 5′2″, 118 lb.)

Trips to the grocery store are part of our everyday routines. Yet for many people, the design of grocery stores and supermarkets can prove frustrating. And with superstores becoming more plentiful throughout American cities, suburbs, and even rural areas, replacing the mom-and-pop corner grocery stores of the past, they have gotten bigger and bigger—but not necessarily better.

Many store products are displayed so high that only the tallest of men can reach them. Short women struggle to grasp that last jar of their favorite tomato sauce perched inconveniently far back on the top shelf. Or they're forced to ask for help. Or they just skip buying it altogether.

REACHING FOR THE STARS: MEN, WOMEN, AND SKYSCRAPERS

"In some cultures, women are not allowed to visit places like unfinished tunnels, even if she is a civil engineer for that project. People say that will cause a calamity." (Female, Asian, age 30, 5′7″, 140 lb.)

Most visible of all commercial environments is the skyscraper, an iconic image of the city itself. Architectural critic Leslie Weisman refers to the office tower as "the cathedral of commerce." Skyscraper design has been almost exclusively the province of signature male architects, many of whom—such as Chicago's Louis Sullivan, Holabird and Root, Daniel Burnham, and Mies van der Rohe—have become classic figures forever etched in urban lore and architectural guidebooks. More recent skyscraper designers such as Helmut Jahn, Phillip Johnson, and Cesar Pelli have been dubbed "starchitects."

For decades, the Empire State Building and the twin towers at the World Trade Center—until their untimely destruction in 2001—represented New York City to the world. The Willis (formerly Sears) Tower and the John Hancock Building still epitomize Chicago, just as the Bank of America Building symbolizes San Francisco.

Many writers view skyscrapers as phallic symbols that keep getting higher and higher, no matter what the consequences for the streetscape and pedestrians below. Starchitects are now designing super-skyscrapers while the United States, the Middle East, and Asia compete for cultural dominance around the world.

The Burj in Dubai, the United Arab Emirates, at more than 828 meters (2,716.5 feet) tall, is the world's tallest freestanding structure. It features the world's fastest elevator, traveling at 59 feet per second. It practically dwarfs the Pearl of the Orient in Shanghai, China (1,535 feet), the tallest tower in Asia before it was surpassed by Taiwan's Taipei 101 (1,671 feet). Although the architectural profession remains male-dominated, with women making up just 17 percent of architecture-firm partners as of 2012, female architects employed in large firms such as Skidmore Owings & Merrill are working behind the scenes on skyscrapers like these around the world.[23]

The male domain of skyscraper design was dealt a big blow with a groundbreaking building that looks at skyscrapers in a new way.

The *Chicago Tribune* featured Jeanne Gang, a Chicago architect of Studio/Gang/Architects, naming her a "rising star" for the cutting-edge design of Aqua, an eighty-two-story skyscraper hotel, apartment, and condominium project in downtown Chicago. Completed in 2009, the $500 million curvilinear structure just north of Millennium Park is the largest commission ever landed by a female-headed architectural firm.

Its undulating balconies, cantilevering anywhere from two to twelve feet outward, offer unique light and stunning views of Lake Michigan, the Chicago River, and city views from each individual apartment unit that would have otherwise been impossible to achieve. And they cost only 1.5 percent of the building's $325 million construction cost.[24] The waves that form across its north and south façades stand in stark contrast to all other buildings in the Chicago skyline. Gang, a graduate of the University of Illinois at Urbana-Champaign's School of Architecture, as well as Harvard's Graduate School of Design, landed the job after sitting next to the developer at a Harvard alumni dinner.

Here's how *Los Angeles Times* architecture critic Christopher Hawthorne critiqued Gang's new Chicago icon:

> In other words: No testosterone!
>
> OK, maybe some testosterone in the ranks of the engineers and construction workers who helped design and building the tower. That much was clear when Gang and I rode the construction elevator to Aqua's top-floor penthouse, stopping every few floors to pick up a new crew of tile-cutters or plumbers. It was like a mobile male locker room in there. . . .
>
> How much of Aqua's substantial appeal, if any, has to do with Gang's gender? Certainly its shape is animated by characteristics that—at the risk of slipping into stereotype—we associate with femininity and even the female form. . . . Aqua seems impatient with the rigidly geometric and overly muscled shapes that surround it in the Chicago skyline as well as with the race to achieve height at the expense of architectural expression.[25]

RETAIL ENVIRONMENTS THAT ADVANTAGE BY DESIGN

Singing Stairways

One of the most innovative staircase designs was installed at the Odenplan subway station near retail shops in Stockholm, Sweden. Volkswagen teamed up with designers to create a stairway that looks like a giant musical keyboard. Every time someone steps a tread, a musical note is played. Even though it's adjacent to an escalator, the unusual stairway is popular with people of all ages, and it even features in a viral video on YouTube.[26]

According to Geek.com, "Will making something fun change a person's behavior? As shown in the video above, the resulting Piano Stairs seem to demonstrate the 'fun theory' rather well as the station's visitors took to the stairs 66 percent more times in a usual day versus the escalator nearby."[27]

In fact, Italian-born artist, engineer, and lighting designer Remo Saraceni first invented the "Walking Piano" that could be played with the feet. It was featured in the 1988 film *Big*, starring Tom Hanks. A Pennsylvania couple who purchased it after the original film release donated the sixteen-foot-long piano keyboard that Tom Hanks and Robert Loggia danced on to the Please Touch Museum in Philadelphia.[28] Saraceni seeks to bring the spirit of childhood back to adults, making life more playful and loosening up our inhibitions.

Super Designs for Supermarkets

An innovative supermarket design in Germany solves many common problems in grocery-store design and incorporates state-of-the-art features, making it exceptionally friendly to people of diverse ages and body types. In East Berlin's Friedrichshain neighborhood, the new Kaiser supermarket is a sharp contrast to the usual cramped inner-city supermarket. Its subtle design details are geared toward the elderly clientele who populate the neighborhood—60 percent of the customers are over fifty—and a senior housing complex is right across the street. So the company tore down a Cold War–era Kaiser's and replaced it with the new store, about double in size, in 2006. In-house brainstorming and market studies identifying the shopping needs of the elderly led to several simple, savvy, sensitive innovations and age-sensitive details.

Long metal steps run along the lower edge of the dairy and frozen-food cases, making it easy to reach items on the top shelves. Forgot your reading glasses? At the end of each of the grocery store's short aisles is a small eye-level station with a magnifying glass and a button that customers can use to summon help. Large, clear signage is visible throughout the store. Aisles are broad, allowing slower customers to take their time.

Shopping carts feature senior-friendly design details. Some are equipped with magnifying glasses; others, with seats and locking wheels for short rest breaks. Smaller baskets have long handles and wheels to make shopping easier. Curved seated carts were fabricated especially for the "generations-market."

Anti-slip synthetic flooring, brighter and more directed lighting, cheery pastel-yellow walls, and a checkout area allows generous room for maneuvering. Near the entrance is a lounge with couches, a TV and computer screen, a water cooler, and a coin-operated massage chair. From the adjacent bakery stand, customers can even have a taxi called for free.

The innovative store design has paid off, with sales 25 percent above forecasted figures. As one seventy-five-year-old customer put it: "Now short people like me can reach the top shelf . . . It's the best supermarket in all of Berlin."

The Kaiser store was modeled after the Adeg Aktiv Market 50+, Europe's first supermarket designed for shoppers over fifty, which opened in 2003 on the outskirts of Salzburg, Austria.[29] Adeg's markets feature big labels, wide aisles, nonskid floors, and plenty of places to sit down. Lights are calibrated to reduce glare on sensitive eyes. Lower shelves make it easy for shoppers to reach all products. In addition to regular shopping carts, some carts hook onto wheelchairs, while other carts double as seats: as soon as a shopper sits down, the wheels lock. A machine allows shoppers to check their blood pressure after waiting in the checkout line.

Although the unusually sensitive details were designed with

seniors in mind, half the customers of the Salzburg store are under fifty, a statistic that surprised the company. The first store proved to be so successful that a branch store in Vienna was renovated with similar 50+ features, and a third store opened in Vienna.

Chapter 10

AN APPLE A DAY: THE DESIGN OF HEALTHCARE SETTINGS

"*Oh yesss*, those flattened breast torture machines known as breast imaging. After nearly a decade of mammograms, I have had it. No more! I am no sissy, but I am sick and tired of having to go along with what I *know* is a bad design. There *has* to be a better way of imaging. I feel as if unless women stop putting up with all the pain and invasive stuff from industrialized medicine and complain loudly enough, these designs and protocols are not going to change!" (Female, age 54)

They're the places where we are born and the places where we die. Healthcare designs form the backdrop to life-changing events. The trauma of an accident, a heart attack or stroke, the end of a long-term illness, or the excitement of a newborn hurls us into an unfamiliar environment where life hangs in the balance. Compared with any other type of designed environment, here is where we're most fearful, vulnerable, and dependent upon others. In these circumstances—where minutes can seem like hours—the impact of the designed environment on patients, their families, friends, and visitors is exaggerated, influencing us to feel more desperate or hopeful.

Like so many others around the world, I know these feelings all too well. For over seven years, I accompanied my late husband to hundreds of gut-wrenching medical appointments, lab tests, blood transfusions, hospital visits, surgical procedures, chemotherapy and radiation treatments, and clinical trials to test out cutting-edge anti-angiogenesis treatments to combat his rare, unpredictable, and virulent form of cancer, an experience we chronicled in our book, *Running for Our Lives: An Odyssey with Cancer.* Our medical journey captured the attention of national media including *Time,* the *Chicago Tribune,* and even the national television evening news (ABC Evening News, NBC Nightly News). Patience, persistence, and perseverance were essential during our grueling emotional roller-coaster ride across five states, eight medical institutions, and scores of doctors, nurses, and medical staff. As one doctor put it, we were "sitting on a barrel of dynamite."[1]

For those who work here under daily stress and strain, design has the power to help or hinder their ability to complete some of life's most important work. In these emotionally charged environments, the impact of inequitable designs that favor certain patients or healthcare workers over others is magnified.

HOSPITAL MATERNITY WARDS VS. FREESTANDING BIRTH CENTERS

Even with today's technology, most women find mammogram exams unpleasant, if not excruciatingly painful. And if they were not proven to save lives, most of us would rather skip them altogether. Social attitudes are reflected in the design of medical equipment for women's health used in such procedures as mammograms, gynecological exams, childbirth, and abortion. Historically those who designed and manufactured such medical equipment—predominantly men—paid inadequate attention to the comfort of female patients and medical technicians, nurses, and other healthcare workers. And mainly male hospital administrators and physicians purchased the equipment.

As Naomi Wolf argued in her best-selling book, *Misconceptions: Truth, Lies, and the Unexpected on the Journey to Motherhood,* despite recent improvements, designers of hospital maternity wards and hospital beds historically paid greater attention to the comfort of male doctors than the comfort of mothers-to-be.

Childbirth is big business that relies on an infrastructure where the vast majority of mothers give birth in a hospital. According to Trish Wilkinson, a doula in Champaign-Urbana, Illinois, a non-medical professional who provides emotional, physical, and informational support to laboring women and their support system, the role of design in childbirth environments is critical. Wilkinson's fifteen years of experience assisting over four hundred women through the childbirth process, mainly at major regional hospitals, has provided her with unique insights based on her observations of scores of well-designed and poorly designed spaces:

> Creating a safe and intimate birth space can affect how we give birth. Birthing women may react negatively to a sterile and impersonal environment, perceived likelihood of medical interventions, and lack of personal control.
>
> Birth rooms need to be large enough to allow the woman to walk around and adopt different positions, to accommodate her and her support people, and to accommodate a range of equipment and flexible furniture that is light enough to move around. Family members need easy access to food and drink and nearby facilities to prepare refreshments—without straying far from the scene. And a range of equipment that encourages and supports upright position for labor and birth, including a birth stool, ball, ropes, and an upright chair should be available in every birth room.[2]

Privacy is extremely important, because as Wilkinson explains, "the sense of 'being observed' can impede labor." The bed should not be visible from the door, but all too often, it is. Natural daylight, a good view, and proper window coverings are important. Lighting should be adjustable. All too often, bright overhead lighting compounds the stress, as do wall clocks that tick away the time all too slowly. Water immersion in a private, easily accessible bathing area can ease the pain of childbirth—but often none is available. Every birth room should have a shower big enough for a pregnant woman, her partner, and apparatus—an amenity not always found. Some women actually labor on the toilet, so comfortable toilets are needed. Screening from noise and ability to play music helps too. Large windowsills and other horizontal surfaces can provide places to display items of personal significance.

Designers need to understand cultural considerations at this family milestone. Certain ethnic groups have traditions and rituals surrounding childbirth that can occur either indoors or outdoors. Some couples come alone, others bring a parent or two, and still others may bring an entire clan of four to six support people to witness the childbirth or visit the new baby. All need to be accommodated in an environment designed to make them feel welcomed.

In fine-tuning the design of childbirth environments, it's important to get feedback from doulas, midwives, labor and delivery nurses, and mothers themselves. As Wilkinson explains: "They know best what does and doesn't work, as they actually see the mother in labor. Basically doctors are in the room as the baby is crowning in order to catch the baby. Their use of the room is centered around the end of the bed—this is where their instruments are and where they have optimal access to the delivering mother. Otherwise, except in case of emergency, the doctors' use of birthing room facilities is minimal."[3]

Cesarean section (C-section) childbirths have soared to record highs in recent years. According to surveys conducted by the World Health Organization (WHO), and reported by the Associated Press in 2010, nearly half (46%) of all babies in China, over a third (35%) in Latin America, and nearly a third (30%) in the United States are delivered by C-section.[4] According to the WHO, many of these C-sections are unnecessary, costlier than natural births, and pose risks for women's health.

My former doctoral advisee, Chia-Hui Wang, now a professor at the University of Taipei, Taiwan, and Nai-Wen Kuo, professor at Taipei Medical University, and I formed one of the first research teams to systematically examine the impacts of the built environment on women's experiences with childbirth. Our focus was on the role of daylight exposure and window views in women's recovery from C-sections. We examined the impact of the built environment on recovery and patient-controlled analgesic (pain control medication) use, length of stay, perceived pain, and general well-being of new mothers. Chia-Hui recruited nearly three hundred women undergoing C-sections at the obstetrics wards of three large hospitals in

Taipei. She enlisted nineteen physicians and thirty-eight registered nurses to assist us in obtaining patient surveys, focus groups, medical charts, and observations. Using light meters, she measured the light levels in each patient's room, where she also noted the distance between the bed and the window, the size and shape of the windows, and the color of the walls. It took us about two years to collect and analyze our data.

Our results showed that the amount of daylight exposure in the hospital room was statistically significantly associated with improvement of patients' physical well-being, and that patients' satisfaction with the view out their window had a statistically significant, positive impact on improving their perceived levels of pain. Satisfaction with their window view significantly decreased patients' use of pain medication, reduced their perceived pain, and improved some dimensions of well-being. Our findings call for increased attention to designing hospital rooms with maximum daylight exposure and expansive views whenever possible, or if that's not possible, by displaying photos or paintings showing scenes of nature. Incorporating our changes can contribute to future best practices for hospital-room designs that may decrease the use of pain medication and therefore substantially reduce healthcare costs.[5]

Although freestanding birth centers provide a welcome alternative to the institutional atmosphere and high costs of hospital maternity wards, in many states they remain illegal. Most states have not yet developed necessary licensing requirements and construction codes.

Birth centers fall in between the code categories that apply to institutional facilities and those that apply to business occupancy. According to the American Association of Birth Centers website, there were 295 birth centers in 2015. Texas has twenty-one, California has fifteen, and Florida has eleven.[6]

The founding of the American Medical Association in 1848 established state licensing requirements that excluded midwives from medical practice, calling them illegal and "dangerous." The AMA promoted hospital deliveries with centralized, sophisticated medical equipment over home births. Yet back then the health risks to women were much greater when they delivered at a hospital than when they delivered with the assistance of midwives in their own homes. Despite the fact that infection rates in hospitals were higher than in homes, women were led to believe that hospital births were safer than home births. And, not surprisingly, the economic and psychological costs of giving birth at a hospital were far greater than those of giving birth at home.

Until birthing rooms or suites were incorporated into the traditional obstetrical ward in the 1980s, men were excluded from the childbirth process, forced to wait in a separate space, prohibited from contacting the mother until after the baby was born. In many other countries, that is still the case today.

How does the design of birth centers compare with that of typical hospital maternity wards? According to the American Association of Birth Centers, the atmosphere at a birth center is more like a country inn or a well-kept home than a hospital.[7] Jacuzzis are provided for women in labor to relax. Usually only one or two women are giving birth at the same time, and the volume of women is relatively low, so privacy is far greater than in the hospital. Because mothers come to the birth center for all their prenatal care, they're familiar with the facility and its staff. The mother can labor in any position that she finds comfortable—squatting, lying on her side, or sitting in bed. And once the baby is born, mother and baby are not separated, as they would be in the hospital. Any treatment or exam performed for the baby is always done in front of the parents. The same staff that takes care of the mother also takes care of the baby.

Although she was not a flight risk, Shawanna Nelson, a pregnant prisoner serving time in Arkansas for writing bad checks, was forced to give birth while immobilized, with her legs shackled to a hospital bed. International human rights laws state that shackling prisoners during childbirth is tantamount to torture. Yet according to the Center for Reproductive Rights in its 2008 annual report, the practice was common in prisons across the United States.[8] In Illinois, a class-action lawsuit was filed on behalf of eighty prisoners who had been restrained by handcuffs, shackles, and belly chains that circled the waist during childbirth. The suit reached a preliminary settlement on May 22, 2012, with $4.1 million going to inmates.[9]

FAMILY-PLANNING CLINICS: DANGEROUS BY DESIGN

Because many hospitals in the United States are owned by religious entities that oppose abortion, family-planning clinics are prohibited in hospitals. Instead these clinics are usually housed in separate spaces. Yet as freestanding and easily identifiable units, family-planning clinics are especially vulnerable to attacks that would be less likely to occur if these clinics were incorporated into local medical facilities. All too often, women entering family-planning clinics in a highly distraught state of mind are forced to walk through a line of antiabortion protesters. Once they enter the door, women may be confronted with dark, depressing, dilapidated facilities. And doctors performing abortions have often put their lives in danger simply by going into work.

Dr. George Tiller was a physician who performed late-term abortions at his Wichita, Kansas, clinic. In 1986, his clinic was seriously damaged by a bomb. In 1993, he was shot through both arms but survived. Antiabortion activists had picketed outside his clinic for years. On Sunday morning, May 31, 2009, moments after the start of services, Dr. Tiller, age sixty-seven, was gunned down and killed while serving as an usher at Reformation Lutheran Church in Wichita.[10]

According to the US Department of Justice, Tiller's shooting prompted US Attorney General Eric Holder to direct federal marshals to "offer protection to other appropriate people and facilities around the nation." Tiller was the fourth American physician killed over abortion since 1993. One can't help but wonder whether these deaths could have been prevented had these physicians worked within the confines of a much larger multipurpose clinic or medical facility, where their offices would blend in rather than stand out.

By contrast, in China, where abortions are common due to the government's limit on the number of children, population and family planning clinics are an accepted part of the urban landscape, and women and medical staff can proceed in safety. Instead of the term "abortion," the Chinese refer to "population and family planning" programs. The government rewards couples that abide by the official policy and, with few exceptions, fines and penalizes those who do not.[11] In Chinese cities and towns most medium and large public hospitals, as well as private women's hospitals and gynecological clinics, offer abortion services. Following a recent visit to China, I was shocked to learn that abortion services are even advertised on public buses, bus shelters, billboards and kiosks with large signs and big, bold letters saying "3-Minute Painless Abortion – Rest Without Anxiety," "Visible Painless Abortion. Abortion fee 99 yuan [$15]." Another sign has a diagram of a pregnancy test kit, with the message "Oh no! Two red lines. How to deal with unplanned pregnancy? Superconducting visual painless abortion. 480 yuan [$70]."

China's one-child policy, in effect for thirty-five years, officially ended in October 2015, but today's couples are still restricted to two children, so vast numbers of abortions will continue. An unintended result: the one-child policy led to thirty million bachelors, an acute gender imbalance. The policy coincided with the technological ability in the 1990s to determine the gender of the fetus, and Nobel Prize–winning economist Amartya Sen estimated that 100 million baby girls were never born or were killed across Asia. This despite the fact that government regulations called for punishment of an institution or individual performing gender identification of fetus or sex-selective pregnancy termination for non-medical purposes.[12] Of the girls that remain, however, as only children they benefited from their parents' generosity in sending them to college, so that urban women born after 1980 achieved far more professional success than any in prior generations.

HEALTH ISSUES FOR HEALTHCARE WORKERS

"After doing some research on why nursing was such a female domi-nant field, I came to find just how hard it is to be a male nurse. Not only do you as a male need to fit in with all the female nurses and earn respect, but you also need to watch your back when it comes to patients. As a male nurse who has a female patient, it seems you always had to make sure that you had a female nurse with you any time you were doing any sort of exam that may be personal to the patient. [For] male nurses, it seemed that sexual harassment was a problem which patients and coworkers could pin on them easily, which is why you always needed a second person there to make sure nothing unprofessional happened." (Male, white, age 23, 6′2″, 180 lb.)

At a suburban Chicago hospital, a male nurse is placed in a socially awkward situation every time he enters the locker room that he shares with female nurses. He must first knock on the door to make sure the room is empty. The operating room and the emergency room each have just one locker room for nurses, reflecting the assumption that all nurses are female.[13] An outmoded design has not kept pace with changing demographics in the nursing profession.

Women represent a large portion of workers employed in healthcare environments. According to the National Institute for Occupational Safety and Health, women currently constitute 92 percent of 4.3 million nurses and nursing aides in the United States. Healthcare workers not only receive relatively low pay, but also face numerous occupational and safety health hazards. These include musculoskeletal disorders, cardiovascular diseases, psychosomatic and mental health disorders, respiratory diseases, neurotoxic effects, and other illnesses caused by chemical agents to which they're exposed. Exposure to radiation from portable x-ray machines and other diagnostic tests or therapies using radioactive sources or waste can promote occupational cancer.

Each year, about 385,000 to 800,000 needlestick injuries occur among the more than eight million healthcare workers in the United States. Most of these injuries involve nursing staff, but laboratory staff, physicians, housekeepers, and other healthcare workers are also at risk. About half of these injuries go unreported. They can needlessly expose workers to blood-borne pathogens—among the worst are human immunodeficiency virus, hepatitis B virus, and hepatitis C virus—all of which can be life-threatening. Needlestick injuries can be reduced with proper use of needleless systems or newer safety needle devices used as part of a comprehensive program to prevent such injuries.[14]

Allergies to latex gloves among healthcare workers are also a major problem. Of those exposed regularly to latex, 8–12 percent develop sensitivity, which may lead to allergic symptoms such as skin rashes; hives; nasal, eye, or sinus symptoms; asthma; and, although rare, even shock.

BODY ISSUES AND HEALTHCARE DESIGN

"I feel that the design of clinic waiting rooms is poor. They are one large room where you must sit, sometimes for hours at a time. When you have a sprained ankle and the guy next to you had the cold of the century, is it fair for you to have to sit next to him? You are really putting yourself in harm's way by subjecting yourself to contagious individuals who are also in the same room. Can't there be some smaller spaces to wait in where you can subdivide into groups or even be alone while waiting?" (Male, white, age 23, 5'8", 150 lb.)

The design of healthcare facilities and medical equipment has not kept pace with the United States' obesity epidemic, presenting serious problems not only to healthcare workers who must lift and transport patients, but also, at times, to the physical facilities themselves.

People with physical disabilities confront special challenges while using medical facilities. Many find it difficult or uncomfortable to use examination tables, medical chairs, weight scales, exercise equipment, and imaging equipment. In their book *Medical Instrumentation: Accessibility and Usability*, editors Jack Winters and Molly Follette Story voice these concerns. Their book opens with a telling quote from a patient: "It takes a village to get me on and off an exam table, which means I don't go to preventive care appointments."[15]

Principles of universal design are relevant to the design of healthcare equipment, yet to date, they have rarely been applied. Universal design seeks to suit the needs of people of all ages, sizes, and shapes, and abilities. Accessible features are integrated into universal designs from the outset, so they look as if they have always been there.

Serious problems can occur in medical facilities when people are above or below average in size. For example, small, frail elderly people stuck in hospitals and nursing homes are endangered by poor bed-rail design. In the United States, there are about 2.5 million beds in hospitals and nursing homes. According to the US Food and Drug Administration (FDA), between 1985 and 2008, 772 patients were trapped or strangled in beds with rails, and 460 people died.[16] A more recent study by the Consumer Product and Safety Commission showed that from January 2003 to September 2012, 155 fatalities from bedrails occurred, with most victims age sixty or over.[17]

Potential benefits of bed rails include aiding in turning and repositioning, providing a handhold for entering or exiting the bed, providing a sense of comfort and security, reducing the risk of falling out of bed when being transported, and providing easy access to bed controls and personal care items. Yet the potential risks of bed rails include strangling, suffocating, and bodily injury or death when body parts are caught between rails or between the bed rails and the mattress. Serious injuries can occur when patients climb over rails and fall. The FDA believes that most patients can be in bed safely without bed rails.[18]

"OPEN WIDE, PLEASE" FOR THE DENTIST

At the dentist, children and adult patients with small mouths find dental x-rays painful when they are forced to bite down on a hard bitewing that feels much too large. In the past, stiff pieces of film were used to capture dental images, but many dentists lacked film in small sizes. Today, extension cone paralleling (commonly known as XCP) dental x-ray film-positioning devices do the job. In order to capture the most precise images of teeth and gums, an XCP collimator ring is used to position the sensor. Although a marked improvement over the old technology, some patients with small mouths may still experience discomfort as they bite down on the XCP ring.

Anyone who has experienced the dreaded root canal is familiar with the rubber dam that covers your mouth, creating a temporarily sealed, sterile environment in which the oral surgeon performs the procedure. Root canals can be an uncomfortable process from the get-go, but for many patients, the rubber dam—a piece of thin, stretchable latex or nonlatex material—makes matters even worse. The endodontist places a clamp over the tooth and spreads the rubber dam over the clamp to isolate the tooth, preparing it for the operation. The dam is held in place by a floss-secured retainer that keeps your mouth wide open. The dam serves as a shield to keep the tooth sterile and dry; it also prevents disinfecting chemical solutions from entering the rest of the mouth.

But if the rubber dam is too large, it covers your tooth, your mouth, and your nose, causing you to feel asphyxiated. During one of my more memorable root canals, my endodontist asked me to raise my hand if I needed help but within seconds exited the room. By the time I realized that I couldn't breathe, no one was around to help. I now know to insist that the rubber dam be trimmed to my size, ensuring I can breathe through my nose.

According to a recent study by American City Business Journals, dental hygiene is one of the most female-dominated professions in the United States. Women comprise 97.7 percent of dental hygienists and 97.1 percent of dental assistants.[19] A qualitative analysis of dental-hygiene work based on five national focus groups found that dental hygienists are prone to serious musculoskeletal symptoms, especially after ten years on the job. Most common ergonomic problems included instruments and chairs.[20] Studies show that dental hygienists who treat more than eleven clients per day or who work more than thirty-four hours per week are at higher risk than those with fewer clients or fewer hours.[21]

If the workstation for dental hygienists is not set up to allow hygienists to position themselves as close to patients as possible and move the chair and the instrument tray closest to the part of the mouth they're working on, overreaching frequently occurs, placing stress on the lower back. Many dental hygienists sit forward on the edge of their chair, worsening the problem. Another set of problems occurs when the height of dental hygienists' chairs fails to match that of the patients' chairs. Hygienists' chairs should be adjustable with lumbar, thoracic, and arm supports, and the adjustable height range of chairs should accommodate hygienists who are larger or smaller than average.[22]

Many of the same problems that plague the female-dominated dental hygienist profession afflict the male-dominated dentistry profession as well.[23] According to an occupational therapist writing on ergonomics in *Dentistry Today*, both dentists and dental hygienists are at risk for musculoskeletal disorders and repetitive strain injuries. "Many instruments were designed with function in mind, without consideration of ergonomic factors or the possible effect on the body, and are unbalanced and require increased muscular force to manipulate."[24] The following factors may contribute to harm: extreme wrist flexion/extension, repetitive grasping with thumb and fingers, excessive finger movements, firm grasp/excessive force needed to hold instruments, vibration damage from vibrating instruments, and tight gloves that constrict wrists and fingers.[25]

CHANGING DEMOGRAPHICS, CHANGING HEALTHCARE DESIGNS

The design of culturally insensitive hospitals, clinics, and other medical facilities impairs nonnative English speakers' access to healthcare in the United States. Increasing concerns about racial, ethnic, and language disparities in healthcare and the growing need for healthcare systems to accommodate diverse patient populations have led to the national importance of language-access services. The number of individuals who speak a language other than English at home rose from 31.8 million in 1990 to 47 million in 2000. And the number of individuals who speak English less than "very well" increased from 14 million in 1990 to 21.4 million in 2000, a 53 percent gain. Substantial research has shown that minorities receive a lower quality of care, resulting in poorer health.

To what extent have medical environments responded to these changing demographics? In 2005, the American Institutes for Research developed *A Patient-Centered Guide to Implementing Language Access Services in Healthcare Organizations* for the Office of Minority Health, US Department of Health and Human Services.[26] Among its goals were to improve racially and ethnically diverse populations' access to care, quality of care, patient satisfaction, and resource utilization.

A key concern is displaying signage and directions that non-English-speakers can understand. The guide includes detailed information to help institutions decide what type of signage to post, where to display signage, how to determine the quality of signage, and how to train staff on new signage. Signage can include words, symbols, pictures, or a combination of all three, and it should be incorporated in existing facilities as well as facilities under construction. Simple wording is essential for those patients with low literacy.

Changing demographics have also caused healthcare architects to question the design of the typical hospital room. For example, when a Latina grandmother is hospitalized, her extended family of children, grandchildren, nieces, and nephews may all come to visit at the same time—a situation that the typical hospital room can't accommodate. Although economic constraints dictate the size of the standard hospital room, designers are exploring ways to better accommodate visits by extended families.

CAN YOU READ THE FINE PRINT? PATIENT INSTRUCTIONS

"The print on over-the-counter medication packaging is minuscule—especially the really crucial information about dosages. Bleary-eyed with sleep in the middle of the night, when the medicine is in the bathroom and one's reading glasses are back somewhere in the bedroom near a lightly sleeping partner, it's tempting to just guess how much to take. This situation has probably led to a number of dangerous accidental overdoses or useless underdosing. There's a lot of information to pack onto a package back, but what about enclosing a large-print insert with the essentials?" (Female, white, age 53, 5′3″, 120 lb.)

The design of prescription labels and patient instructions, with typically microscopic print, endangers millions of individuals around the world. When someone takes the wrong dosage of a medicine, the consequences can be disastrous. Elderly people and those with even a slight visual impairment are most vulnerable to misreading or misjudging doses.

Although state pharmacy boards specify requirements for the *content* of prescription labels, they do not regulate the *format* of the information. Anyone who has trouble reading prescription labels faces medical-safety issues. Inability to read prescription labels and information sheets, difficulty determining the color, shape, and markings distinguishing a medication, and failure to see markings on measuring or testing devices are among the most serious dangers. People who can't read prescription labels or distinguish different medications must rely on their memory, use special compensatory strategies, or depend upon others while managing their medications.

As the baby-boomer generation matures, age-related eye disease such as macular degeneration, cataracts, diabetic retinopathy, and glaucoma affect increasing numbers of people. According to the National Eye Institute, American Foundation for the Blind, the number of people at risk for age-related eye disease and resulting vision impairment is expected to double by 2050, increasing to more than eight million.[27] Physiological changes in vision also occur with age, causing loss of near focus (presbyopia), reduced contrast sensitivity, and visual-field impairment.

The American Society of Consultant Pharmacists Foundation collaborated with the American Foundation for the Blind to develop Guidelines for Prescription Labeling and Consumer Medication Information for Persons with Vision Loss. These guidelines provide pharmacists and pharmacies with recommendations about how to make medication information accessible to those with vision loss, and they serve as a resource for the visually impaired. But in the meantime, the rest of us just may need magnifying glasses to read our prescriptions.

HEALTHCARE THAT ADVANTAGES BY DESIGN

Motorbike Ambulances Make Childbirth Safer

In many developing countries, countless women die on the way to childbirth. They live far away from medical facilities and rely on primitive means of transportation. Poor road conditions, or no roads at all, make it difficult for women needing emergency support to reach clinics. This is the case in the remote Eastern Equatoria region of South Sudan. According to Atem Nathan Riek, director-general of primary healthcare in South Sudan, which has one of the highest rates of maternal mortality in the world (a one-in-six chance of dying during pregnancy or delivery), "We have a problem bringing critically sick people to the few referral facilities available."[28]

There, in 2009, UNICEF donated five powerful scrambler motorbikes with sidecar "beds" in a pilot effort to help cut the high rates of maternal mortality. The Ministry of Health deploys the motorbikes to boost access to health facilities for pregnant women. Compared with heavier vehicles, bikes can more easily negotiate narrow paths around flooded tracks. They're also cheaper and easier to maintain. The service is free for pregnant women, and if successful, it could be extended to the rest of the country. The motorcycles cost about $6,000 each and provide space for the patient to sit or lie down on a cushioned bed on wheels that has seat belts for legs and waist, as well as a space for a health worker to sit behind the patient.

Similar bikes have been introduced in Uganda and Malawi. According to UNICEF, in Malawi, bikes helped raise the number of women giving birth at health facilities from 25 percent to 49 percent over a four-year period and helped reduce maternal mortality rates from 586 to 236 per 100,000 live births.

Lighting Up the Maternity Ward

Some of the most innovative medical-facility designs can be found in children's hospitals. Compared with healthcare facilities for adults, pediatric facilities are cheerful, fun, and even festive. Architects, interior designers, and landscape architects stretch the envelope in creating uplifting spaces for children.

At Mercy Medical Center in Rogers, Arkansas, anxious families awaiting the birth of a child can "paint with light," using an entire spectrum of colors and shapes on Philips Electronics' Imagination Light Canvas, a fourteen-foot-long by six-foot-high interactive wall featuring 1,420 LEDs animated by touchscreen. It's an innovative way to help both kids and adults alleviate stress and boredom.[29]

A Visit to the Hospital and a Journey to the Milky Way

Children's Hospital at Montefiore was founded in 2001, a $123 million addition to the Montefiore Medical Center serving southern Westchester County and the Bronx, New York. It combines Dr. Irwin Redlener's agenda of excellence in pediatric care for disenfranchised children with cutting-edge design; the latest technology; and the worldview of the late astronomer, author, and scientific philosopher Carl Sagan.[30] The hospital's unusual mission is to take children on a journey to health, discovery, and possibility. As one writer describes it, "The effect is part high-tech classroom, part cutting-edge science museum, and part futuristic playground. Combined, it is a powerful statement of what a children's hospital needs to be."[31]

Redlener engaged the expertise of David Rockwell and his design team at the Rockwell Group, known for Cirque du Soleil's Orlando headquarters and sets for theatrical productions of *The Rocky Horror Show Live* and *Hairspray*. According to Rockwell, "Children are explorers on a journey to health." His idea was to uncover "all of those moments in your experience as a child in a hospital that are terrifying, dehumanizing, and lacking in information and to use those as interventions to provide information, insight, and a sense of wonder and delight."[32]

A glowing glass mural of the Milky Way, swirling blues and purples surrounding a white-hot center marked with a tiny red "you are here" dot dominates the hospital's lobby. Each of the seven floors for patients has a theme and design palette. Instead of numbers, patients' rooms feature constellations, animals, or aquatic creatures, depending upon the floor's theme. The Big Dipper room may house a teenager, while an infant might occupy the Bumblebee room. Child-height exhibits feature artwork from young children around the city and encourage patients to create their own drawings, collages, and sculptures in fully supplied lounges on each floor.

Seniors-Only Emergency Rooms

Emergency rooms designed specifically for people age sixty-five and up have been making their debut in a growing number of American hospitals. They include special accommodations such as nonskid floors, rails along the walls, extra heating units, thicker mattresses to prevent bedsores, and artificial skylights to combat "sundowning." Because elderly patients account for 15–20 percent of emergency-room visits, a number expected to rise as baby boomers age, hospitals have strong incentives to update their designs.[33]

One of the first senior-only emergency rooms to open was at Holy Cross Hospital in Silver Spring, Maryland, in 2008. Since then, its parent organization, Trinity Health System, opened several more.

At St. Joseph's Regional Medical Center in Paterson, New Jersey, Chairman of Emergency Medicine Mark S. Rosenberg led the effort to create a senior emergency department after his mother had experienced many unpleasant emergency-room visits near her home in South Florida. As Dr. Rosenberg explained, "She was so afraid to be in the ED because of the gang-violence patients and the screaming and people in pain. . . . She would sometimes even lie to [ED staff] just to get out of there. She said to me, 'Why don't we build an emergency department that's designed for seniors, just like we do for kids?'"[34] Rosenberg, his mother, two aunts, and friends from her bridge group met to talk about what they'd like to see there. In 2009, St. Joseph's opened its first geriatric emergency department, an eleven-bed space on the hospital's third floor. It features natural lighting on three sides and a much more orderly and quiet environment than a typical adult emergency department. Patient satisfaction has increased, while return visits and admissions have decreased.

Avoiding admissions is key, because, as Rosenberg says, "Seniors often don't do well when admitted to the hospital."[35] Research shows that hospitalized seniors face special risks, such as worsening functional status, delirium, falls, medication toxicity, infections, and pressure ulcers. In 2012, the geriatric emergency department was relocated downstairs next to the adult emergency department, enabling it to expand to twenty-four beds. Harps and aromatherapy contribute to a calm environment.

The geriatric emergency department at St. Joseph's served as a model for the one at the 1,171-bed Mount Sinai Hospital in New York City. Mount Sinai's geriatric emergency department has fourteen treatment spaces, nonskid and nonglare floors, handrails, and high-back chairs that are easy for patients to get in and out of. Other special features include reading glasses, hearing devices, and pressure-reducing mattresses.

As of 2016, there are more than one hundred geriatric emergency departments in the United States. As people age eighty-five and older are now the fastest growing population, emergency-medicine experts believe that such facilities could soon double in number.[36]

Balance Beam Makes Safer Nighttime Trips to the Bathroom

According to designers at HOK and HOK Product Design, "a recovering patient's steps should be celebrated, not prompt fear and anxiety associated with falls, prolonged lengths of stay, or legal woes. Every step should reinforce a patient's autonomy, assist hospital staff with care delivery, and symbolize that a patient is on the road to recovery."[37]

The "balance beam," a touch-sensitive lighted handrail, guides hospital patients from their bed to the bathroom. The io™ Balance Beam received a Silver Award and an Innovation Award at the Best of NeoCon™ Awards in 2011.[38] If widely adopted, it can prevent millions of patients from having dangerous falls, costly injuries, and hip fractures. Among people over sixty-five years old, most falls occur in hospitals and nursing homes. Among hospitalized patients, the most common adverse event is a fall. Falls increase patients' pain and distress, can cause new injuries and disabilities, and can even be fatal. Falls increase healthcare costs and often lead to costly litigation. In the England and Wales, about 250,000 hospital falls are reported annually, and in the United States perhaps as many as one million patients fall each year. Most falls occur from the bed, from bedside chair, or while transferring between the two. But many also occur while patients are on their way to the bathroom, or are in the bathroom itself.[39] Falls are a huge safety threat, especially for acutely ill and elderly patients.[40]

According to the Centers for Disease Control, the situation is even worse in nursing homes. As many as half the nation's 1.5 million nursing home residents fall at least once a year, and many fall more often than that. To make matters worse, many falls are not seen and may go unreported. Falls in nursing homes kill about 1,800 patients each year. At both nursing homes and hospitals, the rate of falls far exceeds the rate for elderly people who live in their own homes.[41]

In both hospitals and nursing homes, some of the most dangerous design issues concern the distance and path from the bed to the bathroom, a bed that is convenient for medical staff but too high for patients, and insufficient floor lighting at night. Many patients call for assistance to use the restroom, but if a nurse or aide does not arrive right away, they will try to go by themselves and risk a fall along the way.

A team of healthcare designers at HOK and HOK Product Design and a design researcher in professional practice developed the balance beam to improve patient safety and streamline the work of healthcare staff. Nursing staff benefit by using the balance beam to assist with patient-to-bathroom transfers and also as an unobtrusive light source to check on sleeping patients.

A simple touch of the hand activates the LED-illuminated bar, which lights the way to the patient's destination. The light stays on for a predetermined amount of time. So that a patient's sleep will not be disturbed when the room is dim, small amber-colored lights indicate where the patient should grab the bar to activate it. Using "double-touch" activation, caregivers can turn the light off without waiting for the time delay.

The balance beam can be adapted for use in the home. It would be a boon to seniors most vulnerable to injury during nighttime trips to the bathroom, and it could keep elderly people living longer, healthier, independent lives in their own homes.

Chapter 11

A CALL TO ACTION

"I think the difficulty lies in the economics of trying to supply something for everyone. For clothing, I think stores like Big and Tall are a great start. These types of stores specialize in proper clothing. But how can you possibly apply this to airlines, for example? Is it even possible to make a seat that is completely customizable while still maintaining cheap flights? I think there will always be a gray line that everyone must come to grips with. As humans, we have an uncanny ability to adapt to varying environments. The real question is where to draw that gray line?" (Male, white, age 39, 5'11", 230 lb.)

It's time for a seismic shift in the world of fashion, product, and building design, one that is long overdue.

In his preface to *A Woman's Nation Changes Everything*, John Podesta argues, "Our policy landscape remains stuck in an idealized past, where the typical family was composed of a married-for-life couple with a full-time breadwinner and full-time homemaker who raised the children herself."[1] The same is true for design. As our society becomes increasingly diverse in gender, age, and body size, it's time to become unstuck.

You can help make that happen.

You can help improve the design of products, spaces, and places to keep up with today's changing times. *Designs that reduce, minimize, or eliminate gender, age, and body biases can provide equal opportunities for all.* Together we can help create safer, healthier designs that better respond to diversity. Together we can help stamp out future fashions, products, and buildings that disadvantage us by design.

WHAT YOU CAN DO TO CHANGE THE DESIGN PROFESSIONS

If you are anything other than an average-sized, college-age white male, if you use a wheelchair, cane, or other mobility device, or if you are visually impaired, contact the design department at your local college or university and volunteer to serve as a sample consumer. You can be involved in the students' design process from the outset, as a desk critic throughout the term, or during their review process in the middle or at the end of the term. Design schools need more diverse consumers to critique students' work. You can play an important role in students' design education.

If you have daughters, ethnically underrepresented children, or children who are exceptionally petite or large, or happen to be transgender, encourage them to become designers. We need people of all genders, shapes and sizes to become industrial designers, architects, builders, contractors, and other members of the building professions who can shape the design of future products, spaces, and places.

WHAT YOU CAN DO FOR YOUR CHILDREN

Routinely check the US Consumer Product Safety Commission (CPSC) website, Parents.com, and ConsumerWatch.com for product recalls and news alerts for products currently on the market or previously available worldwide. The CPSC has a Google+ Hangout as well as Facebook and Twitter accounts.

Monitor Safekids.org, the site of Safe Kids Worldwide, a global organization of more than four hundred coalitions and chapters in the United States that partners with organizations in thirty countries dedicated to preventing injuries in children. Unintentional injuries are the number one killer of kids in the United States; around the world, a child dies from an unintentional injury every thirty seconds.[2] Safe Kids Worldwide brings together health and safety experts, educators, corporations, foundations, governments, and volunteers to educate families in order to prevent injuries at home, at play, and on the way.[3] Sign up for a monthly e-mail alert that tells you the latest juvenile-product recalls.

Consult the wealth of information found in *Child Product Safety Guide: Potentially Dangerous Products* published by the European Child Safety Alliance. It lists dangerous products and summarizes relevant literature and available data from EU countries, the CPSC, and Health Canada documenting injuries and deaths. For each product, the following information is included: why the product poses a problem, how it can be dangerous for children, what to look for when buying or prior to using, and how to use it safely.[4]

Exercise caution when buying secondhand children's toys or play equipment. Recalled items may still be found in homes, in secondhand markets, and in e-commerce venues such as eBay. Hand-me-downs are especially vulnerable.

If you own a recalled product, follow the government's instructions that may require you to stop using the product, repair it, or return it for a refund or replacement. And be sure to inform friends or family members who may own it, too. Share recall info on your social networking sites.

WHAT YOU CAN DO TO IMPROVE FASHION AND PRODUCT DESIGN

When shopping for a purse or bag, purchase one made of lightweight material and avoid overstuffing it. Empty out your purse at least once a week. If your bag needs to carry heavy contents, alternate shoulders every ten or fifteen minutes or carry it in front with two hands.

Men should downsize their wallets, carrying only the minimum number of credit cards and necessary cash.

Call upon manufacturers to eliminate "wrap rage" and dangerous clamshell packaging that needlessly injures thousands each year. Tell them you refuse to buy their products if they can't find a safe way to package them. Designing packaging that's safe for everyone—not just able-bodied adults—to use should be a greater priority than the efficiency of shipping and stacking. If the European Union can regulate packaging design and waste, so can we. A more immediate solution: If you think you'll have difficulty opening something that you're about to purchase in a store, have the cashier open it at the cash register right after you pay for it. Say that otherwise you won't buy it. That's what I do!

Ask for safer product design and more rigorous safety standards from the American National Standards Institute/Outdoor Power Equipment Institute to prevent more than nine thousand children from needless injuries while mowing their lawns each year.

Call for the safer design of snowblowers, which cause more than fifty-three hundred emergency department visits and one thousand amputations per year.

Speak out for power saws and tools to be designed to accommodate both left-handed and right-handed people. No longer should power-saw accidents be the most common cause of amputating hand injuries.

High-end designer beds that perch sleepers high above the floor must be equipped with warning labels about falls that can injure people for life. Product descriptions both in stores and on websites should include the height of beds with different-size mattresses. Consumers must be aware of just how high off the ground they'll be when they wake up in the middle of the night to find their way to the bathroom in the dark.

Parents must lobby car-seat manufacturers to test child car seats at higher speeds and in side-impact collisions, not just simulations of front-end collisions at thirty-five miles per hour.

New federal safety regulations are needed to require vendors to include anchoring attachments with the sale of flat-panel TVs and heavy furniture, to prevent serious injuries to children who inadvertently knock them over. Parents should do a walk-through of their home to check for tipping hazards and anchor them, just as they would to protect their home from an earthquake.

WHAT YOU CAN DO IN YOUR COMMUNITY

If you live in a suburban neighborhood without sidewalks, ask your local governing agency to consider installing them to encourage more pedestrian activity and reduce obesity. Cite some of the findings from active-living research.

If you live on a busy street in an urban neighborhood, suggest that your street become a candidate for traffic-calming devices that can make it safer for children.

Call for changes in the timing of traffic lights, to allow pedestrians more time to cross the street without fear of getting run over. Make suburbs safer places for pedestrians of all ages.

If your child has attention deficit/hyperactivity disorder, try to integrate more green time into his or her daily activities. Spending time outdoors can reduce children's need for medication by one dose per day.

Participate in the design-review process for proposed new residential and school buildings, and stress the need to pay greater attention to the view out the window, as it can have an enormous effect on people's competence and civility. As environmental psychologists Stephen and Rachel Kaplan have argued, views of nature provide cheap remedies to many social problems and are linked to many positive psychological outcomes for children.

Learn about laws governing your city and state to assist you in asserting your restroom rights. Some business establishments may prohibit customers from using their restrooms. Depending upon where they're located, those businesses may be breaking the law. As a business owner, you should be aware of those laws. If you're required to provide toilet access to customers, you need signs clearly indicating where restrooms are located.

If you're a parent of a child in diapers, try to plan your trips in advance. Call ahead to find out whether diaper-changing stations are available at your destination, and if so are they in both men's and women's restrooms? If they're not, ask to speak with the manager and explain why you and your friends will boycott their business.

Inform your civic leaders about the importance of making attractive public restrooms available in your city or town. Point out the success of Japanese public restrooms, the best in the world. Public restrooms can play a major role in revitalizing America's downtowns.

If a new public restroom is proposed for a park or other public facility in your area, ask city officials to see the preliminary designs before they issue a building permit. Get involved in the design-review process.

WHAT YOU CAN DO IN YOUR SCHOOLS

Inform teachers and school administrators of the need to stamp out infrastructure bias in classroom settings from preschools to universities. Ensure that furniture replacements serve left- and right-handed students equally.

Propose a nondiscrimination policy for classroom design and desk-purchase criteria that stipulate that no side-biased tablet-arm desks be purchased.

Ensure that left-handed students sit at a full desk or table for important timed tests such as the SAT, GRE, and TOEFL.

Call upon classroom-furniture manufacturers to design and distribute classroom desks and chairs that provide a healthy fit with students' bodies, preventing musculoskeletal disorders later in life.

Protest school administrators who propose eliminating school lockers without understanding the serious health consequences of millions of children forced to carry heavy backpacks to and from school every day. Ask administrators to either maintain existing lockers or replace them with new clear acrylic materials.

Raise money or make a donation to your local school to remedy minor but annoying noise problems that can interfere with students' and teachers' ability to concentrate. Simple short-term solutions such as placing felt pads under desks and chairs and lubricating squeaky drawers, desk covers, and door hinges can go a long way.

As public schools face ever-increasing budget cuts, start a local campaign to raise funds to redesign school restrooms, making them safer and cleaner for boys and girls alike and discouraging restroom bullying. Simple changes such as full-length partitions between urinals or entrances with an open maze rather than a closed doorway are good starts.

If restrooms in your child's school are poorly maintained and barely usable, seek out your city, county, or state legislators to craft an effective ordinance clarifying enforcement provisions to school restrooms in bad repair. Point to Tom Keating's efforts at Project CLEAN and the new law in DeKalb County, Georgia, as a model for how to do it.

If you're the parent of a school-age child and you're moving to a new school district, check out both the quality of the school as well as its location relative to serious noise or odor problems. Avoid sending children to noisy schools along busy streets, under flight paths, or near trains and industrial noise.

If your son plays football, check to make sure that he and his teammates are no longer forced to wear helmets that don't protect them properly and that make them vulnerable to concussions and traumatic brain injuries that can last a lifetime. If he's wearing a reconditioned helmet, be sure to ask how long it has been since it was reconditioned, and make sure that it has been reconditioned within the past year. Newer, safer helmet design should be required of all football players, whether they be in the National Football League or a peewee league.

If your daughter plays sports, call your school administrators to make sure that she and her teammates are treated fairly, and as is legally required by Title IX of the Education Amendments of 1972.[5] Female high school and college athletes must no longer lag behind males in the provision of equitable resources like equipment, uniforms, and facilities.

WHAT YOU CAN DO IN YOUR WORKPLACE

Become more aware of how space and resources are allocated—how they influence your ability to do your job. Raise your antennas and make sure that you are assigned a workspace design that treats you fairly compared with others on the job. Here are some questions to ask yourself and your employer:

> *Do those of us doing the same kind of work have workspaces relatively equal in size?*
>
> *Do some people work in thermal comfort while others do not? If some workstations are too hot or too cold, how are these issues addressed?*
>
> *Do any employees show symptoms of sick building syndrome? If so, what steps are taken to remedy the issue?*
>
> *Are some people given proportionately greater access to daylight than others? Who decides and how?*

How are resources such as computers and printers distributed? Who decides and how?

How do the age, size, and speed of computers compare? Who decides on computer replacement cycles and how?

How do chairs, desks, and other amenities compare?

Do new mothers have easy access to lactation spaces on the job? Is your workplace located in a state whose law requires employers to provide reasonable accommodations—other than a toilet stall—where mothers can express their milk? If so, is that law being enforced? If your workplace is in a state without such a law, can you and your coworkers bring this issue to the attention of your state legislators—and to your employer?

Can your workplace be designated "infant friendly?"

If you believe you're being disadvantaged by the design of your workspace, ask your employer to remedy the situation. Federal employment-discrimination laws prohibit employers from disparate treatment of employees based on race, color, religion, sex, or national origin. Many employers unknowingly engage in disparate treatment when the design of their physical work environment systematically disadvantages one or more of these groups.

If your place of employment requires a uniform, smock, or apron, make sure it fits. If it doesn't come in your size, ask whether your apparel can be altered. Regarding occupational health and safety issues, call for new laws worldwide mandating that manufacturers design and produce clothing and tools that fit everyone properly.

CALL FOR NEW LEGISLATION AND REVISED BUILDING CODES

Find out what building codes are in effect in your state or municipality and when they're due to be updated. Get involved in that process by voicing your opinion to building-code officials. Use the power of social networks to encourage family and friends to join in.

Call for legislation similar to that passed in 2000 by San Francisco that prohibits discrimination based on weight. Legal cases must continue to ensure that diverse constituencies are treated fairly in built environments for workplace, healthcare, and sport.

Ask for the incorporation of better ventilation standards in hair-styling, manicure, and pedicure salons to prevent stylists from being at increased risk of serious respiratory illness. Improve working environments for historically female-dominated jobs.

Call for the incorporation of large-scale exercise and fitness facilities in fire stations, to encourage greater physical activity and to reduce the numbers of firefighters with serious heart conditions. New fire-station designs should offer flexibility, privacy and more unisex facilities, to accommodate increasing gender diversity on the job.

Prod your legislators and building-code officials to improve our nation's infrastructure by designing and building twenty-first-century public restrooms that make cities safer, friendlier places for all people to enjoy—regardless of gender, age, and body size. The award-winning unisex restrooms at Kellogg Park in La Jolla, California, are prototypes that can be replicated in warm climates. Space-saving unisex restrooms like these must become the norm in indoor environments as well.

Stress to your legislators and building-code officials that potty parity for women and girls is a right, not a privilege. Pregnant women and young children who have frequent need and sudden emergencies for restrooms must be able to relieve themselves without waiting in long lines. Recognize late-term pregnancy as a serious form of disability for women. Just as is the case with the Americans with Disabilities Act, laws and codes about potty parity are needed at the federal level. Our biological needs do not vary by state or by country.

Push for child-height toilets and sinks in new public restrooms or for the installation of products like Step 'n Wash that allow children to be more independent and keep their parents from getting splashed during hand-washing. Just as men's rooms often include low urinals to accommodate young boys, women's rooms need to accommodate young girls.

Call for building-code changes providing greater privacy between urinal stalls to reduce bullying behavior among young boys and teenagers and to provide greater dignity for males of all ages.

Call for increased family restrooms not only in major places of assembly such as sports stadiums but also in smaller venues like restaurants and libraries. A grandmother should no longer have to send her young grandson alone into the men's room. A single father or a gay father should not have to take his young daughter with him into the men's room.

Renew the call to legislators and building-code officials for diaper-changing stations in both men's and women's restrooms in most or all public places. Parents should no longer be forced to change their children's diapers on dirty bathroom floors, in parking lots, or in their cars. Double standards in design that assume only mothers, but not fathers, change babies' diapers, should be dropped.

Request more physical activity–friendly buildings that feature attractive, safe, and accessible stairways. Adding lighting, music, artwork, and air conditioning into existing fire exits can transform them into pleasant spaces to be enjoyed daily, just like the subway exit in Stockholm. Incorporating stairways into light-filled atrium spaces promotes increased physical activity. Designing stairways filled with natural light, even along the edges of building facades, can make them pleasant, welcoming spaces.

Press for mandated minimal natural-lighting requirements in work and school settings and greater access to the outdoors during the workday. Time spent outdoors is critical to our mental and physical health. Medical staff, the office secretarial pool, and sales associates who work in indoor shopping malls and big-box stores should no longer be forced to spend years on end in cavernous spaces that can cause seasonal affective disorder and vitamin D deficiency. Widespread daylighting legislation would benefit everyone, not only the disproportionately large numbers of women and ethnic minorities who work in windowless environments.

Mandate greater access to natural light through more slender building profiles that place more workers closer to windows, and more skylights and atrium spaces to allow light from above to promote a much healthier workforce.

WHAT YOU CAN DO IN THE REALM OF PUBLIC TRANSPORTATION

Call for the redesign of a small portion of replacement seats on subways, trains, and buses to accommodate overweight passengers and their seatmates, increasing comfort for all.

Urge the Federal Aviation Administration (FAA) to recognize the aircraft cabin as a workplace and to design better-proportioned galleys, service carts, latch handles, grips, overhead bins, handholds, and shock-absorbing seating to make them safer for flight attendants, who come in different shapes and sizes. Injury and illness rates of flight attendants should no longer be double that of construction workers.

Call upon the FAA to regulate the accepted decibel level in airline cockpits, as is the case in Europe, in order to reduce industrial deafness in airline pilots.

Implore your local transportation authority to replace dangerous turnstiles and decrepit, rusted-out stairways in our nation's antiquated subway systems and replace them with state-of-the-art features that encourage people to take public transit.

Support efforts to create more child-friendly public-transit design that can make taking a trip just as fun as riding the monorail at Disneyland. Be willing to pay taxes to modernize our nation's trains and subways so that we can match the high standards found across Europe and Asia.

If you live in a large city where taxicabs have floor-to-ceiling partitions separating drivers from passengers, call upon your local taxi company to replace these with digital cameras.

Whether it's the design of safe car seats or toys for children, or packaging that even the elderly can open—as with so many other instances of disadvantaging by design—complying with the minimum standard requirements is simply not enough. We must demand that designers go well beyond the minimum to provide safe, high-quality products and buildings that work well for an increasingly diverse set of people, regardless of gender, age, and body size.

We can celebrate those products, spaces, and places whose winning designs already advantage us all. We simply need more of them: more 3D body scanners that provide clothing to fit our diverse body types, more walk stations so that we can all exercise during work, more Segways to take us on short trips and out of our cars, more infant-friendly workplaces so that new mothers can enjoy going back to work, more workspaces that spark creativity and innovation on the job, more super designs for supermarkets so that at any age we can continue to shop for ourselves, more TOTO Washlets so that at any age we can continue to take care of our bodily needs by ourselves.

"We shape our buildings, and afterwards our buildings shape us." So said Sir Winston Churchill. Throughout the world, designers will continue to create the spaces in which we live and work, from those where we're born to those where we die. The built environment remains one of culture's most lasting and influential legacies.

Fashion, product, and building designs shape our lives every day in surprising, powerful ways. And whether we're aware of it or not, they affect everything we feel, think, and do. We must all continue to question, to challenge, and to no longer settle for designs that favor and empower one group of people over another through hidden gender, age, and body biases.

As French sociologist and philosopher Henri Lefebvre argued, "Change life! Change Society! These ideas lose completely their meaning without producing an appropriate space . . . new social relations demand a new space, and vice-versa."[6]

Be aware of your rights. Remember that design is only a tool. But it has the power to transform our lives. For better or for worse, we can be disadvantaged—or advantaged—by design every day. Nonetheless, we must no longer be defined by design. Design doesn't make changes. People do. And with your new set of lenses, so can you.

NOTES

INTRODUCTION

1. Amanda L. Valdez et al., "Pediatric Exposure to Laundry Detergent Pods," *Pediatrics* 134, no. 6 (2014), doi: 10.1542/peds.2014-0057.

2. Tara Haelle, "'Pretty Poison' Laundry Detergent Pods Cause Increase in Poisonings, Serious Effects," *Forbes*, April 25, 2016, http://www.forbes.com/sites/tarahaelle/2016/04/25/pretty-poison-laundry-detergent-pods-cause-increase-in-poisonings-serious-effects/#637cac045da7.

3. Adam Suchy, "Product Instability or Tip-Over Injuries and Fatalities Associated with Televisions, Furniture, and Appliances: 2014 Report," US Consumer Product Safety Commission, 2014, https://www.cpsc.gov/PageFiles/171154/InstabilityorTipoverReport2014Stamped.pdf.

4. Duaa Eldeib and Michelle Stoffel, "TV Tips Over, Kills 6-Year-Old Boy: Death Spotlights Dangers Posed by Heavy Furniture, Safety Advocates Say," *Chicago Tribune*, November 1, 2011, http://articles.chicagotribune.com/2011-11-01/news/ct-met-child-tv-safety-20111101_1_flat-screen-televisions-tvs-head-injuries.

5. James Levine, "Killer Chairs: How Desk Jobs Ruin Your Health," *Scientific American*, November 1, 2014, http://www.scientificamerican.com/article/killer-chairs-how-desk-jobs-ruin-your-health/.

6. Acropolis Museum, *A Highlights Report: Year Seven,* June 2015 –May 2016, https://issuu.com/theacropolismuseum/docs/acropolis_museum_englishannual_repo/1.

7. Elizabeth Johnson, "Glass Staircase Not Dress Friendly," *CNN's This Just In*, June 9, 2011, http://news.blogs.cnn.com/2011/06/09/glass-staircase-not-dress-friendly/.

8. Associated Press, "Opponents Seeing Red over Iowa's Pink Locker Room," ESPN, September 28, 2005, http://sports.espn.go.com/ncb/news/story?id=2174828.

9. Henri Lefebvre, "Reflections on the Politics of Space," *Antipode* 8, no. 2 (1976): 31.

CHAPTER 1: SKIN TIGHT

1. Todd Sinett and Sheldon Sinett, *The Truth about Back Pain* (New York: Penguin, 2008), pp. 80–81.

2. Jonathan G. Hobbs, Jacob S. Young, and Julian E. Bailes, "Sports-Related Concussions: Diagnosis, Complications, and Current Management Strategies," *Journal of Neurosurgery* 40, no. 4 (2016): E5, doi: 10.3171/2016.1.FOCUS15617.

3. Erik Brady, "Why Are High School Football Players Dying?" *USA Today*, November 30, 2014, http://www.usatoday.com/story/sports/highschool/2014/11/30/high-school-football-deaths-damon-janes/19712169/.

4. Kaylin Kahler and Dan Greene, "The Game's Tragic Toll," *Sports Illustrated*, November 24, 2015, http://mmqb.si.com/mmqb/2015/11/24/high-school-football-deaths-2015.

5. Travis Waldron and Erick Fernandez, "Why High School Football Is Just as Deadly Now as It Was 35 Years Ago," *Huffington Post*, October 26, 2015, http://www.huffingtonpost.com/entry/high-school-football-deaths_us_562a1a7be4b0aac0b8fc72a0.

6. Ibid.

7. Ibid.

8. Jason M. Breslow, "High School Football Players Face Bigger Concussion Risk," PBS, October 31, 2013, http://www.pbs.org/wgbh/frontline/article/high-school-football-players-face-bigger-concussion-risk/.

9. Ken Reed, "Concussion Focus Needs to Shift from NFL to Youth and High School Football," *Huffington Post*, December 22, 2015, http://www.huffingtonpost.com/ken-reed/concussion-focus-needs-to_b_8865518.html.

10. University of Colorado Anschutz Medical Campus, "High School Football Helmets Offer Similar Protections Despite Different Prices," *ScienceDaily*, February 24, 2016, https://www.sciencedaily.com/releases/2016/02/160224151209.htm.

11. Scott L. Zuckerman et al., "Recovery from Sport-Related Concussion: Days to Return to Neurocognitive Baseline in Adolescents Versus Young Adults," *Surgical Neurology International* 3 (October 27, 2012): 130, http://www.ncbi.nlm.nih.gov/pmc/articles/PMC3513851/.

12. Peter Keating, "After the Aftermath," *ESPN The Magazine*, May 17, 2012, http://espn.go.com/nfl/story/_/id/7930585/nfl-junior-seau-suicide-raises-more-questions-nfl-handling-concussions-espn-magazine.

13. "NFL Faces New Concussion Lawsuit by More Than 100 Ex-Players," *CBSNews*, May 3, 2012, http://www.cbsnews.com/8301-400_162 -57427518/nfl-faces-new-concussion-lawsuit-by-more-than-100-ex-players/; Kia Kokalitcheva, "New Evidence Stacks Up in Case against the NFL's Former Helmet Maker," *Fortune*, February 16, 2016, http://fortune .com/2016/02/16/riddell-helmet-lawsuit/.

14. Ken Belson, "Appeals Court Won't Revisit NFL Concussion Settlement," *New York Times*, June 1, 2016, http://www.nytimes.com/2016/06/ 02/sports/football/nfl-concussion-settlement-appeals-court-ruling.html ?rref=collection%252Ftimestopic%252FHead%20Injuries%20in%20 Football&action=click&contentCollection=sports&region=stream&module =stream_unit&version=latest&cont&_r=1.

15. Ibid.

16. Reed, "Concussion Focus Needs to Shift."

17. For more information on the Brain Injury Association, see http:// www.biausa.org. For more information on the American Academy of Neurology, see http://www.aan.com.

18. University of Colorado, "High School Football Helmets."

19. Travis Waldron, "Congressmen Push for Study of High School Football Deaths: New Legislation Would Require the Government to Recommend Ways to Prevent Such Tragedies," *Huffington Post*, November 6, 2015, http://www.huffingtonpost.com/entry/congress-high-school -football-deaths_us_563cd978e4b0307f2cad2b5d.

20. Bob Shephard, "UAB Study Shows that Injury Rates from Wearing High-Heeled Shoes Have Doubled," University of Alabama at Birmingham News, December 9, 2015 (story originally published May 21, 2015), https://www.uab.edu/news/innovation/item/6071-uab-study-shows-that -injury-rates-from-wearing-high-heeled-shoes-have-doubled; Justin X. Moore et al., "Epidemiology of High-Heel Shoe Injuries in US Women: 2002 to 2012," *Journal of Foot and Ankle Surgery* 54, no. 4 (2015): 615–19, doi: http://dx.doi.org/10.1053/j.jfas.2015.04.008.

21. "Experts Warn of High-Heel Danger," BBC News, August 1, 2006, http://news.bbc.co.uk/2/hi/health/5235630.stm.

22. Jill McIntosh, "Why You Need to Stop Driving in High Heels and Flip Flops," *Toronto Metro Canada*, July 9, 2013, http://www.metronews.ca/ drive/2013/07/10/why-you-need-to-stop-driving-in-high-heels-and-flip -flops.html.

23. "High Heels, Flip-Flops Could Put Drivers at Risk Behind the Wheel," CBS Los Angeles, June 27, 2013, http://losangeles

.cbslocal.com/2013/06/27/high-heels-flip-flops-could-put-drivers
-at-risk-behind-the-wheel/.

24. Jeff Bartlett, "Fatal Tragedy Highlights Dangers of Inappropriate
Driving Footwear," *Consumer Reports News*, August 11, 2011, http://www
.consumerreports.org/cro/news/2011/08/fatal-tragedy-highlights
-dangers-of-inappropriate-driving-footwear/index.htm.

25. Alyssa B. Dufour et al., "Foot Pain: Is Current or Past Shoe-
wear a Factor?" *Arthritis & Rheumatism (Arthritis Care & Research)* 61,
no. 10 (2009): 1352–58, http://www3.interscience.wiley.com/cgi-bin/
fulltext/122612113/PDFSTART.

26. Ibid.

27. Jeanna Bryner, "Fix Me: Nips and Tucks Soar," *LiveScience*, April
15, 2008, http://www.livescience.com/health/080415-crimes-against
-nature.html.

28. Jason Averill et al., *Federal Building and Fire Safety Investigation of
the World Trade Center Disaster: Occupant Behavior, Egress, and Emergency Communications*, NCSTAR 1-7, NIST (National Institute of Standards and Technology), Gaithersburg, MD, 2005, http://www.mingerfoundation.org/
downloads/mobility/nist%20world%20trade%20center.pdf; Christopher
F. Hardej, "Escape from the 82nd Floor," *Guard Times* 9, no. 6 (2001),
http://dmna.ny.gov/gdtimes/novdec2001.html#escape.

29. Sinett and Sinett, *Truth about Back Pain*, p. 84.

30. J. Courtney Sullivan, "Ouch! My Bag Is Killing Me," *New York Times*,
December 7, 2006, http://www.nytimes.com/2006/12/07/fashion/
07ouch.html.

31. Ibid.

32. Johnny Acton, Tania Adams, and Matt Packer, *Origin of Everyday
Things* (New York: Sterling Publishing, 2006), p. 272.

33. Bo Runeman et al., "Investigative Report: The Vulvar Skin Micro-
environment: Impact of Tight-Fitting Underwear on Microclimate, pH and
Microflora," *Acta Derm Venereol* 85 (2005): 118–22.

34. "Your Underwear, Your Health," *Berkeley Wellness*, April 12, 2016,
http://www.berkeleywellness.com/self-care/sexual-health/article/your
-underwear-your-health.

35. Martha K. Terris, Subbarao V. Cherukuri, and Christopher A.
Hathaway, "Urethral Syndrome," *Medscape*, http://emedicine.medscape.
com/article/451683-overview.

36. Hayley Phelan, "Young Women Say No to Thongs," *New York Times*,
May 27, 2015, http://www.nytimes.com/2015/05/28/fashion/young
-women-say-no-to-thongs.html.

37. Kate Abnett, "Inside the Economics of Your Underwear: Under-wear Is a $110 Billion Market. Which Companies Are Most Successfully Getting into our Bras and Briefs?" *Business of Fashion*, June 22, 2015, https://www.businessoffashion.com/articles/intelligence/inside-the-economics-of-your-underwear.

38. This section is based in part on Sharra Vostral, *Under Wraps: A History of Menstrual Hygiene Technology* (Lanham, MD: Lexington Books, 2008), pp. 21, 26–27, 63–65, 130–131, 155–58, & 161.

39. Vostral, *Under Wraps*, p. 64.

40. Ibid., p. 26.

41. Ibid., p. 131.

42. Ibid., p. 161.

43. Ann Schofield, "The Fashion of Mourning," in *Representations of Death in Nineteenth-Century US Writing and Culture*, ed. Lucy Elizabeth Frank (Burlington, VT: Ashgate Publishing, 2013), p. 160.

44. Monica McGoldrick, "Gender and Mourning," in *Living Beyond Loss. Death in the Family*, 2nd ed., ed. Froma Walsh and Monica McGoldrick (New York: W. W. Norton, 2004), p. 100.

45. Mohamed Boubekri, *Daylighting, Architecture and Health: Building Design Strategies* (Oxford, UK: Architectural Press, 2008), pp. 67–68; see also M. R. El-Sonbaty and N. U. A. M. A. Abdul-Ghaffar, "Vitamin D Deficiency in Veiled Kuwaiti Women," *European Journal of Clinical Nutrition* 50, no. 5 (1996): 338–39; M. H. Gannage-Yared et al., "Hypovitaminosis in a Sunny Country: Relation to Lifestyle and Bone Markers," *Journal of Bone and Mineral Research* 15, no. 9 (2000): 1856–62; M. Z. Ekral et al., "High Prevalence of Vitamin D Deficiency, Secondary Hyperparathyroidism and Generalized Bone Pain in Turkish Immigrants in Germany: Identification of Risk Factors," *Osteoporosis International* 17, no. 8 (2006): 1133–40.

46. Peter Barss et al., *Injury Prevention: An International Perspective: Epidemiology, Surveillance, and Policy* (New York: Oxford University Press, 1998), pp. 66 & 183.

47. Tarek Basley, "3D Body Scanning Set to Disrupt Clothing Industry: Cheap Yet Advanced Body-Scanning Technology Looks Set to Reshape the Online and Tailored Clothing Industries," Al Jazeera, September 3, 2015, http://www.aljazeera.com/news/2015/09/3d-body-scanning-set-disrupt-clothing-industry-150903112712046.html.

48. "The 3D Body Scanner," *Cornell University, College of Human Ecology*, http://www.bodyscan.human.cornell.edu/scene0037.html.

49. Chris Gayomali, "Here's What It's Like to Step into a 3-D Body

Scanner for a Custom-Made Suit: Startups Like Alton Lane Are Using 3-D Modeling to Mold Clothes to Their Clients' Bodies. Welcome to the Future of Bespoke Design," *Fast Company*, September 3, 2014, http://www .fastcompany.com/3035092/heres-what-its-like-to-step-into-a-3d -body-scanner-for-a-custom-made-suit.

50. Ibid.

51. "The 3D Body Scanner: Made-to-Measure," Cornell University, College of Human Ecology, http://www.bodyscan.human.cornell.edu/ scene0605.html.

52. Greg Moore, personal e-mail communication, July 22, 2016.

53. "Simon Fraser Students Create Adjustable High-Heeled Shoes," CTV News, April 3, 2012, http://www.ctvnews.ca/simon-fraser-students -create-adjustable-high-heeled-shoes-1.791412.

CHAPTER 2: PLAY AT YOUR OWN RISK

1. Steve Mills, "Is Your Backyard Play Set Unsafe? Tribune Watchdog: Federal Agency Has Yet to Alert Parents to Design Flaw Tied to Boy's 2006 Death," *Chicago Tribune*, August 30, 2009, http://www.chicagotribune .com/news/chi-playsetaug30,0,6828223.story.

2. Michelle Esteban, "Magnetic Toys to Carry New Warning Labels," KOMONews, March 1, 2007, http://komonews.com/archive/magnetic -toys-to-carry-new-warning-labels.

3. Michael Oneal, Patricia Callahan, and Evan Osnos, "Mattel Recalls 18 Million Toys," *Chicago Tribune*, August 15, 2007, http://www.chicago tribune.com/business/chi-toysaug15-story.html; see also, Eric C. Lipton and David Barboza, "As More Toys Are Recalled, Train Ends in China," *New York Times*, June 19, 2007, http://www.nytimes.com/2007/06/19/ business/worldbusiness/19toys.html?_r=0; David Schaper, "Thomas Tank Engine Toy Recall Angers Parents," NPR, June 22, 2007, http://www.npr .org/templates/story/story.php?storyId=11271805.

4. Nancy Cowles, "The Year of the Nursery Product Recall: Nursery and Sleep Environment Products Pose a Serious Threat; CPSC Sharpens Its Teeth," press release, Kids in Danger, March 29, 2010, http://www .kidsindanger.org/docs/news/Recall_Report_2009_Release.pdf (accessed December 2, 2016).

5. Esteban, "Magnetic Toys."

6. *Ms.* magazine, "Moms Fight Toxic Toy Makers," *Mother Warriors*

Voice, Winter 2008, http://www.welfarewarriors.org/mwv_archive/w08/ w08moms.htm (accessed December 2, 2016).

7. E. Marla Felcher, *It's No Accident: How Corporations Sell Dangerous Baby Products* (Monroe, ME: Common Courage Press, 2001).

8. Linda Ginzel and Boza Keysar, in a review of Felcher's *It's No Accident: How Corporations Sell Dangerous Baby Products,* http://www.amazon .com/Its-No-Accident-Corporations-Dangerous/product-reviews/ 1567512046/ref=dp_top_cm_cr_acr_txt?ie=UTF8&showViewpoints=1.

9. The complete *Chicago Tribune* series that won the 2007 Pulitzer Prize in Investigative Reporting, "Hidden Hazards: Kids at Risk," can be found at http://www.chicagotribune.com/news/watchdog/chi-safety -storygallery-storygallery.html?page=1.

10. "Consumer Product Safety Improvement Act (CPSIA) Compliance Solutions," Intertek, http://www.intertek.com/cpsia/.

11. Rachel Weintraub, Testimony before the Subcommittee on Commerce Trade and Consumer Protection, Committee on Energy and Commerce, US House of Representatives, Hearing on the Consumer Product Safety Enhancement Act, April 29, 2010, http://www.consumerfed.org/ elements/www.consumerfed.org/file/cps%20enhancement%20act%20 testimony%204%2010.pdf.

12. Cowles, "Nursery Product Recall."

13. "Toy Recall Statistics," US Consumer Product Safety Commission, November 20, 2014, http://www.cpsc.gov/en/Safety-Education/ Toy-Recall-Statistics/.

14. Ibid.

15. Personal interview with North Shore Chicago pediatrician, Chicago, IL, February 12, 2010.

16. NRDC Staff, "Smarter Living: Chemical Index: Arsenic," Natural Resources Defense Council, August 27, 2008, http://www.simplesteps.org/ es/node/183.

17. Mills, "Is Your Backyard Play Set Unsafe?"

18. "Adventure Playsets Recall to Repair Backyard Swing Sets Due to Fall Hazard," US Consumer Product Safety Commission, November 5, 2009, http://www.cpsc.gov/en/recalls/2010/adventure-playsets -recall-to-repair-backyard-swing-sets-due-to-fall-hazard/.

19. "Trampoline Safety," US Consumer Product Safety Commission, CPSC Safety Alert, http://www.cpsc.gov/pagefiles/137868/085.pdf.

20. "Toy Recall Statistics."

21. American Academy of Pediatrics, Committee on Injury and Poison

Prevention and Committee on Sports Medicine and Fitness, "Policy State-ment: Trampolines at Home, School, and Recreational Centers," *Pediatrics* 103, no. 5 (1999): 1053–56 (quote on p. 1053), http://pediatrics .aappublications.org/content/103/5/1053.full.pdf. Statement of reaffir-mation for this policy published May 1, 2006, http://pediatrics.aap publications.org/content/117/5/1846.full.pdf+html?sid=2e4e392d -f6c8-4630-8d2e-151149a542ab.

22. Ibid.

23. Shari Rudavsky, "Home Trampoline Danger: 1M Visits to ER, Study Says," *USA Today*, May 7, 2014, http://www.usatoday.com/story/ news/nation/2014/05/07/home-trampoline-hospital-visits/8820793/.

24. "Child Restraint Systems NPRM," Regulations.gov, https://www .regulations.gov/docketBrowser?rpp=25&so=DESC&sb=commentDueDate &po=0&dct=PS&D=NHTSA-2014-0012.

25. Emily A. Mathews, "More Change Needed for Car Seat Side-Impact Protection: Proposed Standards Are a Big Step Forward, but They're Not Quite There Yet," *Consumer Reports*, September 29, 2015, http://www.consumerreports.org/cro/carseats/child-seat-side -impact-protection.

26. Ibid.

27. "Child Seat Research," National Highway Traffic Safety Adminis-tration, http://www.nhtsa.gov/Research/Child+Seat+Research.

28. Patricia Callahan, "When Car-Seat Safety, Commerce Collide," *Chicago Tribune*, July 14, 2007, http://www.chicagotribune.com/news/ specials/chi-carseats-special,0,7167915.story.

29. US Department of Transportation, "Traffic Safety Facts: 2008 Data: Children," National Highway Traffic Safety Administration, DOT HS 811 157, http://www-nrd.nhtsa.dot.gov/Pubs/811157.pdf.

30. US Department of Transportation, "Children Injured in Motor Vehicle Traffic Crashes," National Highway Traffic Safety Administration, DOT HS 811 325, May 2010, http://www-nrd.nhtsa.dot.gov/Pubs/811325.PDF.

31. Callahan, "When Car-Seat Safety, Commerce Collide."

32. "Child Safety Seat Ease of Use Ratings," National Highway Traffic Safety Administration, http://www.nhtsa.gov/nhtsa_eou/info.jsp ?type=infant.

33. "Register Your Car Seat," Parents Central, http://www.safercar .gov/parents/CarSeats/Car-Seat-Registration.htm?view=full.

34. Patti Neighmond, "Falling TVs: A Growing Threat for Young Kids," *NPR: Morning Edition*, May 4, 2009, http://www.npr.org/templates/

story/story.php?storyId=103769777; see also "Safe Kids USA: Preventing Accidental Injury," http://www.usa.safekids.org/.

35. Duaa Eldeib and Michelle Stoffel, "TV Tips Over, Kills 6-Year-Old Boy: Death Spotlights Dangers Posed by Heavy Furniture, Safety Advocates Say," *Chicago Tribune*, November 1, 2011, http://articles.chicagotribune.com/2011-11-01/news/ct-met-child-tv-safety-20111101_1_flat-screen-televisions-tvs-head-injuries.

36. Ibid.

37. Adam Suchy, "Product Instability or Tip-Over Injuries and Fatalities Associated with Televisions, Furniture, and Appliances: 2014 Report," US Consumer Product Safety Commission, August 2014, https://www.cpsc.gov/PageFiles/171154/InstabilityorTipoverReport2014Stamped.pdf.

38. Ibid.

39. Abha Bhattaral, "Ikea Recalls 35 Million Dressers That Can Tip Over on You," *Washington Post*, June 28, 2016, https://www.washingtonpost.com/news/business/wp/2016/06/28/ikea-recalls-35-million-dressers-that-can-tip-over-on-you/.

40. Ibid.

41. "NAPPA Honors Winner: Quick Change Crib," Parenthood, http://www.parenthood.com/NAPPA/PR_quickchangecrib.php.

42. "2008 Toy of the Year (TOTY) Awards," Toy Industry Association, Inc., http://www.toyassociation.org/Events2/TOTY_Awards/2008_TOTY_Winners.aspx#.V27NCd77VuU.

43. "2014 Toy of the Year (TOTY) Awards," Toy Industry Association, Inc., http://www.toyassociation.org/Events2/TOTY_Awards/2014_TOTY_Winners.aspx#.V27LW977VuV.

44. "Meet Our Inventor and CEO, Debbie Sterling," GoldieBlox, http://www.goldieblox.com/pages/about.

45. Molly McDonald, "Equal Pay Day 2016: .79 Just Doesn't Make Sense," *GoldieBlox: The Blog*, April 11, 2016, http://blog.goldieblox.com/2016/04/happy-equal-pay-day/.

CHAPTER 3: BIG TOYS FOR BIG BOYS AND GIRLS

1. ICT Facts & Figures, "The World in 2015," International Telecommunication Union, https://www.itu.int/en/ITU-D/Statistics/Documents/facts/ICTFactsFigures2015.pdf. Note that these statistics reflect the number of subscriptions, not people; individuals with multiple

cellular subscriptions can be double counted, while others may share phones.

2. Fnu Deepinder, Kartikeya Makker, and Ashok Agarwal, "Cell Phones and Male Infertility: Dissecting the Relationship," *Reproductive BioMedicine Online* 15, no. 3 (2007): 266–70, http://www.clevelandclinic.org/Reproductive ResearchCenter/docs/agradoc250.pdf; Kartikeya Makker et al., "Cell Phones: Modern Man's Nemesis?" *Reproductive Biomedicine Online* 18, no. 1 (2009): 148–57; Joan Raymond, "Is That a Phone in Your Pocket? A New Study Finds that the Radiation Emitted by Cell Phones Can Lower Sperm Quality," *Newsweek*, September 18, 2008, http://www.newsweek.com/id/159624.

3. Anna Almendrala, "How Your Cell Phone Might Be Hurting Your Sperm," *Huffington Post*, June 16, 2014, http://www.huffingtonpost .com/2014/06/12/mobile-phone-sperm_n_5486067.html.

4. David Gorski, "No, Cell Phones Are Not 'Cooking Men's Sperm,'" *ScienceBlogs*, February 24, 2016, http://scienceblogs.com/insolence/ 2016/02/24/no-cell-phones-are-not-cooking-mens-sperm/.

5. Cairna Storrs, "Cell Phones and Risk of Brain Tumors: What's the Real Science?" CNN, July 28, 2015, http://www.cnn.com/2015/07/28/ health/cell-phones-brain-tumor-risk-berkeley/; "Cell Phones and Cancer Risk," National Cancer Institute, National Institutes of Health, May 27, 2016, http://www.cancer.gov/about-cancer/causes-prevention/risk/ radiation/cell-phones-fact-sheet.

6. Grace Dobush, "How Mobile Phones Are Changing the Developing World," Consumer Technology Association, July 27, 2015, https:// www.cta.tech/News/Blog/Articles/2015/July/How-Mobile-Phones-Are -Changing-the-Developing-Worl.aspx.

7. National Safety Council, "National Safety Council Estimates that at Least 1.6 Million Crashes Are Caused Each Year by Drivers Using Cell Phones and Texting," PRNewswire, January 12, 2010, http://www .prnewswire.com/news-releases/national-safety-council-estimates-that-at -least-16-million-crashes-are-caused-each-year-by-drivers-using-cell-phones -and-texting-81252807.html.

8. "Cell Phones: Challenges of Collecting and Reporting Reliable Crash Data. From the National Safety Council," National Safety Council, 2013, http://www.nsc.org/DistractedDrivingDocuments/NSC-Under -Reporting-White-Paper.pdf.

9. Michael Green, "Distraction and Teen Crashes: Even Worse than We Thought," AAA NewsRoom, March 25, 2015, http://newsroom.aaa .com/2015/03/distraction-teen-crashes-even-worse-thought/.

10. "Drivers on Cell Phones Clog Traffic: Longer Commutes Due to Fewer Lane Changes, Slower Speed," News Center, University of Utah, January 2, 2008, http://archive.unews.utah.edu/news_releases/drivers-on-cell-phones-clog-traffic/.

11. "Cell Phone Driving Laws: August 2016," Governors Highway Safety Association, June 2016, http://www.ghsa.org/html/stateinfo/laws/cellphone_laws.html.

12. "Countries that Ban Cell Phones While Driving," *Cellular News*, June 6, 2009, http://www.cellular-news.com/car_bans/.

13. Loyola University Health System, "Laptops Linked to Male Infertility," *ScienceDaily*, June 13, 2009, http://www.sciencedaily.com/releases/2009/06/090612202347.htm.

14. Todd Sperry, "EPA to Remove Vapor-Capturing Rubber Boot from Gas Pump Handles," CNN, May 10, 2012, http://www.cnn.com/2012/05/10/politics/epa-gas-pump-handles/.

15. Eric Loveday, "EPA Says Outdated Gas Vapor Recovery Nozzles No Longer Required," *Autoblog*, July 12, 2011, http://www.autoblog.com/2011/07/12/epa-says-outdated-gas-vapor-recovery-nozzles-no-longer-required/.

16. "Women Design Concept Car for Volvo," *USA Today*, March 2, 2004, http://www.usatoday.com/money/autos/2004-03-02-ycc_x.htm.

17. Roy Schwartzman and Merci Decker, "A Car of Her Own? Volvo's Your Concept Car as a Vehicle for Feminism?" *Studies in Popular Culture* 30, no. 2 (2008): 100–118. http://roypoet.com/files/volvo_article.pdf; "Women Design Concept Car."

18. David Thomas, "2014 Chevy Impala Marks End of Front Bench Seats in Cars," *Cars*, April 4, 2012, http://blogs.cars.com/kickingtires/2012/04/2014-chevy-impala-marks-end-of-front-bench-seats-in-cars.html.

19. Daniel S. Watson et al., "Golf Cart-Related Injuries in the US," *American Journal of Preventive Medicine* 35, no. 1 (2008): 55–59. The next few paragraphs are based on this study.

20. Gerald McGwin Jr. et al., "Incidence of Golf Cart-Related Injury in the United States," *The Journal of Trauma: Injury, Infection, and Critical Care* 64, no. 6 (2008): 1562–66.

21. "Segway FAQ," Segway, http://www.segway.com/support/faqs.php.

22. Jacques Steinberg, "Easy Rider, Part II: The Self-Balance Years," *New York Times*, January 8, 2010, http://travel.nytimes.com/2010/01/08/travel/escapes/08segway.html.

23. "Segway FAQ."

24. John Ashurst and Benjamin Wagner, "Injuries Following Segway Personal Transporter Accidents: Case Report and Review of the Literature," *Western Journal of Emergency Medicine* 16, no. 5 (2015): 693–95, http://www.ncbi.nlm.nih.gov/pmc/articles/PMC4644037/.

25. Dan Childs and ABC News Medical Unit, "Segway Boss Jimi Heselden Dies on Segway: Are Segways Safe?" ABC News, September 27, 2010, http://abcnews.go.com/Health/Wellness/segway-accident-kills -jimi-heselden-segway-boss/story?id=11736855.

26. "Wii: The Top-Selling Wii Games," VGChartz, http://www .vgchartz.com/platform/2/wii/.

27. "Nintendo Wii Most Popular Console among Female Gamers: Around 80 Percent of Female Gamers Prefer the Wii to Other Consoles, Says Nintendo," *Telegraph*, November 29, 2009, http://www.telegraph .co.uk/technology/video-games/nintendo/6672402/Nintendo-Wii-most -popular-console-among-female-gamers.html.

28. Jennifer Van Pelt, "Exercise as Medicine," *Aging Well* 3, no. 1 (2010): 18, http://www.agingwellmag.com/archive/020110p18.shtml.

29. Medical College of Georgia, "Nintendo Wii May Enhance Parkinson's Treatment," *ScienceDaily*, June 12, 2009, http://www.sciencedaily .com/releases/2009/06/090611120744.htm.

CHAPTER 4: WRAP RAGE

1. Kate Bertrand Connolly, "Facing Off against 'Wrap Rage,'" *Brand Packaging*, October 1, 2006, http://www.brandpackaging.com/articles/ facing-off-against-wrap-rage; Steve Freiss, "Tales from Packaging Hell," *Wired*, May 22, 2006, http://archive.wired.com/science/discoveries/new s/2006/05/70874?currentPage=all; Chris Nippert, "A Plastic Clamshell Packaging Alternative That Is Consumer Friendly, Cost Efficient, and Theft Resistant? It's Finally Here," *Loss Prevention*, September–October 2006, pp. 87–88; Gary Strauss, "Open at Your Own Risk," *USA Today*, July 13, 2001, http://www.usatoday.com/money/general/2001-07-13-cd-usat .htm.

2. Kate Browne, "Can't Open Your Own Purchase?" *Choice*, September 14, 2014, https://www.choice.com.au/shopping/packaging -labelling-and-advertising/packaging/articles/wrap-rage.

3. Steve Friess, "A Gift Can Leave You in Stitches," *USA Today*,

December 20, 2006, http://usatoday30.usatoday.com/news/health/2006
-12-20-gifts-packaging_x.htm.

4. Connolly, "Facing Off against 'Wrap Rage'"; Freiss, "Tales from
Packaging Hell"; Nippert, "A Plastic Clamshell Packaging Alternative."

5. Friess, "A Gift Can Leave You in Stitches."

6. Nick Britten, "60,000 Are Injured by Opening Packaging," *Telegraph*, February 11, 2003, http://www.telegraph.co.uk/news/uknews/
1421698/60000-are-injured-by-opening-packaging.html.

7. Stephanie Clifford, "Devilish Packaging, Tamed," *New York Times*,
June 1, 2011, http://www.nytimes.com/2011/06/02/business/energy
-environment/02packaging.html?_r=2&ref=business.

8. "Amazon Certified Frustration-Free Packaging FAQs," http://
www.amazon.com/gp/help/customer/display.html?ie=UTF8
&nodeId=200285450.

9. Browne, "Can't Open Your Own Purchase?"

10. Stephanie Rosenbloom, "Solution, or Mess? A Milk Jug for a
Green Earth," *New York Times*, June 30, 2008, http://www.nytimes.com/
2008/06/30/business/30milk.html?pagewanted=1&th&emc=th.

11. "Important Facts about Falls," Centers for Disease Control and
Prevention, http://www.cdc.gov/HomeandRecreationalSafety/Falls/adult
falls.html.

12. National Center for Injury Prevention and Control, "Preventing
Falls: A Guide to Implementing Effective Community-Based Fall Prevention Programs," Centers for Disease Control and Prevention, 2015, http://
www.cdc.gov/homeandrecreationalsafety/pdf/falls/fallpreventionguide
-2015-a.pdf.

13. National Center for Injury Prevention and Control, "Check for
Safety: A Home Fall Prevention Checklist for Older Adults," Centers for
Disease Control and Prevention, 2016, http://www.cdc.gov/steadi/pdf/
steadi_checkforsafety_brochure-a.pdf.

14. American Academy of Orthopaedic Surgeons and the Orthopaedic Trauma Association, "Falls Awareness and Prevention Guide,"
http://orthoinfo.aaos.org/falls/media/AAOSFallPrevention.pdf.

15. M. Sengölge and J. Vincenten, *Child Product Safety Guide: Potentially
Dangerous Products* (Edgbaston, Birmingham, UK: European Child Safety
Alliance, 2013), http://www.childsafetyeurope.org/publications/info/
product-safety-guide.pdf.

16. Kelley Colihan, "Fall from Bunk Bed Can Land Kid in ER: Study
Shows Bunk Bed-Related Injuries Common," WebMD, June 2, 2008,

http://children.webmd.com/news/20080602/fall-from-bunk-bed
-can-land-kid-in-er.

17. Penny Sparke, *As Long as It's Pink: The Sexual Politics of Taste* (Oakland, CA: Pandora Press, 1995).

18. Linda Tischler, "Introducing the Femme Den: Going Beyond 'Shrink It and Pink It,'" *Fast Company*, September 17, 2009, https://www.fastcodesign.com/1361553/introducing-the-femme-den-going -beyond-shrink-it-and-pink-it.

19. Leading type of injury was a laceration (41 percent), followed by a soft tissue injury (21 percent), burn (16 percent), and fracture (10 percent). Most common body region injured was the hand or finger (35 percent), lower extremity (19 percent) and foot/toe (18 percent), with 97 percent of the amputation injuries occurring to the foot/toe and hands/ finger. See David Vollman and Gary A. Smith, "Epidemiology of Lawn Mower-Related Injuries to Children in the United States, 1990–2004," *Pediatrics* 118, no. 2 (2006): 273–78.

20. Christopher Ingraham, "People Keep Sticking Their Hands in Snowblowers without Turning Them Off First, Data Show," *Wonkblog, Washington Post*, January 27, 2015, https://www.washingtonpost.com/news/ wonk/wp/2015/01/27/people-keep-sticking-their-hands-in-snowblowers -without-turning-them-off-first-data-show/.

21. John S. Taras, Michael J. Behrman, and Gregory G. Degnan, "Left-Hand Dominance and Hand Trauma," *Journal of Hand Surgery* 20A, no. 6 (1995): 1043–45.

22. Duke Medicine News and Communications, "Consumer Nail Gun Injuries Spike," *Duke Medicine*, April 13, 2007, http://corporate.duke medicine.org/news_and_publications/news_office/news/10039.

23. National Institute for Occupational Safety and Health, "Nail Gun Safety," February 19, 2014, http://www.cdc.gov/niosh/topics/nailgun/; Centers for Disease Control and Prevention, "Nailing Down the Need for Nail Gun Safety," December 15, 2014, http://www.cdc.gov/features/nail gunsafety/index.html.

24. Claudia Parcells, Manfred Stommel, and Robert P. Hubbard, "Mismatch of Classroom Furniture and Student Body Dimensions: Empirical Findings and Health Implications," *Journal of Adolescent Health* 24, no. 4 (1999): 265–73.

25. K. H. Berquet, *Sitz- und Haltungsschäden, Auswahl und Anpassung der Schulmöbel [Seating and Posture Problems, Selection and Adaption of School Furniture]* (Stuttgart, Germany: Thieme, 1988), p. 17.

26. Parcells, Stommel, and Hubbard, "Mismatch of Classroom Furniture," p. 3.

27. Yvette Doss, "Labor Pains: Hotel Housekeepers Push for Healthier Work Conditions and Better Pay," *Ms. Magazine* (Winter 2008): p. 16; Hotel Workers Rising! Lifting One Another above the Poverty Line, http://www.hotelworkersrising.org/.

28. National Institute for Occupational Safety and Health, "Women's Safety and Health Issues at Work," http://www.cdc.gov/niosh/topics/ women/; Irene Padavic and Barbara F. Reskin, *Women and Men at Work*, 2nd ed. (Thousand Oaks, CA: Pine Forge Press, 2002).

29. Linda M. Goldenhar and Marie Haring Sweeney, "Tradeswomen's Perspectives on Occupational Health and Safety: A Qualitative Investigation," *American Journal of Industrial Medicine* 29, no. 5 (1996): 516–20.

30. "Lefty Workers 'At Risk of Injury,'" BBC News, August 12, 2000, http://news.bbc.co.uk/2/hi/health/876012.stm.

31. Stanley Coren, *The Left-Hander Syndrome: The Causes and Consequences of Left-Handedness* (New York: Vintage Books, 1993), p. 258.

32. Lynne Melcombe, "The Left Hand of Research," *University of British Columbia Alumni Chronicle* 47, no. 1 (1993): 12–13.

33. This section is excerpted from Kathryn H. Anthony, "Rethinking Power through Podium Design," in *Diversity and Design: Understanding Hidden Consequences*, ed. Beth Tauke, Korydon Smith, and Charles Davis (London: Routledge Press, 2016), pp. 191–208.

34. OPEN NY, "The Measure of a President," *New York Times*, October 6, 2008, http://www.nytimes.com/interactive/2008/10/06/opinion/ 06opchart.html?_r=0.

35. Gregg R. Murray, "It's Weird, Candidate Height Matters in Elections: Why Does Candidate Height Matter? Not for the Reasons Many People Think," *Caveman Politics* (blog), *Psychology Today*, October 30, 2012, http://www.psychologytoday.com/blog/caveman-politics/201210/it-s -weird-candidate-height-matters-in-elections. See also Gregg R. Murray and J. David Schmitz, "Caveman Politics: Evolutionary Leadership Preferences and Physical Stature," *Social Science Quarterly* 92, no. 5 (2011): 1215–35.

36. This section is excerpted from Anthony, "Rethinking Power through Podium Design," in *Diversity and Design*, pp. 191–208.

37. "Lifting Column DL4S," Linak Company, http://www.linak.com/ products/lifting-columns.aspx?product=DL4S.

38. Sophie Hardach, "Wasabi Fire Alarm a Lifesaver for the Deaf," Reuters, March 17, 2008, http://www.reuters.com/article/idUKT294

21020080318; Tim Hornyak, "Wasabi Smoke Alarm Raises a Stink in Japan," CNET, January 29, 2010, http://news.cnet.com/8301-17938_105 -10443919-1.html.

39. "About the Ig Nobel Prizes," Improbable Research, http://www .improbable.com/ig/.

40. National Center for Health Statistics, "Table 53: Selected Health Conditions and Risk Factors, by Age: United States, Selected Years 1988– 1994 through 2013–2014," Centers for Disease Control and Prevention, April 27, 2016, http://www.cdc.gov/nchs/fastats/obesity-overweight.htm.

41. Steve Lohr, "Taking a Stand for Office Ergonomics," *New York Times*, December 1, 2012, http://www.nytimes.com/2012/12/02/ business/stand-up-desks-gaining-favor-in-the-workplace.html?_r=0.

42. Jen Weiczner, "Falling Down on the Job? Workstations Designed to Help You Get Fit May Make You Type Poorly, Even Fall," *Wall Street Journal*, January 29, 2013, http://www.wsj.com/articles/SB10001424127887324539 304578263650060635048.

43. Lohr, "Taking a Stand for Office Ergonomics."

44. Kate Rockwood, "Forget 'Shrink It and Pink It': The Femme Den Unleashed," *Fast Company*, October 1, 2009, http://www.fastcompany .com/1353548/forget-shrink-it-and-pink-it-femme-den-unleashed.

45. Tischler, "Introducing the Femme Den."

46. Rockwood, "Forget 'Shrink It and Pink It.'"

CHAPTER 5: TOO CLOSE FOR COMFORT

1. Cynthia L. Ogden et al., "Prevalence of Obesity in the United States, 2009–2010," Centers for Disease Control, National Center for Health Statistics Data Brief No. 82, January 2012, http://www.cdc.gov/ nchs/data/databriefs/db82.pdf.

2. University of Illinois at Urbana-Champaign, "Weight Gain of US Drivers Has Increased Nation's Fuel Consumption," *ScienceDaily*, October 25, 2006, http://www.sciencedaily.com/releases/2006/10/061025183256 .htm.

3. Bureau of Labor Statistics, "Labor Force Statistics from the Current Population Survey: Household Data Annual Averages—11. Employed Persons by Detailed Occupation, Sex, Race, and Hispanic or Latino Ethnicity," last modified February 10, 2016, http://www.bls.gov/ cps/cpsaat11.htm.

4. "Federal Appeals Court Dismisses Flight Attendants' Lawsuit Seeking Coverage under OSHA," Ford Harrison, Airline Management Newsletter, September 1, 2007, http://www.fordharrison.com/3193.

5. Flight Safety Foundation Editorial Staff, "Study of Airline's Flight Attendants Finds More Than Half of Injuries Affect Muscles and Bones in Back, Neck, Shoulders," *Cabin Crew Safety* 37, no. 4 (2002), http://flight safety.org/ccs/ccs_jul-aug02.pdf.

6. Ibid.

7. Per Arva and Anthony S. Wagstaff, "Medical Disqualification of 275 Commercial Pilots: Changing Patterns over 20 Years," *Aviation, Space and Environmental Medicine* 75, no. 9 (2004): 791–94.

8. Vilhjalmur Rafnsson et al., "Cosmic Radiation Increases the Risk of Nuclear Cataract in Airline Pilots: A Population-Based Case-Control Study," *Archives of Ophthalmology* 123, no. 8 (2005): 1102–05, http://archopht.ama-assn.org/cgi/content/abstract/123/8/1102?ck=nck.

9. Daisy Carrington, "Airbus Could Seat Obese Passengers on Benches," CNN, February 23, 2016, http://www.cnn.com/2016/02/23/aviation/airbus-patent-could-bench-obese-passengers/.

10. "London Underground: Avoiding Stairs Tube Guide," Transport for London, June 2016, http://content.tfl.gov.uk/avoiding-stairs-tube-guide.pdf.

11. Robert Davis, "Bulletproof Shield Left Out of Taxi Safety Bill: Few Are Happy after City Council Ok," *Chicago Tribune*, October 15, 1992, http://articles.chicagotribune.com/1992-10-15/news/9204030263_1_safety-measures-cabdrivers-cab-owners.

12. Dawn N. Castillo and E. Lynn Jenkins, "Industries and Occupations at High Risk for Work-Related Homicide," *Journal of Occupational Medicine* 36, no. 2 (1994): 125–32; Jonathan Rosen, "A Labor Perspective of Workplace Violence Prevention: Identifying Research Needs," *American Journal of Preventive Medicine* 20, no. 2 (2001): 161–68; Martha J. Smith, "Robbery of Taxi Drivers," US Department of Justice, Office of Community Oriented Policing Services, Problem-Oriented Guides for Police, Problem-Specific Guides Series, No. 34, March 14, 2005, http://www.popcenter.org/problems/pdfs/robberytaxidrivers.pdf.

13. Gabrielle Birkner, "Doctors Predict Fewer Taxi Craniofacial Injuries," *New York Sun*, April 2, 2007, http://www.nysun.com/new-york/doctors-predict-fewer-taxi-craniofacial-injuries/51639/.

14. Ibid.

15. Chicago cab driver, in interview with author, February 12, 2010.

16. Department of Business Affairs and Consumer Protection, City of Chicago, "Backgrounder: Security Cameras," http://www.cityofchicago.org/content/dam/city/depts/bacp/publicvehicleinfo/medallion owners/Securitycameras070209.pdf.

17. Sean McCarthaigh, "Security Cameras in Taxis Met with Widespread Opposition by Drivers," *Irish Examiner*, February 29, 2016, http://www.irishexaminer.com/ireland/security-cameras-in-taxis-met-with-widespread-opposition-by-drivers-384572.html.

18. Bureau of Justice Statistics, Office of Justice Programs, "Location," US Department of Justice, http://www.bjs.gov/index.cfm?ty=tp&tid=44.

19. Robert Greenwald, *Walmart: The High Cost of Low Price* (film) (Culver City, CA: Brave New Films, 2005), 1 hour, 37 min., 26 sec., http://www.bravenewfilms.org/walmartmovie.

20. Chris E. McGoey, "Parking Lot Security: Security Planning for Families," Crimedoctor, http://www.crimedoctor.com/parking.htm.

21. Yonah Freemark, "Sao Paulo Tries New Station Seats . . . for the Obese," *TransportPolitic*, August 25, 2009, http://www.thetransportpolitic.com/2009/08/25/sao-paulo-tries-new-station-seats-for-the-obese.

22. Rachel Glickhouse, "'Supersize It': Seats Widen to Accommodate Brazil's Growing Obese Population," *Christian Science Monitor*, September 7, 2012, http://www.csmonitor.com/World/Americas/Latin-America-Monitor/2012/0907/Supersize-it-seats-widen-to-accommodate-Brazil-s-growing-obese-population.

23. "Wider Seats for Obese Train Passengers: Special Enlarged Seats for Obese People Have Been Installed at Underground Stations in Sao Paulo, Brazil," *Telegraph*, August 24, 2009, http://www.telegraph.co.uk/news/newstopics/howaboutthat/6080374/Wider-seats-for-obese-train-passengers.html.

24. Ibid.

25. Associated Press, "WC Special Seats to Be Set Aside for Obese," ESPN FC, March 4, 2013, http://www.espnfc.com/story/1363115/brazil-cup-to-be-1st-to-offer-seats-for-obese-fans.

26. Jen Mills, "An Airline Has Designed Special Seats for Obese People," *Metro*, February 21, 2016, http://metro.co.uk/2016/02/21/an-airline-has-designed-special-seats-for-obese-people-5709564/#ixzz4CYR9Qnuw.

27. See also Shannon Sanders McDonald, *The Parking Garage: Design and Evolution of a Modern Urban Form* (Washington, DC: Urban Land Institute, 2007).

28. Mary S. Smith, "Crime Prevention through Environmental Design in Parking Facilities," *National Institute of Justice: Research in Brief*, April 1996, https://www.ncjrs.gov/pdffiles/cptedpkg.pdf.

27. "Stockholm," Metrobits, http://mic-ro.com/metro/metrocity .html?city=Stockholm.

30. "Accessibility: Tips for Travelers with Disabilities," Visit Seoul, http://www.visitseoul.net/en/article/article.do?_method=view&art_id =66593&lang=en&m=0004023002005&p=07.

CHAPTER 6: A TABOO TOPIC

1. This chapter is based in part on Kathryn H. Anthony and Meghan Dufresne, "Putting Potty Parity in Perspective: Gender and Family Issues in Restroom Design," *Journal of Planning Literature* 21, no. 3 (2007): 267–94.

2. Sheila L. Cavanagh, "You Are Where You Urinate," *Gay & Lesbian Review Worldwide*, July 1, 2011, http://www.glreview.org/article/you-are -where-you-urinate/; Sheila L. Cavanagh, *Queering Bathrooms: Gender, Sexuality, and the Hygienic Imagination* (Toronto, Ontario: University of Toronto Press, 2010).

3. Elizabeth Nolan Brown, "Why Aren't There More Unisex Bathrooms?" *Reason*, July 2014, http://reason.com/archives/2014/06/28/ why-arent-there-more-unisex-ba.

4. This paragraph is excerpted from Anthony and Dufresne, "Putting Potty Parity in Perspective," excerpts from pp. 269–70.

5. Katie Nodjimbadem, "Apartheid, Twenty-Five Years after Its Repeal: Segregated Public Facilities, Including Beaches, Were Commonplace, but Even Today, the Inequality Persists," *Simthsonian*, October 15, 2015, http://www.smithsonianmag.com/history/what-did-apartheid -south-africa-look-180956945/?no-ist.

6. This paragraph and the next two paragraphs are excerpted from Anthony and Dufresne, "Putting Potty Parity in Perspective," excerpts from pp. 269–70.

7. "Attorney General Loretta E. Lynch Delivers Remarks at Press Conference Announcing Complaint Against the State of North Carolina to Stop Discrimination against Transgender Individuals," US Department of Justice, May 9, 2016, https://www.justice.gov/opa/speech/attorney -general-loretta-e-lynch-delivers-remarks-press-conference-announcing -complaint.

8. Philip Elliott, "North Carolina Gov. Pat McCrory Blames Congress for Transgender Bathroom Controversy," *Time*, May 19, 2016, http://time.com/4341150/north-carolina-transgender-bathrooms-governor-pat-mccrory/; Amber Phillips, "The Legal Fight over North Carolina's Transgender Bathroom Law, in 4 Questions," *Washington Post*, May 9, 2016, https://www.washingtonpost.com/news/the-fix/wp/2016/05/09/the-legal-fight-over-north-carolinas-transgender-bathroom-law-explained-in-4-questions/.

9. Barbara Penner, *Bathroom* (London: Reaktion Books, 2013), p. 22.

10. Nick Haslam, "How the Psychology of Public Bathrooms Explains the 'Bathroom Bills,'" *Washington Post*, May 13, 2016, https://www.washingtonpost.com/posteverything/wp/2016/05/13/how-the-psychology-of-public-bathrooms-explains-the-bathroom-bills/.

11. Ben Mathis-Lilley, "Hillary Clinton Makes First Known Presidential Debate Reference to How Long It Takes Women to Pee," *Slate*, October 13, 2015, http://www.slate.com/blogs/the_slatest/2015/10/13/hillary_clinton_bathroom_break_you_know_it_does_take_me_a_little_longer.html.

12. Amy Chozick, "Finally, an Explanation for Hillary Clinton's Long Bathroom Break," *New York Times*, December 20, 2015, http://www.nytimes.com/politics/first-draft/2015/12/20/finally-an-explanation-for-hillary-clintons-long-bathroom-break/?_r=0.

13. Jenna Johnson, "Donald Trump Says Clinton's Bathroom Break during the Debate Is 'Too Disgusting' to Talk About," *Washington Post*, December 21, 2015, https://www.washingtonpost.com/news/post-politics/wp/2015/12/21/donald-trump-calls-hillary-clinton-disgusting-for-using-the-restroom-during-a-debate/.

14. Junda Woo, "'Potty Parity' Lets Women Wash Hands of Long Loo Lines," *Wall Street Journal*, February 24, 1994, A-1, A-19.

15. Jerry Gillam, "March Fong Eu Quits as Secretary of State," *Los Angeles Times*, February 11, 1994, http://articles.latimes.com/1994-02-11/news/mn-21734_1_march-fong-eu (accessed November 28, 2016).

16. ICC G3-2011, "Global Guideline for Practical Public Toilet Design," International Code Council, Inc., 2011, http://shop.iccsafe.org/media/wysiwyg/material/7053S11-toc.pdf.

17. Jay Peters, "Code Council, Global Organizations Advance Toilet Design," PRWeb, October 21, 2010, http://www.prweb.com/releases/2010/10/prweb4676224.htm.

18. Douglas P. Shuit and Daniel Yi, "At the Getty, Art in Loo of Bathrooms," *Los Angeles Times*, March 26, 1998, http://articles.latimes.com/1998/mar/16/news/mn-29536 (accessed November 28, 2016).

19. Sarah A. Moore, "Facility Hostility? Sex Discrimination and Women's Restrooms in the Workplace," *Georgia Law Review* 36, no. 599 (2002).

20. Ibid.

21. *Restroom Gender Parity in Federal Buildings Act*, HR 4869, 111th Congress (2009–2010), https://www.congress.gov/bill/111th-congress/house-bill/4869?q=%7B%22search%22%3A%5B%22HR+4869%22%5D%7D&resultIndex=4.

22. Brian Montopoli, "Lawmakers Introduce 'Potty Parity Act,'" CBSNews, March 18, 2010, http://www.cbsnews.com/8301-503544_162-20000722-503544.html?tag=contentMain;contentBody.

23. *Restroom Gender Parity in Federal Buildings Act*, HR 693, 110th Congress (2007–2008), https://www.congress.gov/bill/110th-congress/house-bill/693 (accessed November 28, 2016).

24. Transcript of the testimony of the Honorable Sharon Pratt before the House Committee on Oversight and Government Reform, https://oversight.house.gov/wp-content/uploads/2012/02/20100512Pratt.pdf.

25. Transcript of Kathryn H Anthony's testimony before the Committee on Oversight and Government Reform, United States House of Representatives, "In support of HR 4869, The Bipartisan Restroom Gender Parity in Federal Buildings Act," Washington, DC, May 12, 2010, http://oversight.house.gov/wp-content/uploads/2012/01/20100512Anthony.pdf.

26. *Restroom Gender Parity in Federal Buildings Act*, H.R. 1361, 112th Cong. (2011–2012), https://www.congress.gov/bill/112th-congress/house-bill/1361.

27. "Committee Holds Hearing on Restroom Parity," Women's Policy, Inc., n.d., http://www.womenspolicy.org/source/committee-holds-hearing-on-restroom-parity.

28. Anne Paine, "Coliseum Potty Ratio Makes Guys Squirm," *Tennessean*, December 20, 1999.

29. John Branch, "New Ballpark Statistic: Stadium's Toilet Ratio," *New York Times*, April 12, 2009, http://www.nytimes.com/2009/04/13/sports/baseball/13potty.html?_r=0.

30. Fran Spielman and Andrew Herrmann, "Bears Ask for Potty Break: Opening Women's Rooms to Men during Games Is Suggested," *Chicago Sun-Times*, April 23, 2004; Andrew Herrmann, "Soldier Field Evens the Score with More Men's Restrooms," *Chicago Sun-Times*, August 29, 2004, p. 3.

31. "Long Lines at Women's Toilets? It's the Law," NPR, May 12, 2008, http://m.npr.org/news/front/90365900?singlePage=true.

32. Jacob Demmitt, "Amazon's Potty Problem: Too Many Dudes, Not Enough Toilets, Workers Complain to State Officials," *GeekWire*, September 14, 2015, http://www.geekwire.com/2015/amazon-employees-biggest -complaint-not-enough-mens-bathrooms-for-all-the-dudes/.

33. Dany Westneat, "Potty Parity 2015: Too Many Dudes, Not Enough Toilets at Amazon," *Seattle Times*, September 18, 2015, http://www .seattletimes.com/seattle-news/potty-parity-2015-too-many-dudes -not-enough-toilets-at-amazon/.

34. "At Amazon, Employees Treat the Bathroom as an Extension of the Office," *Motherboard*, August 17, 2015, https:// motherboard.vice.com/en_ca/read/at-amazon-employees-treat-the -bathroom-as-an-extension-of-the-office.

35. Branch, "Ballpark Statisticians."

36. Ibid.

37. Kathryn Anthony et al., "How Gender and Family Friendly are Public Restrooms at the University of Illinois at Urbana-Champaign Campus? An Evaluation of Eleven Major Campus Buildings Based on the Gender Equity Design Checklist," A Report by the Provost's Gender Equity Council, May 13, 2011, University of Illinois at Urbana-Champaign, May 9, 2011.

38. Muhammad Taimur and Sana Taimur, "Battling Out with Babies," unpublished report, School of Architecture, University of Illinois at Urbana-Champaign, 2015.

39. "California Governor Rejects Bills to Help Men Change Diapers," Reuters, September 20, 2014, http://www.reuters.com/article/us -usa-diaper-california-idUSKBN0HF05M20140920.

40. Michele Richinick, "Ashton Kutcher: Men's Restrooms Need More Diaper-Changing Stations," MSNBC, March 10, 2015, http:// www.msnbc.com/msnbc/ashton-kutcher-calls-diaper-changing -stations-mens-restrooms#56369.

41. Caroline Bologna, "Men's Restrooms Will Now Require Baby Changing Stations. Thanks, Obama!" *Huffington Post*, October 10, 2016, http://www.huffingtonpost.com/entry/mens-restrooms-will-now -require-baby-changing-stations-thanks-obama_us_57fbe25ee4b068 ecb5e0d3b0.

42. "Senate Bill S5473," New York State Senate, 2015–2016 Legislative Session, https://www.nysenate.gov/legislation/bills/2015/s5473#.

43. *Bathrooms Accessible in Every Situation (BABIES) Act*, HR 5147, 114th

Cong. (2015–2016), https://www.congress.gov/bill/114th-congress/house-bill/5147.

44. Harold Kiewel, e-mail correspondence with the author, May 2009 and December 2, 2016.

45. Beth Finke, interview with the author, November 23, 2016.

46. Dana Milbank, "A Senator's Wide Stance: 'I Am Not Gay,'" *Washington Post*, August 29, 2007, http://www.washingtonpost.com/wp-dyn/content/article/2007/08/28/AR2007082801664.html.

47. Kim Hubbard, Anne-Marie O'Neill, and Christina Cheakalos, "Out of Control: Weight-Obsessed, Stressed-Out Coeds Are Increasingly Falling Prey to Eating Disorders," *People*, April 12, 1999, http://www.people.com/people/archive/article/0,,20127911,00.html.

48. Ibid.

49. Steven Soifer, *Shy Bladder Syndrome: Your Step-by-Step Guide to Overcoming Paruresis* (Oakland, CA: New Harbinger Publications, 2001), p. 2.

50. National Center for Education Statistics, US Department of Education, "Fast Facts," *Digest of Education Statistics*, 2014 (NCES 2016-006), Chapter 2, https://nces.ed.gov/fastfacts/display.asp?id=84.

51. Jenny Perez, "Minimum Standards for School Toilets Are Needed to Improve Child Health," *Nursing Times*, June 22, 2010, http://www.nursingtimes.net/minimum-standards-for-school-toilets-are-needed-to-improve-child-health/5016204.fullarticle.

52. Tod Schneider, "Violence and Crime Prevention through Environmental Design," in *Safe and Healthy School Environments*, ed. Howard Frumkin et al. (New York: Oxford University Press, 2006), pp. 251–69, quote on p. 262.

53. "Project CLEAN and World Toilet Day in the Media," Project Clean, http://projectclean.us/publications.php.

54. Tom Keating, "Flushed with Respect for Restrooms," *School Planning & Management*, August 1, 2013, https://webspm.com/Articles/2013/08/01/Improving-School-Restrooms.aspx.

55. Andrew Cauthen, "County's Clean Restroom Ordinance Gets an Update," *Champion*, November 24, 2015, http://thechampionnewspaper.com/news/local/countys-clean-restroom-ordinance-gets-an-update/.

56. Sharon LaFraniere, "Another School Barrier for African Girls: No Toilet," *New York Times*, December 23, 2005, http://www.nytimes.com/2005/12/23/international/africa/23ethiopia.html?pagewanted=all.

57. "It Is Time to Talk about Toilets! Despite Continued Progress 36 Percent of China without Safe Toilets," Media Center, UNICEF, November

19, 2012, http://www.unicef.cn/en/index.php?m=content&c=index&a =show&catid=53&id=3665.

58. Sharon LaFraniere, "For Chinese Women, a Basic Need, and Few Places to Attend to It," *New York Times*, February 29, 2012, http://www .nytimes.com/2012/03/01/world/asia/chinese-women-demand-more -public-toilets.html?_r=1.

59. Josie Delap, "Flushing away Unfairness: Hanging On Too Long for Porcelain Parity Is More Than a Nuisance for Women," *Economist*, July 8, 2010, http://www.economist.com/node/16542591.

60. Ann Schraufnagel, "India's Need for School Toilets," Pulitzer Center on Crisis Reporting, February 15, 2016, http://pulitzercenter.org/ reporting/school-toilets-india.

61. Haikel Fahim, "World Toilet Organization Won Gates Foundation's Support of USD 270,000," press release, World Toilet Organization, November 1, 2011, http://worldtoilet.org/documents/gates_foundation.pdf.

62. "Check a Toilet App," *Accessible Japan*, http://www.accessible-japan .com/check-a-toilet-app/. See also "Wheelchair Accessible Toilets in Japan," *Accessible Japan*, https://www.accessible-japan.com/wheelchair -accessible-toilets-in-japan/.

63. Anna Fifield, "How Japan's Toilet Obsession Produced Some of the World's Best Bathrooms," *Washington Post*, December 15, 2015, https://www.washingtonpost.com/news/worldviews/wp/2015/12/15/ how-japans-toilet-obsession-produced-some-of-the-worlds-best-bathrooms/.

64. "Cities, Firms Clean Up with Wins at Japan's First Toilet Awards," *Japan Times*, September 5, 2015, http://www.japantimes.co.jp/news/ 2015/09/05/national/cities-firms-clean-wins-japans-first-toilet-awards/ #.V3YKdt77Wis.

65. Gabriel Wildau, "China Flush with Toilets after Campaign to Boost Tourism: Government Officials Tout a Loo Revolution to Help Promote Travel as New Economic Growth Engine," *Financial Times*, April 3, 2016, https://next.ft.com/content/2aa1b16e-f960-11e5-8e04-8600cef2ca75.

66. World Toilet Organization, http://worldtoilet.org.

67. American Restroom Association, http://americanrestroom.org.

68. "Water, Sanitation and Hygiene: Strategy Overview," Bill and Melinda Gates Foundation, http://www.gatesfoundation.org/What -We-Do/Global-Development/Water-Sanitation-and-Hygiene.

69. Fakim, "World Toilet Organization Won."

70. "What Is UN World Toilet Day?" World Toilet Organization, http://worldtoilet.org/what-we-do/world-toilet-day/.

71. Ceri Au, "Fighting for the Right to Flush," *Time*, July 31, 2007, http://www.time.com/time/nation/article/0,8599,1648349,00.html.

72. Kim Bellware, "Gender-Neutral Bathrooms Are Quietly Becoming the New Thing at Colleges," *Huffington Post*, July 18, 2014, http://www.huffingtonpost.com/2014/07/18/gender-neutral-bathrooms-colleges_n_5597362.html.

73. JoAnn Hindmarsh Wilcox and Kurt Haapala, "Why Architects Must Rethink Restroom Design in Schools," *Metropolis*, November 3, 2016, http://www.metropolismag.com/Point-of-View/November-2016/Why-Architects-Must-Rethink-Restroom-Design-in-Schools/; see also JoAnn Hindmarsh Wilcox and Kurt Haapala, "How to Design School Restrooms for Increased Comfort, Safety, and Gender Inclusivity," *ArchDaily*, November 15, 2016, http://www.archdaily.com/799401/how-to-design-school-restrooms-for-increased-comfort-safety-and-gender-inclusivity.

74. Jason Renner, "Facilities for Families: Family Restrooms Make Facilities More Accessible," *Buildings*, January 7, 2004, http://www.buildings.com/Articles/detail.asp?ArticleID=1701.

75. Port of Seattle, "Restroom Renovations, 2005," http://www.port seattle.org/seatac/expansion/restrooms.shtml (accessed November 22, 2005) (site discontinued).

76. Step 'n Wash, http://stepnwash.com.

77. For more information, see "Step 'n Wash: A Big Step for Little Feet," http://www.stepnwash.com. To see how it works, see http://www.stepnwash.com/video/SNW_CBS46_720x480_4B_S45.wmv.

CHAPTER 7: HELPFUL OR HARMFUL TO YOUR HEALTH

1. Christina Mooney and Kathryn H. Anthony, "Housing Hidden Helpers: Domestic Servant Spaces in Three Frank Lloyd Wright Masterpieces" (unpublished manuscript).

2. Farnsworth quoted in Alice T. Friedman, *Women and the Making of the Modern House: A Social and Architectural History* (New York: Harry N. Abrams, 1998), p. 141.

3. Friedman, *Women and the Making of the Modern House.*

4. Naomi Wolf, *Misconceptions: Truth, Lies, and the Unexpected on the Journey to Motherhood* (New York: Doubleday, 2001), p. 209.

5. Reid Ewing et al., "Relationship between Urban Sprawl and Physical Activity, Obesity, and Morbidity," *American Journal of Health Promotion* 18, no. 1 (2003): 47–57.

6. Lawrence D. Frank, Martin A. Andresen, and Thomas L. Schmid, "Obesity Relationships with Community Design, Physical Activity, and Time Spent in Cars," *American Journal of Preventive Medicine* 27, no. 2 (2004): 87–96.

7. "James F. Sallis," Active Living Research, August 24, 2012, http://activelivingresearch.org/about/programstaff/sallis.

8. Gina Jacobs, "City Dwellers Worldwide Healthier Than Suburban Counterparts: SDSU Study Finds People Who Live in City Neighborhoods Twice as Likely to Get Exercise," San Diego State University News Center, June 16, 2009, http://newscenter.sdsu.edu/sdsu_newscenter/news.aspx?s=71384; see also James F. Sallis, "Measuring Physical Activity Environments: A Brief History," *American Journal of Preventive Medicine* 36, no. 4, Supplement (2009): S86–S92, http://www.ajpm-online.net/article/S0749-3797(09)00005-1/abstract; see also Reed Ewing et al., "Relationship between Urban Sprawl and Physical Activity, Obesity, and Morbidity— Update and Refinement," *Health & Place* 26 (March 2014): 118–26.

9. M. Nakashian, *Active Living Research: An RWJF National Program*, Robert Wood Johnson Foundation, January 12, 2015, http://www.rwjf.org/en/library/research/2011/07/active-living-research.html.

10. Jeffrey Levi et al., *F as in Fat: How Obesity Policies Are Failing in America: 2009* (Washington, DC: Robert Wood Johnson Foundation, 2009), p. 87, http://healthyamericans.org/reports/obesity2009/Obesity2009Report.pdf.

11. Susan Goltsman and Daniel Iacofano, *The Inclusive City: Design Solutions for Buildings, Neighborhoods and Urban Spaces* (Berkeley, CA: MIG Communications, 2007).

12. Gary W. Evans, "The Environment of Childhood Poverty," *American Psychologist* 59, no. 2 (2004): 77–92.

13. Andrea Faber Taylor, Frances E. Kuo, and William Sullivan, "Views of Nature and Self-Discipline: Evidence from Inner-City Children," *Journal of Environmental Psychology* 22, nos. 1–2 (2002): 49–63.

14. Children and Adults with Attention-Deficit/Hyperactivity Disorder, http://www.chadd.org.

15. Frances E. Kuo and Andrea Faber Taylor, "A Potential Natural Treatment for Attention-Deficit/Hyperactivity Disorder: Evidence from a National Study," *American Journal of Public Health* 94, no. 9 (2004): 1580–86.

16. Centers for Disease Control and Prevention, "10 Leading Causes of Nonfatal Injuries, United States," WISQARS Leading Causes of Death Reports, 2001–2014, http://webappa.cdc.gov/sasweb/ncipc/nfilead2001.html; see also CDC Foundation and MetLife Foundation, Department of Health and Human Services, "Check for Safety: A Home Fall Prevention Checklist for Older Adults,"

Centers for Disease Control and Prevention, 2005, http://www.cdc.gov/Home
andRecreationalSafety/pubs/English/booklet_Eng_desktop-a.pdf.

17. Hamish Simpson et al., "Does the Type of Flooring Affect the Risk
of Hip Fracture?" *Age and Ageing* 33, no. 3 (2004): 242–46, http://ageing
.oxfordjournals.org/cgi/reprint/33/3/242.

18. Ibid.

19. Allied Dunbar survey 1992, cited in Canada Mortgage and
Housing Corporation, "Preventing Falls on Stairs," https://www.cmhc-schl
.gc.ca/en/co/acho/acho_012.cfm.

20. Cohousing: Building a Better Society, One Neighborhood at a
Time, http://www.cohousing.org; see also Kathryn McCamant and Charles
Durrett, *Creating Cohousing: Building Sustainable Communities* (Gabriola
Island, British Columbia: New Society Publishers, 2011).

21. Nessa Winston, "Urban Regeneration for Sustainable Development: The Role of Sustainable Housing?" *European Planning Studies* 17, no.
12 (2009): 1781–96, http://www.tandfonline.com/doi/abs/10.1080/
09654310903322306. For more about ecovillages, also see Global Ecovillage Network, http://gen.ecovillage.org/; Jan Bang, *Ecovillages: A Practical Guide to Sustainable Communities* (Edinburgh, UK: Floris Books, 2005);
Diana Leafe Christian, *Creating a Life Together: Practical Tools to Grow Ecovillages and Intentional Communities* (Gabriola Island, British Columbia:
New Society Publishers, 2003); Diana Leafe Christian, *Finding Community:
How to Join an Ecovillage or Intentional Community* (Gabriola Island, British
Columbia: New Society Publishers, 2007); Jonathan Dawson, *Ecovillages:
New Frontiers for Sustainability* (Devon, UK: Green Books, 2006).

22. Ecovillage at Ithaca, http://ecovillageithaca.org/evi/. See also Liz
Walker, *Ecovillage at Ithaca: Pioneering a Sustainable Culture* (Gabriola Island,
British Columbia: New Society Publishers, 2005).

23. Los Angeles Eco-Village, http://www.laecovillage.org/.

24. Clare Foran, "How to Design a City for Women: A Fascinating
Experiment in 'Gender Mainstreaming,'" *Atlantic CityLab*, http://www
.citylab.com/commute/2013/09/how-design-city-women/6739/.

25. "Women Friendly City Project," Seoul Solution, November 6,
2014, https://seoulsolution.kr/content/women-friendly-city-project
?language=en; see also "Women Friendly City Project," Women Friendly
City, http://www.womenfriendlycity.or.kr/about/about_03.html.

26. TOTO, "TOTO Washlet Sales Top 40 Million Units Globally,"
PRNewswire, November 11, 2015, http://www.prnewswire.com/news
-releases/toto-washlet-sales-top-40-million-units-globally-300176569.html.

27. For more about TOTO Washlet toilet seats, see: http://www .washlet.com; TOTO representatives, in discussion with the author, March 25, 2009.

28. TOTO, "TOTO Washlet Sales."

29. Ibid.

30. Ibid.

CHAPTER 8: HIDDEN POWER

1. "Dear Abby: Breast-Feeding Laws May Come to the Rescue of New Mom," *San Diego Union-Tribune,* June 18, 2009, Night & Day Section, p. 4.

2. US Bureau of Labor Statistics, *Women in the Labor Force: A Databook,* Report 1049, Table 11, May 2014, http://www.bls.gov/cps/wlf-data book-2013.pdf.

3. Alexa Pazniak, "Backpacks Too Heavy for Small Kids," ABC News, January 23, 2002, http://abcnews.go.com/Health/story?id=117024.

4. Mette Harreby et al., "Are Radiographic Changes in the Thoracic and Lumbar Spine of Adolescents Risk Factors for Low Back Pain in Adults?" *Spine* 20, no. 21 (1995): 2298–302.

5. David Siambanes et al., "Influence of School Backpacks on Adolescent Back Pain," *Journal of Pediatric Orthopaedics* 24, no. 2 (2004): 211–17.

6. "Backpack Misuse Leads to Chronic Back Pain, Doctors of Chiropractic Say," American Chiropractic Association, http://www.prnewswire .com/news-releases/backpack-misuse-leads-to-chronic-back-pain-doctors -of-chiropractic-say-72397057.html.

7. Rotraut Walden, "The School of the Future: Conditions and Processes—Contributions of Architectural Psychology," in *Schools for the Future: Design Proposals from Architectural Psychology,* ed. Rotraut Walden (Cambridge, MA: Hogrefe & Huber Publishers, 2009), p. 83.

8. Igor Knez, "Effects of Indoor Lighting on Mood and Cognition," *Journal of Environmental Psychology* 15, no. 1 (1995): 39–51.

9. Markus Dederich, *In den Ordnungen des Leibes. Zur Anthropologie und Padagogik von Hugo Kukelhaus [In the Orders of the Body: On the Anthropology and Pedagogy of Hugo Kukelhaus]* (Münster, Germany: Waxmann, 1996).

10. Walden, "School of the Future," p. 86.

11. University of Southern California/Keck School of Medicine, "Traffic-Related Pollution near Schools Linked to Development of Asthma in Pupils, Study Suggests," *ScienceDaily,* April 9, 2010, http://www.science

daily.com/releases/2010/04/100409142431.htm. See also Rob McConnell et al., "Childhood Incident Asthma and Traffic-Related Air Pollution at Home and School," *Environmental Health Perspectives* 118, no. 7 (2010): pp. 1021–26, https://www.ncbi.nlm.nih.gov/pmc/articles/PMC2920902/.

12. "Basic Facts about Hearing Loss," Hearing Loss Association of America, http://www.hearingloss.org/content/basic-facts-about -hearing-loss.

13. "Researchers Find Increase in Hearing Loss among Adolescents," *BWH Bulletin*, September 10, 2010, http://www.brighamand womens.org/about_bwh/publicaffairs/news/publications/Display Bulletin.aspx?articleid=4952; see also J. Shargorodsky et al., "Change in Prevalence of Hearing Loss in US Adolescents" (abstract), *JAMA* 304, no. 7 (2010): 772–78.

14. "Researchers Find Increase in Hearing Loss"; Shargorodsky et al., "Change in Prevalence of Hearing Loss in US Adolescents" (abstract); Lorraine E. Maxwell and Gary W. Evans, "Design of Child Care Centers and Effects of Noise on Young Children," http://www.designshare.com/ Research/LMaxwell/NoiseChildren.htm.

15. J. A. Lackney, *Thirty-Three Educational Design Principles for Schools and Community Learning Centers* (paper, Mississippi State University, MS, Educational Design Institute, 2000); Robert Gifford, "Educational Environmental Psychology," in *Environmental Psychology: Principles and Practice*, 3rd ed. (Colville, WA: Optimal Environments, 2002), pp. 296–36.

16. Walden, "School of the Future," p. 103.

17. US Bureau of Labor Statistics, "Economic News Release, Table 6, Employment Status of Mothers with Own Children under 3 Years Old by Single Year of Age of Youngest Child and Marital Status, 2014–15 Annual Averages," US Department of Labor, http://www.bls.gov/news.release/ famee.t06.htm.

18. Kirsten Berggren, "What You'll Need," Work and Pump.com, 2005, http://www.workandpump.com/needs.htm.

19. Jake Marcus, "Lactation and the Law Revisited," Breastfeeding Law, http://breastfeedinglaw.com/articles/lactation-and-the-law -revisited/; "Laws and Legislation," NYS Breastfeeding Coalition, https:// www.nysbreastfeeding.org/laws-and-legislation.

20. US Department of Labor, "Wage and Hour Division: Fact Sheet #73: Break Time for Nursing Mothers under the FLSA," revised August 2013, http://www.dol.gov/whd/regs/compliance/whdfs73.htm.

21. LaLeche League International, http://www.lalecheleague.org.

22. "Breastfeeding State Laws," National Conference of State Legislatures, August 30, 2016, http://www.ncsl.org/research/health/breast feeding-state-laws.aspx.

23. Carol Garvan, "The Natural Goodness of Mom: The Rights of Mothers Who Breastfeed," *Portland Press Herald,* June 10, 2014, http:// contributors.pressherald.com/business/on-the-job/natural-goodness -mom-rights-mothers-breastfeed-2/.

24. Marcus, "Lactation and the Law Revisited."

25. Garvan, "Natural Goodness of Mom."

26. Irene Padavic and Barbara Reskin, *Women and Men at Work,* 2nd ed. (Thousand Oaks, CA: Pine Forge, 2002).

27. "Healthy Ideas," *Consumer Reports on Health,* 10580832, 13, no. 5 (2001); Ginny Graves, "Danger at Your Local Salon," *Health,* December 22, 2008, http://www.health.com/health/article/0,,20411389,00.html.

28. Jonas Brisman et al., "The Incidence of Respiratory Symptoms in Female Swedish Hairdressers," *American Journal of Industrial Medicine* 44, no. 6 (2003): 673–78, http://onlinelibrary.wiley.com/doi/10.1002/ ajim.10293/abstract, doi: 10.1002/ajim.10293.

29. Maria Albin et al., "Incidence of Asthma in Female Swedish Hairdressers," *Occupational and Environmental Medicine* 59, no. 2 (2002), pp. 119–23.

30. Deborah Condon, "Chemical Warning to Hairdressers," *Irish-Health,* February 8, 2002, http://www.irishhealth.com/article.html ?id=4109.

31. CDC's National Asthma Control Program Grantees, *Asthma Facts* (Chamblee, GA: CDC, 2013), http://www.cdc.gov/asthma/pdfs/asthma _facts_program_grantees.pdf; Rob Stein, "Childhood Asthma Rates Level Off, but Racial Disparities Remain," *Morning Edition,* NPR, December 28, 2015, http://www.npr.org/sections/health-shots/ 2015/12/28/460845335/childhood-asthma-rates-level -off-but-racial-disparities-remain.

32. Michelle Conlin and John Carey, "Is Your Office Killing You? Sick Buildings Are Seething with Molds, Monoxide—and Worse," *Business Week,* June 5, 2000, http://www.anapsid.org/mask/sbsbusweek.html (accessed November 23, 2016).

33. Monika Bullinger et al., "The Sick Building Syndrome: Do Women Suffer More?" *Zentralblatt für Hygiene und Umweltmedizin* 202, no. 4 (1998): 235–41, http://www.ncbi.nlm.nih.gov/pubmed/10507131; Sabine Brasche et al., "Why Do Women Suffer from Sick Building Syndrome More Often

than Men? Subjective Higher Sensitivity versus Objective Causes," *Indoor Air* 11, no. 4 (2001): 217–22, http://www.ladep.es/ficheros/documentos/Why%20do%20Women%20Suffer%20from%20Sick%20Building%20Syndrome.pdf; Michelle Conlin with John Carey, "Is Your Office Killing You? Sick Buildings Are Seething with Molds, Monoxide—and Worse," *Business Week*, June 5, 2000, http://www.anapsid.org/mask/sbsbusweek.html.

34. Dee Dee Myers, *Why Women Should Rule the World* (New York: HarperCollins, 2008); Dee Dee Myers in lecture at the University of Illinois, December 2, 2008. See also Jay MacDonald, interview with Dee Dee Myers, *BookPage*, March 2008, https://bookpage.com/interviews/8447-dee-dee-myers#.WEWHZrIrK1t (accessed December 5, 2016).

35. Donald A. Ritchie, historian emeritus, US Senate Historical Office, e-mail correspondence, December 2, 2008, December 4, 2008, December 5, 2008, December 8, 2008.

36. Nancy McKeon, "Women in the House Get a Restroom," *Washington Post*, July 28, 2011, http://www.washingtonpost.com/lifestyle/style/women-in-the-house-get-a-restroom/2011/07/28/gIQAFgdwfI_story.html.

37. Ruth Bader Ginsburg, American Sociological Association Annual Meeting, Montreal, August 11, 2006, https://www.supremecourt.gov/publicinfo/speeches/viewspeech/sp_08-11-06; Jennifer Lee, "A 'Women Only' Restroom Renovation Tips the Balance at Grand Central," *New York Times*, July 18, 2008, http://www.nytimes.com/2008/07/18/nyregion/18bathrooms.html?_r=1.

38. Elizabeth S. Scott, N. Dickon Reppucci, and Mark Aber, "Children's Preferences in Adjudicated Custody Decisions," *Georgia Law Review* 22 (1988): 1035–78.

39. "Children's Waiting Rooms and Day Care Centers: Courthouse Design and Finance, State Links," National Center for State Courts, http://www.ncsc.org/Topics/Courthouse-Facilities/Courthouse-Design-and-Finance/State-Links.aspx?cat=Childrens%20Waiting%20Rooms%20and%20Day%20Care%20Centers#Federal%20Courts.

40. For an overview of which state courts offer children's waiting rooms and daycare centers, see "Courthouse Design and Finance Resource Guide," National Center for State Courts, http://www.ncsc.org/Topics/Courthouse-Facilities/Courthouse-Design-and-Finance/Resource-Guide.aspx.

41. 2009 California Rules of Court, Standard 10.24 Children's Waiting Room. Standard 10.24 renumbered effective January 1, 2007; adopted as sec. 1.3 effective January 1, 1987, http://www.courts.ca.gov/documents/JDCA2008V2Ch6.pdf.

42. Bobbie L. Welling and Susan Mather, eds., *Gender and Justice: Implementing Gender Fairness in the Courts, Implementation Report,* Judicial Council of California: Advisory Committee on Access and Fairness, Gender Fairness Subcommittee, July 1996, http://www.courts.ca.gov/documents/imp_rept.pdf.

43. "Children's Waiting Rooms and Day Care Centers: Courthouse Design and Finance, State Links," http://www.ncsc.org/Topics/Courthouse-Facilities/Courthouse-Design-and-Finance/State-Links.aspx?cat=Childrens%20Waiting%20Rooms%20and%20Day%20Care%20Centers#Illinois.

44. Ellen Lupton, *Mechanical Brides: Women and Machines from Home to Office* (New York: Princeton Architectural, 1993).

45. "Leaders of 9 Universities and 25 Women Faculty Meet at MIT, Agree to Equity Reviews," Massachusetts Institute of Technology News Office, January 30, 2001, http://web.mit.edu/newsoffice/2001/gender.html; Members of the First and Second Committees on Women Faculty in the School of Science, "A Study on the Status of Women Faculty in Science at MIT: How a Committee on Women Faculty Came to Be Established by the Dean of the School of Science, What the Committee and the Dean Learned and Accomplished, and Recommendations for the Future," *MIT Faculty Newsletter,* March 1999, http://web.mit.edu/fnl/women/women.html.

46. Carey Goldberg, "MIT Admits Discrimination against Female Professors," *New York Times,* March 23, 1999, http://www.nytimes.com/1999/03/23/us/mit-admits-discrimination-against-female-professors.html.

47. Stacie Bloom, "In the Debate of Sex and Science, Summers, Hopkins, and the X Chromosome Battle It Out," *Journal of Clinical Investigation* 115, no. 5 (2005): 1107–08, http://www.jci.org/articles/view/25238.

48. "Fire Stations," City of Chicago, 2011, https://data.cityofchicago.org/Public-Safety/Fire-Stations/28km-gtjn.

49. Jill Sederstrom, "Just Part of the Team: Female Firefighters," *Kansas City Star,* January 26, 2016, http://www.kansascity.com/news/local/community/joco-913/article56575658.html; S. Nikki Sprenger and Gerald M. Bates, "Pregnant Pause," *Fire Chief,* April 1, 2003, https://i-women.org/wp-content/uploads/2014/04/Fire-Chief-Pregnant-Pause.pdf. Note that California has the highest number of female firefighters, followed by Florida, Texas, Maryland, and Virginia. But many large fire departments have no female firefighters at all.

50. Denise Smith et al., "Firefighter Fatalities and Injuries: The Role of Heat Stress and PPE," University of Illinois Fire Service Institute, July

2008, http://www.fsi.illinois.edu/documents/research/FFLSRC_Final Report.pdf; Richard Cowen, "Firefighter Health a Cause for Alarm, Lack of Fitness Sometimes Proves Fatal," *FireRescue1 News*, April 26, 2006, http://www.firerescue1.com/fire-rehab/articles/103555-Firefighter -health-a-cause-for-alarm-lack-of-fitness-sometimes-proves-fatal/.

51. John K. Murphy, "Firefighter Fitness and Medical Evaluations: A Difficult Journey," *Fire Engineering*, December 2008, pp. 67–68, http://www .fireengineering.com/articles/2008/12/firefighter-fitness-and-medical -evaluations-a-difficult-journey.html.

52. Ibid.

53. Cowen, "Firefighter Health."

54. International Association of Women in Fire & Emergency Services, "Reproductive Safety and Pregnancy: Sample Fire Department Policy Language," National Resources Defense Council, https://i-women.org/ wp-content/uploads/2014/04/repropack.pdf.

55. Tony Saavedra, "Female Firefighters Win Discrimination Suit," *Orange County Register*, August 20, 2013, http://www.ocregister.com/tax dollars/city-521504-firefighters-long.html.

56. Ibid.

57. Federal Emergency Management Agency, *The Changing Face of the Fire Service: A Handbook on Women in Firefighting* (2013), p. 54.

58. Ibid., p. 9.

59. iWomen Staff Office, "Position Statement: Facilities," International Association of Women in Fire & Emergency Services, August 1, 2012, http://old.i-women.org/position_statements_sogs/Facilities%20 Position%20Statement.pdf.

60. Walden, "The School of the Future," p. 86; see also *Freie Waldorfschule Köln* (German), http://www.waldorfschule-koeln.de/; Peter Blundell Jones, "Social Engagement: Peter Hubner's Design of the Waldorf School in Cologne, Germany," *Architectural Review*, February 1999.

61. Jude Garvey, "Archipod's Pod Is an Energy Efficient, Eco-Friendly Garden Office," *Gizmag*, January 31, 2010, http://www.gizmag.com/ archipods-pod-is-an-energy-efficient-eco-friendly-garden-office/14041/. See also Archipod, http://www.archipod.com.

62. Ally Marotti, "Google Debuts New West Loop Office Space: Take a Tour," *Crain's Chicago Business*, December 3, 2015, http://www.chicago business.com/article/20151203/NEWS12/151209896/google-debuts -new-west-loop-office-space-take-a-tour.

63. Information about Chicago's new Google headquarters based on

our private office tour with John Musnicki, facilities manager at Google Chicago, on April 15, 2016.

64. Nico Saleh, "Google EMEA Engineering Hub/Camezind Evolution," *ArchDaily*, November 22, 2009, http://www.archdaily.com/41400/google-emea-engineering-hub-camezind-evolution/.

CHAPTER 9: SHOPPING, SPENDING, AND REACHING FOR THE STARS

1. Amili Vesilind, "Fashion's Invisible Woman: Even as Americans Get Larger, Designers and Retailers Cling to the Idea that Style Comes in One Size: Small," *Los Angeles Times*, March 1, 2009, http://articles.latimes.com/2009/mar/01/image/ig-size1.

2. Ginia Bellafante, "Plus-Size Wars," *New York Times Magazine*, July 28, 2010, http:// nytimes.com/2010/08/01/magazine/01plussize-t .html?referer=&_r=0.

3. Ibid.

4. Joanne Muniz and Kathryn H. Anthony, "The Plus-Size Displacement: Store Design and the Plus Size Consumer Experience" (unpublished manuscript).

5. Leslie Weisman, *Discrimination by Design: A Feminist Critique of the Man-Made Environment* (Champaign: University of Illinois Press, 1992).

6. Mohamed Boubekri, *Daylighting, Architecture and Health: Building Design Strategies* (Oxford, UK: Architectural Press, 2008), p. 54.

7. Russel J. Reiter, "Oxidative Processes and Antioxidative Defense Mechanisms in the Aging Brain," *FASEB Journal* (*Journal of the Federation of American Societies for Experimental Biology*) 9, no. 7 (1995): 526–33.

8. National Multiple Sclerosis Society, http://www.nationalmssociety .org.

9. William B. Grant, "Insufficient Sunlight May Kill 45,000 Americans Each Year from Internal Cancer," *Journal of Cosmetic Dermatology* 3, no. 4 (2004): 176–78; Sunlight, Nutrition and Health Research Center, http:// www.sunarc.org.

10. Oliver Gillie, *Sunlight Robbery: Health Benefits of Sunlight Are Denied by Current Public Health Policy in the UK* (London: Health Research Forum, 2004).

11. Raymond L. Lam, ed., *Seasonal Affective Disorder and Beyond: Light Treatment for SAD and Non-SAD Conditions* (Arlington, VA: American Psychiatric Publishing, 1998); Roxanne Dryden-Edwards and Melissa Conrad Stöppler,

"What Is Seasonal Affective Disorder (SAD)?" MedicineNet.com, http://www
.medicinenet.com/seasonal_affective_disorder_sad/article.htm.

12. "Roy Raymond, 47; Began Victoria's Secret," *New York Times*, September 2, 1993, http://www.nytimes.com/1993/09/02/obituaries/
roy-raymond-47-began-victoria-s-secret.html.

13. "'Men Buy, Women Shop': The Sexes Have Different Priorities When Walking down the Aisles," *Knowledge @ Wharton, University of Pennsylvania*, November 28, 2007, http://knowledge.wharton.upenn.edu/article
.cfm?articleid=1848.

14. Jennifer Pittman, "Hardware Store Chains Target Women Customers," *Sacramento Business Journal*, October 21, 2005, http://www.biz
journals.com/sacramento/stories/2005/10/24/focus8.html.

15. Sherond Glover, "How to Build a Woman-Friendly Dealership: A Key Ingredient When Selling to Women," Car-Buy-Her, http://www.car
-buy-her.com/woman-friendly-dealership-article.html.

16. "Escalator Accidents & Deaths," ConsumerWatch.com, http://
consumerwatch.com/workplace-public-safety/escalators; David W. White, "Death of 82-Year-Old Woman in MBTA Escalator Accident in Boston Investigated," *Massachusetts Injury Lawyer Blog*, February 25, 2009, http://
www.massachusettsinjurylawyerblog.com/2009/02/death-of-82-year-old
-woman-on.html.

17. Jennifer McGeehan et al., "Escalator-Related Injuries among Children in the United States, 1990–2002," *Pediatrics* 118, no. 2 (2006): e1–e6, doi: 10.1542/peds.2005-1822.

18. Joseph O'Neil et al., "Escalator-Related Injuries among Older Adults in the United States, 1991–2005" (abstract), *Accident Analysis & Prevention* 40, no. 2 (2008): 527–33, http://www.ncbi.nlm.nih.gov/pub
med/18329403; see also Tara Parker-Pope, "Surge in Escalator Injuries among Elderly," *New York Times*, March 14, 2008, http://well.blogs.nytimes
.com/2008/03/14/surge-in-escalator-injuries-among-elderly/.

19. Nicole A. Kerr, "Increasing Stair Use in a Worksite through Environmental Changes," *American Journal of Health Promotion* 18, no. 4 (2004): 312–15.

20. Ishak A. Mansi et al., "Stair Design in the United States and Obesity: The Need for a Change," *Southern Medical Journal* 102, no. 6 (2009): 610–14; Avril Blamey, Nanette Mutrie, and Tom Aitchison, "Health Promotion by Encouraged Use of Stairs." *British Medical Journal* 311, no. 7000 (1995): 289–90; Karen J. Coleman and Eugenia C. Gonzales, "Promoting Stair Use in a US–Mexico Border Community," *American Journal of Public Health* 91, no. 12 (2001): 2007–9; Kerri N. Boutelle et al., "Using Signs, Artwork, and Music

to Promote Stair Use in a Public Building," *American Journal of Public Health* 91, no. 1 (2001): 2004–6; T. Bungum, M. Meacham, and N. Truax, "The Effects of Signage and the Physical Environment on Stair Usage," *Journal of Physical Activity and Health* 4, no. 3 (2007): 237–44.

21. Mansi et al., "Stair Design."

22. Mikaela Conley, "Obesity Grows alongside Oversized Caskets," ABC News, January 4, 2011, http://abcnews.go.com/Health/obesity -grows-alongside-oversized-casket-demand/story?id=12531885.

23. Amanda Kolson Hurley, "Would There Be More Women Architects If There Were More Women Developers?" *Architect*, September 17, 2012, http://www.architectmagazine.com/design/would-there-be -more-women-architects-if-there-were-more-women-developers_o; see also Lamar Anderson, "How Women Are Climbing Architecture's Ladder," *Curbed*, March 17, 2014, http://www.curbed.com/2014/3/17/10131726/ how-women-are-climbing-architectures-career-ladder.

24. Cliff Kuang, "Chicks with Bricks: The World's Tallest Female-Designed Skyscraper," *FastCompany*, November 23, 2009, https://www .fastcompany.com/1466189/chicks-bricks-worlds-tallest-female -designed-skyscraper.

25. Christopher Hawthorne, "Jeanne Gang Brings Feminine Touch to Chicago's Muscled Skyline," *Los Angeles Times*, January 17, 2010, http:// www.latimes.com/entertainment/news/arts/la-ca-aqua17-2010 jan17,0,7701136.story.

26. "Pianotrappan—rolighetsteorin.se," YouTube video, 1:47, posted by Rolighetsteorin, September 20, 2009, http://www.youtube.com/ watch?v=ivg56TX9kWI.

27. Doug Osborne, "Piano Stairs Make Ascending and Descending Floors Fun," *Geek*, October 9, 2009, http://www.geek.com/articles/news/ piano-stairs-make-ascending-and-descending-floors-fun-2009109/; see also James Sherwood, "Volkswagen Boffins Turn Staircase into Giant Working Piano Keyboard," *Register Hardware*, October 9, 2009, http://www.reg hardware.co.uk/2009/10/09/volkswagen_stairs_and_bin/.

28. Dave Itzkoff, "Museum Gets Really 'Big' Piano," *ArtsBeat Blog*, *New York Times*, January 19, 2009, http://artsbeat.blogs.nytimes.com/tag/ remo-saraceni/.

29. Tania Ralli, "As Europe Ages, a Grocery Chain Extends a Hand," *New York Times*, December 27, 2003, http://www.nytimes.com/2003/12/ 27/business/international-business-as-europe-ages-a-grocery-chain -extends-a-hand.html?pagewanted=1.

CHAPTER 10: AN APPLE A DAY

1. Kathryn H. Anthony, with Barry D. Riccio, *Running for Our Lives: An Odyssey with Cancer.* (2004). Available on Amazon.com: https://www .amazon.com/Running-Our-Lives-Odyssey-Cancer/dp/1500324256. See also K. H. Anthony, "Environment-Behavior Issues for Cancer Patients and their Caregivers" (abstract) in *Old World-New Ideas, Proceedings of the 32nd Annual Conference of the Environmental Design Research Association (EDRA)*, ed. Martin Edge (Edmond, OK: EDRA, 2001), pp. 180–81; K. H. Anthony, "Our Medical Odyssey: An Environment-Behavior Critique of Cancer Treatment Centers" (abstract), in *The Power of Imagination, Proceedings of the 30th Annual Conference of the Environmental Design Research Association (EDRA)*, ed. Thorbjoern Mann (Edmond, OK: EDRA, 1999), pp. 244–45; John Crewdson, "Test Drug Linked to a Cancer's Remission," *Chicago Tribune*, May 25, 1998, Section 1, p. 3, http://articles.chicagotribune .com/1998-05-25/news/9805250142_1_angiostatin-and-endostatin-dr -m-judah-folkman-cancer-treatment; Christine Gorman, "The Hope and the Hype," *Time*, May 18, 1998, pp. 38–44, http://content.time.com/ time/magazine/article/0,9171,988347,00.html; Leonard Novarro, "The Discoverer: Scripps Scientist's Work Offers Big Hope for Cancer Patients," *San Diego Union-Tribune*, October 4, 1998, Health Section, p. 7.

2. Personal e-mail correspondence with Trish Wilkinson, November 22, 2016.

3. Ibid.

4. Associated Press, "C-section Rates around Globe at 'Epidemic' Levels," updated January 12, 2010, NBC News, http://www.nbcnews.com/ id/34826186/ns/health-pregnancy/t/c-section-rates-around-globe -epidemic-levels/#.WDSnWyMrJHY.

5. Chia-Hui Wang, "Evidence-Based Design for Childbirth Environments: The Impacts of Window View and Daylight Exposure on the Health of Post-Cesarean Section Women," PhD diss., School of Architecture, University of Illinois at Urbana-Champaign, 2015; see also Chia-Hui Wang, K. H. Anthony, and Nai-Wen Kuo, "Evidence Based Design for Childbirth Environments: The Impacts of Daylight Exposure on Analgesia Usage of Post-Cesarean Section Women" (abstract), in *Proceedings of the 46th Annual Conference of the Environmental Design Research Association (EDRA)* (Washington, DC: EDRA, 2015), pp. 249–50; Chia-Hui Wang, Nai-Wen Kuo, and K. H. Anthony, "Impact of Sunlight on Pain Interference," *Natural Energy and Recovery, Advances in Energy Equipment Science and Engineering, Proceed-*

ings of the International Conference on Energy Equipment Science and Engineering (ICEESE 2015) (Guangzhou, China: CRC Press, 2015), pp. 1781–85; Chia-Hui Wang, K. H. Anthony, and Nai-Wen Kuo, "Impacts of Window Views and Daylight Exposure on Recovery: A Prospective Study of Post-Cesarean Section" (abstract), in *Proceedings of the 45th Annual Conference of the Environmental Design Research Association (EDRA)* (Washington, DC: EDRA, 2014).

6. *American Association of Birth Centers (AABC),* http://www.birth centers.org/; "AABC Press Kit," American Association of Birth Centers, January 21, 2015, http://c.ymcdn.com/sites/www.birthcenters.org/ resource/resmgr/About_AABC_-_Documents/AABC_Press_Kit.pdf.

7. "What Is a Birth Center?" American Association of Birth Centers, http://www.birthcenters.org/?page=bce_what_is_a_bc.

8. Center for Reproductive Rights, *Seizing Today, Transforming Tomorrow, 2008 Annual Report* (New York: Center for Reproductive Rights, 2009), p. 17, http://reproductiverights.org/sites/crr.civicactions.net/ files/documents/CRR_2008_ANNUALREPORT.pdf.

9. Colleen Mastony, "$4.1 Million Settlement Set for Pregnant Inmates Who Said They Were Shackled before Giving Birth: Judge Grants Preliminary Approval for Deal to End Class-Action Suit against Cook County Sheriff's Office," *Chicago Tribune,* May 23, 2012, http://articles.chicago tribune.com/2012-05-23/news/ct-met-shackled-pregnant-women -20120523_1_pregnant-women-pregnant-inmates-shackles-and-belly-chains.

10. Joe Stumpe and Monica Davey, "Abortion Doctor Shot to Death in Kansas Church," *New York Times,* May 31, 2009, http://www.nytimes .com/2009/06/01/us/01tiller.html?pagewanted=all&_r=0.

11. "How China's One-Child Policy Led to Forced Abortions, 30 Million Bachelors," *Fresh Air,* NPR, February 1, 2016, http://www.npr.org/2016/ 02/01/465124337/how-chinas-one-child-policy-led-to-forced-abortions -30-million-bachelors; "Regulations of Shanghai Municipality on Population and Family Planning (Adopted at the 9th Session of the Standing Committee of the Twelfth Shanghai Municipal People's Congress on December 31, 2003)," Shanghai Municipal Population and Family Planning Commission, http://www.popinfo.gov.cn/spfpen/dr/lawandrules/2009926/ 00000660406460424420580.html?openpath=spfpen%2Flawandrules.

12. "Regulations of Shanghai Municipality on Population and Family Planning."

13. Based on interviews conducted in October 2008.

14. "Stop Sticks Campaign," National Institute for Occupational Safety and Health, June 26, 2013, http://www.cdc.gov/niosh/stopsticks/

sharpsinjuries.html; National Institute for Occupational Safety and Health (NIOSH), "NIOSH Alert: Preventing Needlestick Injuries in Health Care Settings," *DHHS (NIOSH)* Publication No. 2000-108, Cincinnati, OH, November 1999; Jane Elliott, "My Sister's Injury Inspired My Design," BBC World News America, December 23, 2007, http://news.bbc.co.uk/2/hi/health/7085051.stm.

15. Jack M. Winters and Molly Follette Story, eds., *Medical Instrumentation: Accessibility and Usability* (Boca Raton, FL: CRC Press, 2007).

16. "A Guide to Bed Safety Bed Rails in Hospitals, Nursing Homes and Home Health Care: The Facts," US Food and Drug Administration, October 2000, revised January 2008, revised April 2010, updated April 5, 2010, http://www.fda.gov/MedicalDevices/ProductsandMedical Procedures/GeneralHospitalDevicesandSupplies/HospitalBeds/ ucm123676.htm; "Safety Concerns about Bed Rails," Food and Drug Administration, November 3, 2014, http://www.fda.gov/MedicalDevices/ ProductsandMedicalProcedures/HomeHealthandConsumer/ ConsumerProducts/BedRailSafety/ucm362832.htm.

17. Angie Qin, "Adult Portable Bed Rail-Related Deaths, Injuries, and Potential Injuries: January 2003 to September 2012," US Consumer Product Safety Commission, October 11, 2012, http://www.cpsc.gov/ PageFiles/133466/adultbedrail.pdf; see also "Bed Rail Safety," US Food and Drug Administration, http://www.fda.gov/MedicalDevices/Product sandMedicalProcedures/HomeHealthandConsumer/ConsumerProducts/ BedRailSafety/default.htm.

18. "Guide to Bed Safety Bed Rails."

19. Shaila Dewan and Robert Gebeloff, "More Men Enter Fields Dominated by Women," *New York Times*, May 20, 2012, http://www.nytimes .com/2012/05/21/business/increasingly-men-seek-success-in-jobs -dominated-by-women.html.

20. Lori Crawford, Lori G. Gutierrez, and Philip Harber, "Work Environment and Occupational Health of Dental Hygienists: A Qualitative Assessment," *Journal of Occupational and Environmental Medicine* 47, no. 6 (2005): 623–32.

21. Martha J. Sanders, *Ergonomics and the Management of Musculoskeletal Disorders*, 2nd ed. (St. Louis, MO: Butterworth Heinemann, 2004), p. 455, http://www.sciencedirect.com/science/book/9780750674096.

22. Ibid., p. 456.

23. Mr. Graham, "Ergonomics in Dentistry, Part 1," *Dentistry Today*, April 1, 2002, http://www.dentistrytoday.com/ergonomics/1113.

24. Mr. Graham, "Ergonomics in Dentistry, Part 2," *Dentistry Today*, May 1, 2002, http://www.dentistrytoday.com/ergonomics/1111.

25. Mr. Graham, "Ergonomics in Dentistry, Part 1"; "Ergonomics in Dentistry, Part 2."

26. American Institutes for Research, "A Patient-Centered Guide to Implementing Language Access Services in Healthcare Organizations," submitted to Office of Minority Health, US Department of Health and Human Services, September 2005, http://minorityhealth.hhs.gov/Assets/pdf/Checked/HC-LSIG.pdf.

27. "Visual Impairment, Blindness Cases in US Expected to Double by 2050: NIH-Funded Studies Tease Out Trends by Race, Ethnicity and Sex," National Institutes of Health, May 19, 2016, https://www.nih.gov/news-events/news-releases/visual-impairment-blindness-cases-us-expected-double-2050.

28. "SUDAN: Biking for Safer Childbirth," IRIN: Humanitarian News and Analysis: A Project of the UN Office for the Coordination of Humanitarian Affairs, April 1, 2009, http://www.irinnews.org/Report.aspx?ReportId=83727.

29. Sean Fallon, "LEDs: Philips Imagination Light Canvas Allows You to Paint with LEDs," *Gizmodo*, February 28, 2008, http://gizmodo.com/361603/philips-imagination-light-canvas-allows-you-to-paint-with-leds.

30. Polly LaBarre, "Strategic Innovation: The Children's Hospital at Montefiore," *FastCompany*, December 19, 2007, https://www.fastcompany.com/44832/strategic-innovation-childrens-hospital-montefiore.

31. Ibid.

32. Ibid.

33. Elizabeth Nolan Brown, "The Takeaway: Hospitals Open Seniors-Only Emergency Rooms," *AARP Blog*, April 10, 2012, http://blog.aarp.org/2012/04/10/the-takeaway-hospitals-open-seniors-only-emergency-rooms/.

34. Geri Aston, "Hospitals Offer New Twists on Services, with the Older Patient in Mind: From the Emergency Department to the OR, Hospitals Are Taking a Fresh Approach to Treating an Aging Population," *Hospitals & Health Networks,* January 15, 2016, http://www.hhnmag.com/articles/6771-new-twists-on-services-with-the-older-patient-in-mind.

35. Ibid.

36. Michelle Ponte, "5 Essentials of a Geriatric Emergency Department," *Health Leaders*, May 2016, http://www.healthleadersmedia.com/quality/5-essentials-geriatric-emergency-department#.

37. Susan Grossinger (HOK Product Design) and Nicholas J. Watkins (formerly at HOK), private correspondence with author, November 28, 2016.

38. Contract Design Staff, "Best of NeoCon® 2011 Competition Winners Announced," *Contract Design*, June 13, 2011, http://www.contract design.com/news/Best-of-NeoCon-2011-5424.shtml (accessed November 28, 2016).

39. David Oliver, Frances Healey, and Terry P. Haines, "Preventing Falls and Fall-Related Injuries in Hospitals," *Clin. Geriatr. Med.* 26 (2010): 645–92, https://www.memorialcare.org/sites/default/files/media/Pat%20 Quigley%20Falls%20and%20Fall-related%20injuries%20in%20hospitals%20 -%20D%20Oliver%20May%202014.pdf (accessed November 28, 2016).

40. Rene Samples Twibell et al., "Falls and Fall Prevention among Hospitalized Adults," *American Journal of Critical Care* 24, no. 5 (September 2015), http://ajcc.aacnjournals.org/content/24/5/e78.full.pdf+html (accessed November 28, 2016).

41. Karen Angel, "Nursing-Home Falls a Common and Preventable Cause of Death and Serious Injury," *Huffington Post*, October 1, 2013, http://www.huffingtonpost.com/karen-angel/nursinghome-falls-a -commo_b_3684980.html (accessed November 28, 2016).

CHAPTER 11: A CALL TO ACTION

1. John Podesta, "Preface," in *The Shriver Report: A Woman's Nation Changes Everything*, Maria Shriver and the Center for American Progress, eds. Heather Boushey and Ann O'Leary (Washington, DC: Center for American Progress, 2009), https://www.americanprogress.org/issues/ women/report/2009/10/16/6789/the-shriver-report/.

2. "Who We Are," Safe Kids Worldwide, https://www.safekids.org/ who-we-are.

3. Safe Kids USA, http://www.safekids.org/.

4. M. Sengölge and J. Vincenten, *Child Product Safety Guide: Potentially Dangerous Products* (Edgbaston, Birmingham, UK: European Child Safety Alliance, 2013), http://www.childsafetyeurope.org/publications/info/ product-safety-guide.pdf.

5. Lindsay Hock, "What Is Title IX?" Women's Sports Foundation, July 21, 2014, www.womenssportsfoundation.org/sports/what-is-title-ix/.

6. Henri Lefebvre, *The Production of Space* (Oxford: Blackwell, 1991), p. 59.

INDEX